From Burma to Rome

A remarkable book charting a journey which is unusual in the present age. For anybody asking 'why Catholicism?' this should be essential reading.

Ann Widdecombe

Benedict Rogers has written an enthralling account of his spiritual pilgrimage. It is partly an adventure story of human rights campaigning in dangerous places; partly a series of biographical portraits of the Godly counsellors, particularly Cardinal Bo and Lord Alton, who guided the author on his journey towards Rome; and partly a moving explanation of the stirrings of soul that brought about Benedict's conversion to a committed Catholic faith. It makes a profound and powerful narrative which will surely be an inspiration to many.

Jonathan Aitken

Human rights activists who see the Catholic Church as an obstacle to their work will be astonished by this book. Benedict Rogers explains that he embraced the Catholic faith not in spite of his passion for human rights but because of it. Yet this is not simply a personal conversion story: he also shows that many of those risking their lives to defend the defenceless today are inspired not by secular values but by a living relationship with Jesus Christ.

Luke Coppen, Editor of 'The Catholic Herald'

Benedict Rogers has spent 20 years responding to the human needs of the peoples of Burma and East Asia—their needs for justice, to have their rights respected, and to practice their faith freely. He has the courage and honesty to take seriously the desires this awakens in his heart and to follow them according to their total implications—a sure and beautiful path into the Catholic Church. Through this spiritual memoir shines 'the splendor of the truth'.

Congressman Christopher Smith
US House of Representatives

From Burma to Rome

A Journey into the Catholic Church

To Else,

Benedict Rogers

With prayers and
very best wishes,

Ben Rogers.

GRACEWING

First published in England in 2015
by
Gracewing
2 Southern Avenue
Leominster
Herefordshire HR6 0QF
United Kingdom
www.gracewing.co.uk

ISBN 978 085244 863 2

Typeset by Word and Page, Chester, UK

Cover design by Bernardita Peña Hurtado

Cover image: Kyaiktiyo (Golden Rock) Pagoda

For all those who have inspired and guided me on this journey, and especially for those heroes, Cecil Chaudhry and Shahbaz Bhatti in Pakistan, who are no longer with us but who I believe are smiling from heaven.

CONTENTS

ILLUSTRATIONS

ACKNOWLEDGEMENTS

Several friends, including some of those featured in this book, read the draft manuscript and provided invaluable suggestions for improvement. I am enormously grateful to Liam Allmark, Cherrie Anderson, Nicolas Bellord, Joanna Bogle, Cecil Chaudhry Jr, Fr Peter Edwards, Fr Joseph Evans, Mike and Christine Gibson, Pablo Hinojo, Deacon Michael Hughes, Colonel Chris Keeble, Fr Nicholas King, SJ, Martin Lee, Joseph Loconte, James Mawdsley, Ambassador John McCarthy, Ashley Puglia Noronha, Lucinda Phillips, Nelson Santos, Peter Smith, Mary Kay Turner, Pia Vogler and Chen Wang. I am also indebted to my parents, Parry and Juliet Rogers.

Those who gave their time to be interviewed for this book, to share their experiences, beliefs and ideas, deserve much appreciation. These include Lord Alton, Cardinal Bo, Michelle Chaudry, Colonel Chris Keeble, Martin Lee, George Weigel, Ann Widdecombe and Cardinal Zen. I am also grateful to them for reading the manuscript and providing helpful corrections and suggestions.

Many people inspired me in my faith, as this book describes. But seven people played pivotal parts. The Rt Rev. Christopher Cocksworth, now Anglican bishop of Coventry, was my university chaplain and discipled me when I first embraced the Christian faith. Baroness Cox inspired me into the work of human rights and religious freedom advocacy. And in my specific journey into the Catholic Church, while several Catholic friends generously and patiently answered my questions as I explored the faith and suggested reading material, Pablo Hinojo walked alongside me for much of my journey. My parish priest Fr Peter Edwards guided me, both in our regular personal meetings and in the Evangelium course. Fr Nicholas King, SJ, guided my two retreats, and opened the door to Ignatian spirituality for me. Lord Alton accompanied me, not only to Rangoon to stand alongside me as I was received into the Church but for the two years or more leading up to that day, suggesting reading materials and offering inspirational thoughts. And of course without Cardinal Bo, this story would never have been written.

My colleagues in Christian Solidarity Worldwide, with whom I have worked for over two decades, have given me unlimited encouragement, both in my journey of faith and my work for human rights, a platform to pursue the issues about which I am passionate, and the opportunity to meet many of the inspirational and courageous people whose stories are told in this book.

To all my friends, to all the saints with whom I've been privileged to work and travel, to all, both alive and departed who inspired me in this adventure, I can only say 'thank you'. And most of all, my gratitude and praise to God.

FOREWORD

This lovely book reads like a voyage of discovery.

As Benedict Rogers hoists the main sail he invites us to embark with him on a delightfully intimate *tour d'horizon*, mapping out the landmarks and currents which steered him towards Rome.

When Hilaire Belloc wrote his classic *Path to Rome*—the delightful story of the pilgrimage which he undertook on foot—he said he wrote the book to fulfil a vow he had made to 'see all Europe which the Christian Faith has saved'. As he walked to Rome he discovered a joyful Church, noting that 'Wherever the Catholic sun doth shine, there's always laughter and good red wine. At least I've always found it so. Benedicamus Domino!' His friend, G. K. Chesterton also saw no contradiction between a pint, a pipe and the cross.

Ben Rogers's journey has taken him to many parts of the world which have treasured the Christian faith—and met many people whose lives have been saved by their joyful encounter with Christ—but he has also been in those dark places where today Christians are persecuted and under relentless attack.

That story of the suffering and persecuted church first drew him to Christianity. Perhaps he saw that a faith worth dying for might be worth living for. Describing her very practical living Christian faith, it was Mother Teresa who once said that if you judge people you don't have time to love them. As the pouring out of love throughout her life underlined, the power of any principle or belief lies in the action it inspires: in seeing God in all things and in all people.

President Abraham Lincoln insisted that: 'Nothing stamped with the Divine image and likeness was sent into the world to be trodden on.' Yet, in countless ways and in situations documented by the author of this book, men, women and children have their liberties routinely denied and their lives brutally ended.

Throughout his journey from Burma to Rome Ben Rogers has eloquently argued that the great religions have a duty to promote love of God and love of the people He created; that no religion is above humanity and that no religion should incite hatred, bigotry or violence. His advocacy work stands four square with Pope Benedict XVI's encyclical, *Deus caritas est*, in which he insists that the heart must see where love is needed and must act accordingly. That same advocacy work has led Ben to see that mankind is so fallen and so prone to tyranny—think of Stalin, Hitler, Mao, the Kims—that no single man should ever be trusted with unlimited power over the rest of us. We would be asking the wrong question if, when we think of the horrors of Auschwitz or the contemporary prison camps of North Korea, we were to ask 'where was God?' The correct question to ask is 'where was man?'; 'where were we?'

It is a question which Ben Rogers has asked and his work has taken him to some of the nastiest places in the world—and he has risked his life to do so. Like Belloc he holds that it is pointless to wander aimlessly through life, simply for the sake of distraction. Travel has to be for a purpose—as his has been.

He brings that same rigorous outlook—and a will-ingness to take risks—to this spiritual odyssey. His account reveals an enquiring mind and one which is willing to be surprised. His chapter on the great Catholic thinkers who have influenced him is in itself a wonderful introduction to theologians like Scott

Hahn, Von Balthasar and Joseph Ratzinger; writers and public intellectuals such as George Weigel and Malcolm Muggeridge; poets and novelists like Hopkins, Tolkien and Chesterton; and spiritual giants like Merton, Thérèse of Lisieux, and Jean-Pierre de Caussade. This book introduces us to people who know about God but its writer is clearly a man who wants to know God. There's a difference and he wants us to understand that spiritual fecundity helps us to grow and to thrive.

From first dipping a foot into cold water we are treated to the excitement and exhilaration of a traveller who is discovering small islands, new countries and vast continents. It is the universality of the Catholic Church, and its apostolic origins, which clearly grip his imagination, and captivate and animate his soul—as it once gripped the imagination of John Henry Newman and G. K. Chesterton and others who made the journey before him. Not that, in making their journeys, there weren't obstacles to be overcome—but as Newman finally observed: 'Ten thousand difficulties do not make one doubt.'

It's hard to read this account of the great saints, the teaching encyclicals, the *Catechism* or the *Compendium of the Social Doctrine of the Church* and not want to go back to those sources.

It is reinvigorating and challenging to be reminded of what fresh eyes have seen and of those things that we weary travelers have too often forgotten. It is instructive to see how easily he demolishes to his own satisfaction the old canards about Catholicism— the position of Mary, the role of the saints, the nature of authority and so on. There is a sense here of a man who has discovered his English ancestors and likes what he has found.

There is nothing in this story that is sectarian or triumphalist or which, in his own spiritual quest, disowns what went before. As someone who honours the Christian traditions outside the Catholic Church he reminds us that those rich influences in his own early life prepared him for the voyage which he subsequently felt called to make. To journey confidently into the future you need to know where you have been, and he does.

I am particularly struck that he didn't hold back from making his journey out of fear of what others might say or think or because of the risk of disappointment. His first Oxford retreat was clearly a turning point and a useful reminder that we all need quiet places, quiet times, and a wise guide to navigate us through squalls and shark-laden waters. Saint Benedict said that the spiritual life is a constant movement between the desert and the market place.

I was privileged to be with Ben when he asked Cardinal Charles Bo to receive him into the Church. It was during a political visit to Burma. In Rangoon Cathedral, that day, I was struck that people from many faith backgrounds—and none—had gathered to wish Ben bon voyage and to celebrate with him. It was a moment which deserved to be captured and I encouraged him to write something of his experiences and was delighted when this wonderful book emerged. It's a joy to read.

Lord Alton of Liverpool

PREFACE

A Seeker, A Pilgrim and A Fearless Advocate of the Underdog

BENEDICT ROGERS: a name synonymous with human freedom and freedom of choice in South-East Asia. His relentless campaign for the right to believe (and even right not to believe) has taken him to the dangerous streets of Pakistan, the capricious religious landscapes of Indonesia, and the dark and silent corners of Burma (Myanmar). He has travelled to places shunned by other 'professional human rights activists'. This book narrates with a passion his life and mission.

His work for human dignity has exposed him to numerous risks. It was during one of those heightened moments of risk that Ben Rogers knocked at my door. When I saw him, he was composed, serene, ready to face the consequences. His boldness amidst threatening swirls of evil touched me. I would come to know more of his commitment at that young age. His clarity of vision and hard work inspired me. His relentless pursuit of human rights and dignity reminded me of the words of the great civil rights leader, Martin Luther King Jr: 'Injustice anywhere is injustice everywhere.' His hard work for religious freedom has brought him deep friendships with the victims, an inspiring network of inter-religious groups. In a world torn by inter-religious strife, Ben Rogers brings enduring values of mutual respect and our inter-dependence. Together we stand or together we fall. Gandhi's words of caution: 'An eye for an eye leaves the whole world blind.' People like Ben Rogers wage a relentless war against that kind of hatred and mutual destruction.

It is a joy and a blessing to know people like him. Apart from his religious freedom works, he has been an unceasing seeker. His Christian commitment to human dignity has been uncompromising all along. Our friendship brought him closer to the Catholic social teachings. We were waging our own battles in Burma for human dignity. The social gospel of liberation, the exodus event of the Old Testament, Christ's Galilean manifesto of 'freedom for the oppressed', inspired us to stand with our oppressed people of all creeds. Ben Rogers evinced a great interest in the social mission of the Catholic Church. His forays into our mission inspired him. A chance comment on the Catholic Church and my readiness to receive him if ever he wished to enter that church ended with him requesting baptism in the Catholic Church.

By a strange but graceful turn of events, when the baptism date was fixed, the Catholic Church was having a historic first. A reigning pope had resigned and a new pope was elected. Pope Francis emerged as another great inspiring figure to Ben Rogers. His journey from the night he sought safety in the streets of Burma ended in front of the altar in St Mary's Cathedral in Rangoon (Yangon), witnessed by a crowd of friends of different religious and ethnic backgrounds.

Ben Rogers understands the significance of that baptism and the mission bestowed on him. Christ's baptism was not only in the River Jordan, but it was a baptism of fire. John the Baptist's voice was vanquished by the powers. Christ emerges into an unjust world

with his great manifesto of 'Good news to the poor,
Justice to the oppressed' (Luke 4: 16–19). Ben Rogers's
writing and training and campaigning for the rights
of the underdog has intensified after that sacramental
commitment, all over South-East Asia. He continues
to tread where angels dread to go. South-East Asia's
oppressed individuals are blessed to have an advocate
of great integrity and uncompromising commitment
to their cause.

The story of Ben Rogers's journey is a metaphor of
hope. A small lamp has the 'audacity of hope' to dispel
any suffocating darkness, hope that simple men and
women can dream of a world where there will be 'no
more deaths, suffering, crying or pain. I am making
everything new, a new 'heaven and a new earth' (Revelation 21: 1–5).

I am fortunate and blessed to be part of that journey
of Ben Rogers. I warmly commend this book that tells
the story of his life, which I hope and pray may inspire
thousands in our march towards human freedom.

+ Charles Cardinal Bo, DD, SDB
Yangon, Myanmar

Introduction

THIS IS A BOOK I was reluctant to write. A few days before I was received into the Catholic Church, Archbishop—now Cardinal—Charles Bo of Rangoon, Burma (or Yangon, Myanmar, as it is officially called),[1] said to me: 'I will receive you into the Church, but I want you to do something in return. I want you to write a book about why you have become a Catholic.'

I laughed and politely nodded, while making no firm commitment.

A few nights later, at dinner following my reception into the Church in Rangoon on Palm Sunday, Lord Alton, my sponsor, said: 'I think you should write a book about it.'

When two of the people one respects most in life, who have both had a profound impact on one's faith journey, make a suggestion, one is compelled to at least consider it. But I was not keen. For a start, I did not want to tell 'my' story too much, for fear that an excess of self-promotion turn narcissistic. Secondly, I had written five books in eight years, and was not—for the time being—looking to write another. I welcomed having some weekends and evenings back.

But the prompts kept coming. Back in London, I mentioned the idea to two Catholic friends, both influential and devout. They said: 'Funnily enough, we have been thinking the same.' Then my parish priest, when I mentioned it to him, said, 'I've had the same thought'.

There I was, with five Catholic friends whom I value deeply, one an archbishop, one a peer, one my parish priest, one a distinguished media commentator and the other a teacher—I felt I had little choice but to at least give it further thought and prayer.

I prepared a draft proposal and circulated it among Catholic friends, including several priests, to seek their advice. If they had responded with 'don't bother', I would have readily put it aside. Indeed, I was almost hoping I'd be let 'off the hook'. Instead, without exception, and almost to my disappointment, every friend who read the proposal responded with overwhelming enthusiasm and encouragement.

Then, to my horror, prominent figures such as George Weigel and Fr Timothy Radcliffe saw the proposal and, despite being perceived as coming from different ends of the Catholic spectrum, they both told me to go for it. That was a worrying sign.

And then I went on an Ignatian retreat, at the start of 2014, at Campion Hall, Oxford, with Fr Nicholas King. It was my second such retreat, having made a most wonderful retreat at the beginning of 2013 in preparation for being received into the Church. On this second retreat, several times I felt God speaking to me about this book, and encouraging me to get on and write.

Why had I been reluctant initially? Because I knew that if I wrote 'my' story of why 'I' had become a Catholic, there were inherently two dangers: one was the above-mentioned fear of narcissism, or in other words, the danger of falling into the sin of pride and egoism; the other was the danger of wanting to write so honestly that I would expose all my human frailties too much, in an unseemly 'warts and all' manner. Neither option was appealing. But after much prayer, contemplation and reflection I concluded there was another way to do this. For this, ultimately, is God's story, and I want the emphasis to be on Him, His amazing love and grace, the tug of His Holy Spirit, and the range of people whom He has used to inspire me in this journey of faith. People whom I have had the privilege of knowing personally, in places such as East Timor, Pakistan, Hong Kong and Burma, as well as the United Kingdom and the United States, and people whom I have come to know through their lives and writings: Pope Benedict XVI, Scott Hahn, George Weigel, Thomas Merton, G. K. Chesterton, Blessed John Henry Newman, Hans Urs von Balthasar, Henri de Lubac, Jean-Pierre de Caussade, Malcolm Muggeridge and, since becoming a Catholic, Pope Francis, Gerard Manley Hopkins, Dorothy Day, Thomas More and others. In particular, the *Catechism of the Catholic Church* and the *Compendium of the Social Doctrine of the Church* captured my attention and imagination.

This book, therefore, is less about me and my journey, and much more about God and the people—the signposts—He has used to speak to me on the way. Of course, my story is woven into the narrative, because I am not some detached abstraction but rather an active participant, but I hope that my role is more of a walk-on, part of the narrative of a much bigger story. Far more important and interesting are the stories of the brave, inspiring, amazing people who through their lives and writing inspired me to look at the Catholic Church. They spoke to me, to use Blessed John Henry Newman's phrase, as 'heart speaks unto heart'. Through their testimony and example, the Holy Spirit poured His grace into my soul. In the words of the famous hymn, it was as if I prayed 'Breathe on me breath of God, fill me with life anew'—and He did.

There were four factors in my journey into the Catholic Church, and these can be summarised as follows: I discovered within the Catholic Church the clearest expression of a biblical basis for social justice of any Christian tradition; I found within the Catholic Church a truly historical, comprehensive and intellectually serious articulation of the Christian faith; I was inspired by remarkable individuals, whose stories are told in this book; and I experienced mystery, majesty, reverence and spiritual depth which I had sought for so long. These four factors give shape to the structure of this book and are reference points in this journey.

And so, in the words of a song sung at my rite of election service at St George's Cathedral, Southwark, just over a month before I was received into the Church, I do as I am instructed:

> You are called to tell the story,
> passing words of life along,
> then to blend your voice with others
> as you sing the sacred song.
> Christ be known in all our singing,
> filling all with songs of love.
>
> You are called to teach the rhythm
> of the dance that never ends,
> then to move within the circle,
> hand in hand with strangers, friends.
> Christ be known in all our dancing,
> touching all with hands of love.
>
> May the One whose love is broader
> than the measure of all space
> give us words to sing the story,
> move among us in this place.
> Christ be known in all our living,
> filling all with gifts of love.

Note

[1]   The official name of the country was changed by the military regime in 1989, from Burma to Myanmar, and many place names were changed, notably the largest city and former capital, Rangoon, to Yangon. However, the democracy movement led by Aung San Suu Kyi, as well as many of the ethnic nationalities, still prefer to use 'Burma' and 'Rangoon' because, they argue, the regime had no mandate to change the name. Out of respect and support for them, I use 'Burma' and 'Rangoon' in this book.

Lead, Kindly Light

Lead, kindly Light, amid th' encircling gloom, lead
    Thou me on!
The night is dark, and I am far from home; lead
    Thou me on!
Keep Thou my feet; I do not ask to see
The distant scene; one step enough for me.

I was not ever thus, nor prayed that Thou shouldst
    lead me on;
I loved to choose and see my path; but now lead
    Thou me on!
I loved the garish day, and, spite of fears,
Pride ruled my will. Remember not past years!

So long Thy power hath blest me, sure it still will
    lead me on.
O'er moor and fen, o'er crag and torrent, till the
    night is gone,
And with the morn those angel faces smile, which I
Have loved long since, and lost awhile!

Meantime, along the narrow rugged path, Thyself
    hast trod,
Lead, Saviour, lead me home in childlike faith,
    home to my God.
To rest forever after earthly strife
In the calm light of everlasting life.

John Henry Newman, 1833

ON PALM SUNDAY IN 2013, shortly before the start of the evening Mass in St Mary's Cathedral, Rangoon, Burma, the waters of baptism were poured gently over my head by Archbishop—now Cardinal—Charles Maung Bo, the archbishop of Rangoon, and the bells of the cathedral rang out thunderously, chiming a beautiful message of peace and hope.[1] I was filled with an overwhelming sense of joy, a transcendent sense of calm, and a feeling of homecoming. In the steamy tropical heat, and despite sweat rolling down my cheeks, all I could feel at that moment was the balm that comes from the still small voice of God.

The beautiful ceremony had begun shortly before, with the opening words by the archbishop: 'God, come to my rescue.' The congregation responded: 'Lord, make haste to help me.' He then announced the words from Ezekiel 36: 25: 'I will pour out on you pure water, and you shall be cleansed of all your stains, says the Lord.' We then prayed Psalm 8, including those amazing words: 'When I behold the heavens, the work of your fingers, the moon and the stars which you set in place—what is man that you should be mindful of him, or the son of man that you should care for him?'

Then Archbishop Bo called us to pray:

> Almighty, everlasting God, who enable us, your servants, in our profession of the true faith, to acknowledge the glory of the three Persons in the eternal Godhead, and to adore their oneness of nature, their co-equal majesty; grant, we pray, that by steadfastness in that faith we may ever be guarded against all adversity. We beg you, O Lord, grant that your chosen one Benedict Rogers, well instructed in the holy mysteries,

may be born again in the font of baptism and be added to the household of your Church, through Christ our Lord. Amen.

When he then called my name, I had already been taken up to a higher plane, and was grateful when my sponsor—or 'godfather'—Lord Alton of Liverpool, standing next to me, put a hand on my shoulder and gently whispered a prompt: 'I am present, Your Grace.' I declared my presence, as instructed, and then concentrated fully on the responses I had to make.

> 'Benedict Rogers, what are you asking of God's Church?' asked Archbishop Bo.
> 'Faith,' I answered.
> 'Benedict Rogers, what does faith hold out to you?' he asked.
> 'Everlasting life,' I replied.
> 'If, then, you wish to inherit everlasting life, keep the commandments, "Love the Lord your God with all your heart, with all your soul, and with all your mind; and your neighbour as yourself." On these two commandments depend the whole law and the prophets. Now faith demands that you worship one God in Trinity, and Trinity in unity, neither confusing the Persons one with the other, nor making a distinction in their nature. For the Father is a distinct Person, so also the Son, so also the Holy Spirit; yet all Three possess the one nature, the one Godhead.'

After I had renounced Satan, the archbishop breathed gently on me, saying: 'Receive, by this breath, the good Spirit along with His blessing. Peace be with you.' He then anointed me with the oil of catechumens.

A little later, the archbishop prayed another beautiful prayer:

> Holy Lord, almighty Father, everlasting God,
> source of light and truth, I appeal to your
> sacred and boundless compassion on behalf
> of your servant Ben Rogers. Be pleased to
> enlighten him by the light of your eternal
> wisdom. Cleanse, sanctify and endow him
> with true knowledge. For thus will he be made
> ready for the grace of your baptism and ever
> remain steadfast, never losing hope, never
> faltering in duty, never straying from sacred
> truth, but ready at all times to receive your
> grace, through Christ our Lord.

I was then asked to answer whether I believe in God
the Father, the Creator of heaven and earth, Jesus
Christ, His only Son, our Lord, who was born into
this world and suffered for us, and the Holy Spirit,
the holy Catholic Church, the communion of saints,
the forgiveness of sins, the resurrection of the body,
and the life everlasting. To each question in turn, I
declared: 'I do believe.'

Following the baptism, I was then anointed with
the oil of Sacred Chrism, and presented with a white
robe and a burning candle, symbols of purity and inno-
cence. Then came confirmation, a prayer for the Spirit
of wisdom and understanding, the Spirit of counsel
and fortitude, the Spirit of knowledge and piety and
fear of the Lord. I took as my confirmation saint St
Charles Borromeo, in honour of Archbishop Charles Bo
whose baptismal saint he was, but also in recognition
of the great saint's legacy of revival and reformation. I
was blessed already to have the name Benedict, a saint
I have long admired, and so had delayed choosing
another saint until the very last moment—indeed, only
at Lord Alton's prompting and with Archbishop Bo's
guidance did I choose St Charles. I did not know at

the time, but was delighted to discover subsequently, that he was also the patron saint of Pope St John Paul II and that, furthermore, the Polish pope preferred to celebrate the feast day of St Charles Borromeo rather than his own birthday.[2]

It was the most significant day of my life after becoming a Christian 19 years previously. Joining the occasion were a wonderful assortment of friends from varied backgrounds: Burmese Buddhist dissidents and activists, Baptists from the Karen and Chin[3] ethnic backgrounds, Muslims, and some international friends, of whom some were lapsed Catholics who had not been to Mass for decades, and some were agnostic, secular, non-religious. It was beautiful that such an occasion united people of different beliefs in an atmosphere of celebration.

But what had led to this point, and why did it occur in Burma? To answer these questions, let me go back to my roots.

I was born into a most loving family, with parents whose values, spoken and lived, include integrity, honesty, compassion, hospitality, generosity, knowledge and education, and who have a lively and active interest in the world around them, in international issues, current affairs, history, nature, art and music. Neither my mother nor my father is a churchgoer or professing Christian, but both were raised in Christian homes. My maternal grandparents were devout Anglo-Catholics in the Church of England, and my paternal grandparents were Catholics. Indeed, my father was a practising Catholic for more than 40 years, but left the Church when his first marriage broke down and he divorced. He has eight children by his first marriage.

Interestingly, my brother-in-law was also raised in a large Catholic family, but he also left the Church.

Both my father and my brother-in-law were, therefore, surprised and somewhat intrigued by my decision to become a Catholic.

During my childhood, I was taken to church on Sundays very occasionally when I accompanied my maternal grandparents to their Church of England parish. At the age of about 12, something—I am not entirely sure what—caught my imagination and I decided to go to church every Sunday, by myself. For a few years, I became involved in the local Church of England parish of St Peter's in Shaftesbury, Dorset. I even ended up as a server, or altar boy. A flame of some kind of faith had been lit.

The flame, however, flickered for a few years but then was snuffed out by other teenage preoccupations. I stopped going to church, other than to chapel at school but only because it was compulsory. In my 'gap' year between school and university, aged 18, I went to China to teach English for six months in two schools in Qingdao. One of my students, who became a friend, was a Chinese Christian, but I remember her asking me what I believed and at the time I said that I simply did not know if there was a God. I was never an atheist—I was never prepared to take the step of saying with certainty that God does not exist—but nor was I confident that He did. I took the easy option, the agnostic route, and said I simply didn't know.

In 1993, I started my first year as an undergraduate at Royal Holloway and Bedford New College, University of London. I was reading Modern History and Politics. Some time before the end of my first term, living in the beautiful Founder's Hall modelled on a Loire château, I met three evangelical Christians. They intrigued me. Two of them were particularly zealous and rather eccentric, and my intrigue was probably more from an enjoyment of having interesting debates with them and a harmless and not unkind, but nevertheless hardly pure, mockery of them. I found them so odd that they made me laugh — again, though I laughed at them, it wasn't in a deliberately cruel way, but rather in that somewhat immature way in which young students make fun of each other. The other evangelical Christian was a bit more normal, but still very enthusiastic. I engaged in conversations with them, out of curiosity.

Around the same time, I had become attracted to the College Chapel, more out of a vague appreciation for the music, the tradition and the aesthetics than any deep sense of faith. I started to attend Sunday services regularly. It was an interesting, creative and beautiful exercise in ecumenism, for every Sunday service was conducted by both the Anglican and the Catholic chaplains together, with the two of them alternating the preaching, and with the congregation separating only for Communion: Catholics at one end, Anglicans at the other.

Early in my second term, the journey became a bit more serious. My late-night conversations with my eccentric evangelical friends were leading to deeper thought. They gave me a Bible, and various tracts and books to read. Many of these sat on my shelf unread, but some of them I opened. Then I learned that the Chaplaincy, Anglican and Catholic, together with the Christian Union, were organising a one-week mission on campus, with a well-known Methodist preacher called Dr Donald English. The mission was called 'Making Sense'.

The week-long mission was beautifully and brilliantly structured, engaging both head and heart. Every lunchtime, Donald English would participate in debates with academics on themes such as 'Making

Sense of Christianity and Science', 'Making Sense of Christianity and History', 'Making Sense of Christianity and Politics'; and each evening, he would do a more evangelistic meeting, what I call the 'heart' side, in which there would be testimonies, music and a talk.

I attended almost all of these events, and was inspired and impressed. I planned to go to the last meeting of the week, the grand finale on the Friday night, and some of my Christian friends, who knew I had been to the meetings throughout the week, offered to come over to my room a short time before the event began, so we could walk over together.

At around 6pm, I was feeling exhausted. If I recall correctly, I had probably been out late the night before, drinking in the way students do. I lay down on my bed and decided to pick up the Bible my evangelical friends had given me, but I soon fell asleep.

At 6.45pm, I was awakened by a loud knocking at the door. Bleary-eyed, disoriented and dishevelled, I opened the door. My evangelistic friends were not doing their evangelism very well, for they took one look at me and said: 'Oh Ben, you look exhausted. Perhaps you shouldn't come tonight. Just stay in and have an early night.'

That was precisely what I wanted to do. I didn't really want to go to this Christian meeting anyway. But to my astonishment, while those thoughts were in my mind, out of my mouth came the words: 'No, no, I want to come.' I thought: 'Where did that come from? That's the opposite of what I want to do.' Grumbling to myself, I felt: 'Well, I've said it now, so I'll have to go.'

That night, in early 1994, the Christian faith 'made sense' to me for the first time, and I embraced it. Some converts remember precisely the date of their conversion, even to the hour. I don't, because I don't actually consider the date so important. What mattered was the moment, the act, as the culmination of a process.

Donald English gave a talk, in which he spoke about his childhood desire to play the bugle. The problem was, he never learned. One day, the village band-master called him and told him that the bugler was ill. Would he stand in for him? Young Donald explained that he'd love to, but didn't know how. 'That's ok. Just stand in his position and go through the motions of playing the bugle, but don't actually play — don't let any sound come out. Just pretend,' said the band-master. 'That,' said Donald English, 'is what too many people do with Church. They pretend. They go through the motions, and either no sound comes out, or a fairly ugly sound does. If you're going to do this, do it properly with all your heart. Don't play at Church.'

Those words spoke to me more clearly than any other words that week, or any of the conversations with my evangelical friends, though in a sense it brought together all those previous words with a rousing and stirring crescendo. I realised there and then that I had been 'playing at Church', with a half-hearted seriousness, an appreciation of the beauty within it, but a mocking lack of commitment as well. When Donald English ended the meeting with an invitation to 'give your lives to the Lord', I went forward and prayed the prayer of commitment. I became a Christian, that night in early 1994.

At the end of the meeting, I went to the Anglican chaplain, the Reverend Dr Christopher Cocksworth. He is now the Anglican bishop of Coventry. I told Chris that I had prayed the prayer, that I believed, but I still had many questions. 'What do I do now?'

He smiled. 'Come and have coffee with me on Monday morning.'

For most of the following year, I met with Chris approximately once a week, for coffee and to ask questions. Usually I'd ask him about something I'd read in the Bible, or something I'd heard some Christian say, that didn't make sense or needed further explanation. I recall one of my very first questions, asked rather anxiously, was whether I'd have to give up alcohol. He took me through Christ's first miracle at the wedding of Cana, and St Paul's words to Timothy about taking a little wine for one's health and explained the difference between scriptural teaching on drunkenness and excess, which the Bible warns against, and the enjoyment of wine. I was relieved. The most wonderful characteristic of Chris was that no question for him was too stupid, too pointless, or too inappropriate, but similarly, when there were questions he couldn't answer, he was unafraid to say so. When he felt able to answer a question he'd offer a helpful thought or point me to a passage; when he didn't, he'd admit it. In that way, he helped disciple me and enabled me to grow in my new faith.

Within a month of becoming a Christian, another speaker came to my College Chapel who was to change my life. Baroness Caroline Cox spoke in the Sunday evening service, about the persecution of Christians and the oppression of many other communities in countries such as Sudan, Burma and the tiny war-torn Armenian enclave of Nagorno Karabakh. I had never heard of Nagorno Karabakh, but what she described shocked me. As I listened, I had the most extraordinary sensation. The best way to describe it is that it was as if God was poking me in my ribs with a very sharp instrument. It made me sit bolt upright. I had an overwhelming sense that I could not just hear the words and then walk away. 'Don't just sit there and listen,' said a voice from within. 'Do something.'

I spoke to Baroness Cox afterwards, told her how I felt, and she gave me her card. 'Come and have tea at the House of Lords,' she said. That night, I was filled with a flood of ideas for how to raise awareness on campus for these issues of human rights, religious persecution and the suffering of victims of conflict. I sat down and wrote to her, setting out these ideas. Within a few days, I received a reply saying that I should come and see her soon.

As a result of my conversations with Caroline, I was introduced to Christian Solidarity Worldwide (CSW), the human rights charity of which she was honorary president at the time and is still today patron. I met CSW's national director, Stuart Windsor, at Waterloo station in London. Stuart, an Assemblies-of-God Pentecostal, is a man who, in Caroline's words, has a heart as big as his stomach. At the end of my meeting with him, as we stood in the station concourse, he did something I'd never done before. 'Let's pray,' he said. We bowed our heads and he led us in a prayer. As a new Christian with a combination of English reserve and concern for student reputation, the idea of praying out-loud in the middle of a busy station concourse was uncomfortable to me. It was a moment when my confidence in my young faith was given a boost.

A few weeks later, Caroline called me and said: 'If you're really serious about this, why don't you come with us to Nagorno Karabakh, in August?' Azerbaijan had just signed a ceasefire, she added. So I set off with a baroness, a United States congressman, a nurse, another student and a group of plumbers and electricians going to build a rehabilitation centre for victims of the conflict. The Congressman was Frank Wolf, one of the leading voices for human rights and religious freedom in the United States, and a committed Christian. We flew on a cargo plane laden with humanitarian aid, to Yerevan, Armenia, and then by helicopter to Stepanakert, capital of Nagorno Karabakh.

That visit to Nagorno Karabakh was a key turning point, bringing together in an active way my faith and my growing, burning passion for justice, human rights, freedom and peace. I saw the effects of war for the first time. I visited bombed-out churches and destroyed homes, and met widows and orphans. I heard sporadic gunfire on the frontlines in the distance, even though there was a ceasefire. I almost got married off, ending up dancing with a young lady at an Armenian wedding, only to find her father questioning my companions about my wealth and status. Although amusing, it was in fact no laughing matter—it was a symptom of the fact that most young male Karabakhis had either been killed or were serving on the frontlines, so there was a shortage of young men.

Returning from war-torn Nagorno Karabakh, I knew that I had no choice but to take up a call to be a voice for those who are voiceless, whose suffering is largely ignored by the world.

I returned to university and established a campaign— the 'Appeal for the Forgotten People'—to raise funds and awareness specifically for the work of Baroness Cox and CSW in two places: Nagorno Karabakh, and Sudan.

Meanwhile, I maintained my love of China, travelling during the summer holidays in 1995 to teach English in a hospital in Qingdao. My Chinese Christian friend who had previously asked me what I believed, and to whom I had said I don't know, was delighted to find I knew what I believe. An early conversation with her then, however, set me on a long path of questioning about Catholicism. Walking along the street one day, she asked me what the difference was between Protestantism and Catholicism. Fumbling for a reply, and before I was able to compose one, she then added: 'I think I know.' Pointing at a large Protestant church built by the Germans, in Bavarian architecture, she said: 'That church is for the Prince of Peace.' So far, so good. Then pointing at the Catholic cathedral, she added: 'And that church is for His mother.' Even I knew enough to know that that was not exactly correct—Catholics worship Christ too, and we venerate or honour, rather than worship His mother. But it was an interesting early insight into the misunderstandings between Christian brethren.

After graduating from Royal Holloway, I started a one-year master's degree at the School of Oriental and African Studies (SOAS), in China Studies. In 1997, I was offered my first job, as a journalist in Hong Kong. I immediately asked Caroline Cox, Stuart Windsor and another colleague from CSW if they would pray about whether I should take up this job. I felt very much that I did not want to stop my involvement with CSW.

A few days later, all three came back to me to tell me that they had prayed, they felt I should take the job, and 'by the way, would you start CSW in Hong Kong?' I had my answer, and soon after arriving there in the autumn of 1997, just two months after its handover to China, I began to establish CSW in the territory, in my spare time. It was born in one corner of my small bedroom; today it has an office and two full-time staff.

As part of efforts to establish CSW in Hong Kong, Caroline Cox came out, at my invitation, to do some speaking engagements. While she was with me, we began discussing what areas we might focus on from Hong Kong. She told me she was increasingly concerned about East Timor, a place about which I knew nothing. She asked if perhaps we might look into East Timor from Hong Kong. We discovered, with the help of a foreign correspondent, that there was a large East Timorese presence in Macau, and we were given the details of a Catholic priest from East Timor, Fr Francisco Maria Fernandes, living in exile there. Caroline and I decided to visit him, on her last day.

Do you ever have days when you're trying to do something you think is really important, perhaps for God, and it feels as if the enemy throws every conceivable obstacle in the way to try to stop you? That was how our day in Macau felt. The queue for the ferry was enormous. The queue for immigration in Macau was even longer. We had very limited time. When we finally got through immigration and into a taxi, we told the driver we wanted to go to the cathedral. Caroline, who is proficient in several languages, tried 'catedrale'. The driver understood, or so we thought, but we arrived at the ruins of St Paul's, the famous facade of the old sixteenth-century Jesuit-built cathedral destroyed by fire in a typhoon in 1835. We looked at the facade, and I said, helpfully, 'No, we'd like a whole cathedral'. We then got a tour of virtually every church in Macau, stopping at telephone booths every so often to call Fr Fernandes and receive directions. Finally, we reached the cathedral and Fr Fernandes, but we told him we would have to leave almost immediately, if Caroline was to make it back to Hong Kong in time for her flight to London. We spent a few minutes with him in his office, and then he accompanied us on the bus to the ferry.

That crazy round-the-churches day in Macau in late 1997 sparked several relationships in my heart.

First, a close friendship with Fr Fernandes, or Fr 'Chico' as he was known, and the East Timorese exiles in Macau, whom I visited regularly during the five years I lived in Hong Kong, from 1997 until 2002. Fr Fernandes was the first East Timorese to be exiled from his country, soon after the Indonesian invasion of East Timor in 1975.[4]

Second, a close involvement with the struggle of the East Timorese people, which led me to visit the tiny half-island off the coast of northern Australia many times between 2000 and 2006, and to live there for three months during the transition from UN administration to full independence in 2002. I was privileged to witness the birth of the new nation of Timor-Leste, and to be standing next to Fr Fernandes as the national anthem was sung for the first time and the flag was raised. I will never forget turning to him, my oldest East Timorese friend, whom I had literally bumped into at the independence celebration, and asking: 'Fr Chico, did you ever believe you would live to see this day when your country would be free.' His reply has remained with me ever since. 'Yes, I did. Throughout our struggle, people all over the world said to me "Why do you carry on? You are fighting a losing battle. Indonesia will never give you freedom. The world will never help you. Why don't you just give up?" But we had one thing those people did not know about. We trusted God. This was a victory of faith.' As his words 'victory of faith' echoed around me, the fireworks exploded and lit up the night sky.

Third, working in East Timor I developed close friendships with Catholic friends, perhaps for the first time. I was never anti-Catholic, but until this point I had not particularly had much in-depth exposure to Catholicism. In East Timor, however, I worked closely with an amazing nun, Sister Lourdes, and her Secular Institute of Brothers and Sisters in Christ, where I spent three months in 2002. I had the privilege of meeting the courageous Bishop Carlos Filipe Ximenes Belo, Nobel Peace Prize Laureate, several times. I got to know some wonderful Carmelite Sisters in Dili and Liquica. At the time, I was content to remain an evangelical Anglican, but I was developing a deep respect for the Catholic Church and the brave Catholics of East Timor.

In Hong Kong, I came to know several prominent Catholics who impressed me. Martin Lee, QC, and Christine Loh, both well-known politicians and campaigners for democracy, became supportive of CSW, as did Cardinal Joseph Zen, who inspired me with his forthright and courageous willingness to speak out against injustice and human rights abuses in China.

When I returned to London after five years in Hong Kong, I started to work for CSW full-time, reversing my work priorities so that instead of being employed in journalism and being a human rights activist in my spare time, I would work for CSW full-time, but deploy my journalistic experience to enable me to write about the causes and countries I was campaigning for. For five years, from 2004 to 2009, Pakistan was one of the countries for which I was responsible, and in the course of advocating for religious freedom in Pakistan I worked with two truly heroic Catholics: Group Captain Cecil Chaudhry (Rtd), and Shahbaz Bhatti.

Cecil and Shahbaz became very good friends of mine. Cecil was Shahbaz's mentor. A highly decorated former ace fighter pilot from the Pakistan Air Force, Cecil was a national war hero from the India-Pakistan conflicts. He was someone who should have been promoted to the very top of the armed forces, but his promotion was blocked by the dictator General Zia Ul-Haq, on the grounds that he was a Christian. When he learned this, Cecil resigned on principle, and became one of the country's foremost campaigners for human rights, particularly the rights of religious minorities but also on issues such as women's rights and bonded labour. Cecil died from cancer in 2012.

Shahbaz was a frontline, grassroots activist. He founded the All Pakistan Minorities Alliance (APMA), bringing together all the religious minorities to campaign for religious freedom. We travelled together; we missed a bomb in Islamabad by five minutes; we interviewed a seven-year-old girl, Sharee Komal, who had been raped just because she was a Christian; and we spoke on the phone or by email almost every week, sometimes several times a week, for five years. In 2008, Shahbaz was elected to Parliament, and soon after was appointed Federal Minister for Minorities Affairs. His appointment was a Godsend—the first person to hold that post who would be not simply a token Christian or other minority, but a man of integrity who would genuinely use the position to advance the rights of all the oppressed. But as well as being a Godsend, it was a death sentence. For his brave efforts to introduce reform of the notorious blasphemy laws, on 2 March 2011 Shahbaz was assassinated. His car was ambushed by his assassins, who sprayed it with bullets.

These people, these friends of mine, had long made a profound impact on me. Of course on one level, they were my brothers and sisters in Christ, and I saw the larger body of Christ beyond the Catholic Church and was content to remain in the Church of England, admiring Catholicism and my Catholic friends from across the Tiber. But on a deeper, subconscious level they were drawing me closer to the Catholic faith. Not simply through their courage, for there are a great many Protestant brothers and sisters whose faith and courage inspires too, both those I have known in places of persecution and those in history, such as William Wilberforce, Dietrich Bonhoeffer, Martin Luther King and Archbishop Desmond Tutu. But somehow, somewhere, a deeper, often unconscious, voice was calling me on, speaking through the voices of Fr Chico, Bishop Belo, Sister Lourdes, the Carmelites of East Timor, Cardinal Zen, Cecil and Shahbaz.

In addition to these influences, at the same time I was becoming dissatisfied with the form of worship of evangelical churches. That is not meant in any way as a criticism, and there is much to commend in contemporary, evangelical worship, but I found myself hungry for a style that was more contemplative, reverential and liturgical and I was seeking more of the mystery and majesty of God. I felt a tug towards the Catholic Church which became stronger and stronger. I read some of Pope Benedict XVI's works, and some writings of Thomas Merton and Thomas à Kempis, even before I proactively began exploring the Catholic faith. *Nine Days that Changed the World,* a documentary about Pope John Paul II, which I watched with Lord Alton and Baroness Cox one night in a hotel room in Pyongyang, North Korea, stirred me further. Pope Benedict's visit to the United Kingdom in September 2010 captivated me.

But why Burma?

I became involved in Burma in about 1998, through Christian Solidarity Worldwide, and my interest developed. I first went to the Thailand–Burma border in early 2000, to visit refugees from the Karen and Karenni ethnic nationalities. I was introduced to the situation by my friend Dr Martin Panter, a remark-able British-born doctor who has lived in Australia for over 40 years, who works regularly among the refugees on Burma's borders. We travelled together in 2000 and I subsequently travelled many times across Burma's borders, often illegally, and then started to travel inside, through Rangoon, on a visa. My family became involved six years later, with my mother and sister travelling to the border with me. My sister later brought her string quartet to play in refugee camps and for former political prisoners, and my mother estab-lished a small charity called Support for the Oppressed Peoples of Burma (SOPB).

In 2007, CSW published a new report which I wrote, called *Carrying the Cross: The Military Regime's Cam-paign of Restrictions, Discrimination and Persecution against Christians in Burma*. A few months after the report was published, a Karen nun from Burma who lives in Britain contacted me, saying that the arch-bishop of Rangoon wished to meet me. We arranged to meet at Heathrow airport, just before he flew out.

What struck me most immediately about Archbishop Bo—who became Burma's first cardinal in February 2015—was his quiet, confident courage, combined with wisdom and grace. He is not a rabble-rouser, he hasn't taken to the streets, and his courage could be missed if you're not listening. But it is deep. He told me that when my report was published, the authorities came to him and told him that the Catholic Bishops Conference in Burma had to issue a statement. The government presented him with the text they wished him to use. Knowing that he would have to say some-thing, but determined to assert his independence, he told them that he would make a statement, but that he would draft it. He would not use their draft. The statement that was released was striking in its brilliance. It contained three simple clauses. First, that as Christians, the Church follows the teachings of Jesus Christ. Second, whenever they have problems, they discuss them with the government. And third, the Catholic Church in Burma has no formal relationship with CSW. Who could possibly argue with such a statement? All three points are factual, all three points are good and all three points pose no threat or criticism to the government, but equally do not compromise on truth or undermine our advocacy.

In advocacy, accuracy and doing no harm are two of the most important principles, so I asked Archbishop Bo two vital questions. First, was my report accurate, and second, had it caused the Church more problems? Archbishop Bo could not have been more affirming. He told me my report was completely accurate, and that while in the short-term it might cause some small difficulties, the Church could handle them, and it was important for the world to know the truth.

That was the beginning of my friendship with Archbishop Bo. We met several times on my subsequent visits to Rangoon, when he generously entertained me to dinner and offered beautiful hospitality. And then one evening in March 2011, we had a conversation that changed my life.

As we sat talking over a drink before dinner, I asked whether another Christian leader, a Protestant, was in town. Archbishop Bo said that as far as he knew, he was. He asked whether I wished to meet this person. I said I did, but had not been able to reach him. 'I'll send a note to him now, while you are with me, and ask one of my assistants to take it over to him, letting him know that you're in Rangoon and would like to see him,' said the archbishop. I told him that was extremely kind—

but I asked that he emphasise that I would only want to see this person if he was comfortable meeting me. This was before the new period of relative openness in Burma, when the regime's controls were very tight and fear was pervasive. I recalled that this particular Christian leader had been very nervous when I had met him previously, for understandable reasons. I was a well-known critic of the regime, and had written many articles, produced many reports and given many interviews exposing the dire human rights situation. Furthermore, I had written a biography of the then dictator, *Than Shwe: Unmasking Burma's Tyrant*, published in 2010.

When the archbishop's messenger returned, he was laughing. In fact, it wasn't a laughing matter, but what was striking was how the archbishop and those around him carry their courage so lightly. The messenger said that when the recipient of the note read it, he appeared very nervous. Initially, he said that he was very busy, his schedule was full, and he could not see me. Then he looked around to make sure no one was listening, and whispered: 'Tell Ben I'd love to see him, I wish I could see him, but I am too afraid.' Personally, I fully understand. If I were in his shoes, what would I do? He had been in prison earlier in his life, and didn't want to go back there. But the archbishop laughed. He said: 'Well, I am meeting you. I am having dinner with you. And if the military intelligence came, I would just tell them that you were my friend from London and we were having dinner. So go away. What's the problem?'

Something in my spirit stirred that night. I was so struck by the quiet confidence of the archbishop, in contrast with the fear of the other Christian leader who wouldn't meet me. I say that not in judgment or criticism, but simply as an observation. I then told the

archbishop that I had been thinking of attending the
particular Protestant church on Sunday, but as I did
not want to put that leader in a difficult position if he
was afraid of my presence, perhaps I could attend Sunday Mass instead. His response was remarkable. He
said of course, told me the times, and asked me which
Mass I would come to. I suggested the 5pm Mass, at St
Mary's Cathedral. He told me he would be celebrating
Mass in another parish in the morning, and would
not be celebrating at the cathedral—but that if I was
attending the 5pm, he would come too. I responded
by urging him not to: if he had been visiting parishes
outside Rangoon in the morning, he should rest in the
afternoon and, having already offered me so much
hospitality, he should not even think of coming on my
account. But he graciously shook his head and said no,
if I was going to be attending, he would be there too.

As we continued with dinner and conversation, a
deeper, inner voice—not identifiable, not even clear,
but audible—was prompting me. After dinner, as we
had another drink, I simply asked him a question:
more perhaps out of curiosity, at that stage, than intention. 'If someone who is already a Christian wishes
to become a Catholic, what would they need to do?' I
don't know what I was expecting, but I think I anticipated some long, detailed procedure. Instead, the
archbishop replied with beautiful simplicity: 'When a
person can accept the teachings of the Catholic Church,
he or she is ready to become a Catholic.' But then he
said something I most definitely had not anticipated,
and it opened the doors to an incredible adventure. 'If
you ever find yourself in that position, I would receive
you into the Church in Burma.'

It was unexpected, but it turned my mind from mild
curiosity to active pursuit. It had two effects. First, I

thought what a simply beautiful idea, given my long association with and love for Burma: it would be so symbolic. But second, it isn't by itself a good enough reason to become a Catholic—just because I like one particular archbishop and am committed to a country and its peoples' struggle, that isn't enough. Therefore, I thought, if I want to take this invitation at all seriously, I need to investigate and explore this.

That Sunday, I came for the 5pm Mass. I sat about halfway up the aisle. I looked at the front. I assumed that, as archbishop, he would be seated up at the front beside the altar even if he was not the celebrant. But he was not there and so, I thought, he had after all done the sensible thing and decided to have an evening off.

It was only when I started to walk down the aisle of the cathedral at the end of Mass that I saw him. There he was, a few rows behind where I had been sitting, dressed in a simple white cassock, amongst the congregation. The archbishop among the crowd, the shepherd with his flock. Our eyes met, and he gave me a beaming smile. 'Wait for me outside,' he said.

I did as instructed, and Archbishop Bo came out a few minutes later, embracing the faithful who approached him. 'Have you had a tour of the cathedral?' he asked, as he hugged me. I don't know if anyone had been following me, but if there had been, they would have seen him greet me—yet he showed no fear whatsoever. 'Let me show you around.' He gave me a tour of the beautiful cathedral, and then asked me if I'd come back to his residence for a drink. We continued our conversation about faith, over a glass of whisky, and Archbishop Bo gave me a book of interviews with Pope Benedict XVI, by Peter Seewald, called *Light of the World*. And I embarked on a journey of discovery.

A few days later, on my last night in Rangoon, I finished one of my last meetings of the visit. I then met a friend, a brave Christian Karen, in my hotel. After he left, I was finished for the day. The only appointment left was the most important: my first meeting with Burma's democracy leader, Aung San Suu Kyi, who had been released from house arrest just four months' before. Instead of going to bed, I decided to have a night-cap and listen to the band playing in the hotel bar. I love live music, especially when travelling, and I wanted to unwind for a few moments before going to sleep.

I had just sat down at a table in the bar and ordered a drink when the hotel manager came. 'Are you Mr Rogers?' I said yes. He said the dreaded words that every activist and dissident fears: 'The authorities wish to speak to you.'

The next morning, I was deported from Burma. I did not get to see Aung San Suu Kyi. I was fearful for the friends I had met, including Archbishop Bo. I did not want to draw attention to my deportation, but within an hour or two of arriving in Bangkok I received phone calls and emails from the Burmese exiled media asking me to comment. I asked how they knew, and they simply said they had their sources. I asked for time to think. I checked with some of my closest friends in Burma. They told me they were fine, and what's more, they wanted me to speak to the media. They wanted the world to know that Burma was not changing. Experienced friends advised me that if the media already had the story, I should talk to them, to ensure they report it accurately. So I did. The story is told in more depth in my book *Burma: A Nation at the Crossroads*, in articles I wrote for *The International Herald Tribune*[5] and *Democratic Voice of Burma*,[6] and in interviews I gave.[7]

I thought I would never be able to go back to Burma again. Once deported, I assumed there would be no hope of return. At the time, while very sad, I was resigned to this fact, and thought that I would resume my work with Burma's ethnic nationalities and other exiles along the borders, no longer able to travel to Rangoon but continuing to visit, and cross, the frontier. A few days after my deportation I found myself in Mae La refugee camp on the Thai–Burmese border, hearing an extraordinary choir of Karen refugees giving a beautiful rendition of Handel's *Messiah*. The juxtaposition of the beauty of the music, the surrounding landscape and the people, with the stories of why they had fled their homes in Burma and my own experience of being picked up by military intelligence just a few days before was a living rendition of the Gospel: suffering and joy, pain and beauty, death and life.

I devoured the book Archbishop Bo had given me, *Light of the World*, and fell in love with Pope Benedict. Yes, truly. So much so that when I realised to my horror that I had left the copy of the book on the plane to Mae Sot, I went back to the airline to ask if they had found it. Of course I could have bought another copy, but somehow the fact that this copy was given to me by Archbishop Bo meant so much.

The wonderful thing about the Christian Gospel, though, is that it is the ultimate comeback story. The Crucifixion was not the end of it. There is the Resurrection. There is Easter Sunday. And the same seems to be true with my association with Burma.

I remember not long after my deportation, an evangelical Christian heard what had happened. This woman, whom I did not know personally, told me she felt God was saying to her that I would be back in Burma much sooner than I expected, and that I would meet Aung San Suu Kyi. At the time, I filed this in the back of my mind, not entirely dismissing it, but inclined to think that this woman was perhaps a bit loopy. What did she know?, I thought. Yet I did believe in the God of the seemingly impossible, and I was not prepared to write it off completely.

Towards the end of 2011, Aung San Suu Kyi began a dialogue with the regime, and a series of reforms began. Political prisoners were released, space for civil society increased, progress towards ceasefires with the ethnic nationalities began, and restrictions on the media were lifted. Friends suggested I apply for another visa for Burma. Initially, I said that's ridiculous — I had been deported just a few months before. But my friends, wisely, replied that I had nothing to lose by applying. That was true. And so in December 2011, I applied for a visa — and to my astonishment, it was approved.

During my visit to Burma in January 2012, there were several highlights. Perhaps the two main ones were a meeting with Aung San Suu Kyi, my first; and another evening with Archbishop Bo. In that meeting, he gave me another book: *The Compendium of the Social Doctrine of the Church*. Again, I devoured it.

Aung San Suu Kyi asked me to return as soon as possible after the by-elections on 1 April, to see how the situation had developed, and so I returned in May 2012. On this occasion, I was allowed in by immigration, passed through customs, and literally had one foot in a taxi, when an immigration officer came running out and told me to come back in. As I walked back into the immigration area, I could see, before anyone said a word, that the computer was flashing in big bold letters: 'Black List'. An immigration officer helpfully approached me and, politely, informed me that I was on the black list. I was put back on the plane I had arrived on.

When I reached Bangkok, I had to inform Aung San Suu Kyi's office, as well as the British and US embassies, because I had appointments to see them. I did not request help, I did not seek intervention, I simply informed them. All three decided to raise my case with the authorities. It was so at odds with the supposed 'reforms' taking place in Burma, that they felt it had to be raised. I urged them not to make a fuss about me, but to raise the question of the existence of the 'blacklist' as a whole.

In June 2012, I had the privilege of meeting Aung San Suu Kyi at a reception in the Houses of Parliament after her speech in Westminster Hall. The first thing she said was: 'I am so sorry to hear about your deportation. But I believe you will bounce back. You are like a yo-yo—they throw you out, you come back, they throw you out, you come back!'

Later that summer, I was informed that I was welcome to apply for another visa, and since then I have travelled several times a year without difficulty. In March 2013, my third visit after my second deportation, I arrived in Rangoon, with a particularly personal purpose. In addition to my usual work meeting pro-democracy activists and human rights groups and civil society, I was preparing to be received into the Church. Since that first conversation with Archbishop Bo, my journey of exploration had advanced significantly. I had read the entire *Catechism of the Catholic Church* from start to finish—which, incidentally, had been given to me by my dear friend James Mawdsley, who had been jailed in Burma for pro-democracy protests. I had read the entire *Compendium of the Social Doctrine of the Church*. I had read Pope Benedict XVI's encyclicals and books, and I had read Scott Hahn, George Weigel, Malcolm Muggeridge, G. K. Chesterton, Hans Urs von Balthasar, Henri de Lubac, Jean-Pierre de Caussade, Thomas Merton and many of the great Saints. I had read biographies of Edmund Campion and John Henry Newman. I had had many evenings with Catholic friends, firing questions at them and listening to their replies. I had spent hours with my parish priest, who answered my questions and grounded me in the basic foundations. I attended an 'Evangelium' course as an introduction to Catholicism. I had undertaken an Ignatian retreat at Campion Hall, Oxford. And I was about to become not so much a Roman Catholic as a Burmese one.

Notes

[1]   Although I had been baptised as an infant, in the Church of England, and confirmed as a teenager in the Anglican tradition, both of which are recognised by the Catholic Church, Cardinal Bo decided to give me a 'conditional' baptism.

[2]   Clare Anderson and Joanna Bogle, *John Paul II: Man of Prayer — The Spiritual Life of a Saint* (Leominster, Gracewing, 2014), p. 6.

[3]   There are seven major ethnic nationalities in Burma — Burman or Bamar, Karen, Karenni, Shan, Mon, Rakhine, Chin and Kachin — and many smaller ethnic groups and sub-groups.

[4]   The Guardian, Obituary: Fr Chico Fernandes, 14 October 2005.

[5]   Benedict Rogers, 'Uninvited visitors', *The International Herald Tribune*, 3 April 2011.

[6]   Benedict Rogers, 'Is it a crime to write a book?', *Democratic Voice of Burma*, 7 April 2011.

[7]   'The activist and the uninvited guests', Abhaya: Burma's Fearlessness, 7 April 2011.

✛ **2** ✛

From Retreat to Advance

For it is not knowing much, but realising and relishing
things interiorly, that contents and satisfies the soul.

Annotations, The Spiritual Exercises of
St Ignatius of Loyola

I N MID-DECEMBER 2012, I was at work preparing to
leave for the Christmas break. Several times in the
preceding weeks, I had thought that it would be
good to go on retreat in the New Year, in preparation
for my reception into the Church and my new life as
a Catholic. I had, however, made no plans and got no
further than thinking that it would be a good idea. That
day, Lord Alton and I exchanged emails about other
issues, and in the midst of an email exchange he suggested I consider a retreat, and offered to recommend a
priest. I replied saying that I had indeed had the same
thought, and would like to take up his offer. Within an
hour or two, I was booked in for a five-day Ignatian
retreat at the Jesuit-run Campion Hall, Oxford, with
Fr Nicholas King. After Lord Alton's introduction, Fr
Nicholas replied saying that as it happened, he had
had a cancellation and would be available for precisely
the dates that I was available.

In preparation, I read *Ignatius of Loyola: The Pilgrim
Saint*, an excellent biography by Jose Ignacio Tellechea

Idigoras, and Evelyn Waugh's biography of Edmund Campion. And so, on 2 January 2013, I started my retreat. Just before doing so, I exchanged emails with Colonel Chris Keeble, whose story is told later in this book. Chris and I were arranging to meet for lunch in Oxford at the end of my retreat. In wonderful military language very appropriate for my spiritual journey over the next five days, and especially for Ignatian spirituality, Chris emailed another person in reference to our appointment, saying: 'I will find out what time Ben is ready to advance after his retreat.' The military analogy is appropriate. At times in our lives we need to retreat from the heat of battle, to rearm, procure fresh supplies and more ammunition, and above all consult our commander-in-chief on our strategies. Then, after consulting HQ, we should be ready to advance again. That was how I felt at the end of my five days in Campion Hall, as I returned to the battlefield of life.

I didn't begin the retreat all that well. On New Year's Day, I decided to go to the cinema for the first time in ages. Furthermore, and most unusually, I indulged in the extravagance of watching two films, one directly after the other, and each very different from the other: *The Life of Pi*, which has some moving and amusing religious themes, and the latest James Bond film, *Skyfall*, which doesn't. It was wonderful. I then went home, around midnight, but instead of sensibly going to sleep, I stayed up very late reading a book-length interview with Cardinal Joseph Ratzinger as he then was, called *The Ratzinger Report*, followed by Hans Urs Von Balthasar's *Engagement with God*. Both books were good preparation for the retreat, and one could even argue that the two films were also, but sleep deprivation was clearly not. As a result, I overslept the next morning, and had to apologise to Fr Nicholas for arriving almost an hour late. I blamed Pope Benedict and Von Balthasar, and left 007 out of it.

Many of you will have been on a retreat, but for those who have not, it may be worth introducing the structure, before I then describe the experience.

When I arrived at Campion Hall, I had lunch with Fr Nicholas, followed by a tour. Then we started our first session. I thanked him for making time for this retreat, and said how providential it seemed that his previous retreatant had cancelled. He agreed. 'Where does a 400-pound gorilla sit?' he asked. 'Anywhere it wants to. And it is the same with God. When God says something, there is no argument.'

Fr Nicholas explained that the retreat would be Ignatian—in other words, based on *The Spiritual Exercises* of Saint Ignatius of Loyola. It would also be in silence, apart from one meeting a day with Fr Nicholas in which we would discuss what had gone on and he would give me some suggestions for further contemplation and meditation. He encouraged me to keep the silence, including at meal times. I would be given a table on my own, at the other end of the room from the main table where the community ate, and I was encouraged simply to nod and smile in greeting others in the corridors and avoid getting into conversation. He advised me to spend four 'hours' of contemplative and meditative prayer each day. Each 'hour' did not need to be 60 minutes—but should be a minimum of 20 minutes and no more than 60. In between the hours set aside specifically for prayer, I was encouraged to take regular walks, and to read—but to avoid reading materials that were not directly relevant to a spiritual retreat. I was encouraged to switch off my phone and laptop, and disconnect from the world. I established a discipline whereby I would check my blackberry once in the morning, for just a few moments, and once in the evening, briefly, simply in case of any family emergencies—but I avoided any e-mail or phone contact beyond that. I did not read any newspapers or websites. I was off Facebook and Twitter. For five days, I had no idea what was going on in the world outside— and I did not miss it!

In the four 'hours' each day, Fr Nicholas advised me to use suggested passages from the Holy Bible to reflect on, as a stimulus for prayer, but not to use the time primarily to read. It was to be a time to sit in silence, to talk to God, and most importantly, to listen to Him.

And my first observation, looking back, is this: when we give Him time and space, God speaks. That may sound obvious, but in our busy and noisy daily lives it is easy to forget, or to ignore the 'still small voice of God' as we focus on ourselves and the clamour of the world around us. We need to remember that we are told in 1 Kings 19: 12: 'After the earthquake came a fire, but the Lord was not in the fire. And after the fire came a gentle whisper.' In my normal working life, I start and end each day with a time of prayer, aided by the devotional *Magnificat*[1] which contains a beautiful assortment of hymns, readings, prayers and reflections, and *Bible Alive*,[2] which offers a commentary on the Gospel reading of the day. But these times vary in length, are often rushed, and can feel like I am simply saying 'good morning' and 'good night' to God and little more. On retreat, with nothing to rush to, no phone calls to make or receive or emails to read or write, no appointments, no work, just silence and stillness, God speaks. Not necessarily with thunderbolts or lightning flashes, nor in earthquakes or fire, but with little shooting stars and in that 'still, small voice'.

When one stops to think about it, it is like any relationship. If I see a colleague or a friend or relative, and give them a passing greeting but then rush on, then although we have contact, we have no real communication. It is only when one stops, in a corridor, in the street, at a colleague's desk, taking time with the other person, that a conversation takes place and we can hear the other person's voice. The same is true of God. One of the books I read on retreat was Jean-Pierre de Caussade's *Abandonment to Divine Providence,* in which he writes: 'God still speaks today as he spoke to our fathers.' He lived from 1675 to 1751, but those words are as true now as they were then.

I should explain here that what I experienced on retreat, which I will describe, was deep, private meditation. God speaks through the imagination, in powerful mental images and inaudible words. For the avoidance of doubt or misunderstanding, I make no claim to have had 'visions' of the kind the great mystics received.

In my first session with Fr Nicholas, he gave me two 'exercises' to undertake. The first was to read, prayerfully and reflectively, the 'Annotations' at the beginning of St Ignatius's Spiritual Exercises, and the second was what Fr Nicholas called 'Praying with Pen in Hand'.

'Man is created to praise, reverence and serve God our Lord, and by this means save his soul,' says St Ignatius in the First Principles of his Spiritual Exercises. That is the overarching purpose of life. Too often we forget it, or choose to ignore it, even when we are doing work which 'serves God' — we get so focused on the work, that we forget for whom we are doing it or think we should simply be serving and forget to praise and reverence. Taking a few days on retreat helps to remind one of why we are here.

I read the Annotations walking around a flooded Christ Church Meadow, just across the road from Campion Hall. I was struck by the fifth Annotation, which encourages the reader to enter into the Spiritual Exercises 'with great courage and generosity towards his Creator and Lord, offering Him all his will and liberty, that His Divine Majesty may make use of his person and all he has according to His most Holy will.' I did not necessarily feel that I was being courageous or generous—indeed, it was the generosity of God and of people like Fr Nicholas, and the courage of some of the people who live their faith in places of persecution, oppression and conflict, that was inspiring me in my journey. But perhaps in worldly terms, taking five days out from the world—not to be lotus-eating on a tropical beach or relaxing with friends (both of which can be perfectly good and healthy activities for us all), but instead to spend time in silent prayer and contemplation, trying to be aware that we are in the presence of God—does contain within it an element of 'generosity' (though for me it is based as much on need and desire as generosity) and a degree of 'courage' in opening oneself up to God. And so that was what I intended to do.

And, in my experience it is far from sacrificial. It is an immense privilege. In the twentieth Annotation, St Ignatius names the chief benefits for the retreatant. He writes: 'That being thus isolated, and not having his understanding divided on many things, but concentrating his care on one only, namely, on serving his Creator and benefiting his own soul, he uses with greater freedom his natural powers, in seeking with diligence what he so much desires.' He continues: 'The more our soul finds itself alone and isolated, the more apt it makes itself to approach and to reach its Creator and Lord, and the more it approaches Him, the more it disposes itself to receive graces and gifts from His Divine and Sovereign Goodness.'

As I walked around Christ Church Meadow and reflected on these words, I began to sing in my head and heart two hymns: Blessed John Henry Newman's 'Lead, kindly Light', quoted in the previous chapter, and Garrett Horder's 'Dear Lord and Father of mankind,' an adaptation of John Greenleaf Whittier's poem 'The brewing of soma' to the tune 'Repton', arranged from C. Hubert Parry's *Judith*:

> Dear Lord and Father of mankind,
> Forgive our foolish ways!
> Reclothe us in our rightful mind,
> In purer lives Thy service find,
> In deeper reverence, praise.
>
> In simple trust like theirs who heard
> Beside the Syrian sea
> The gracious calling of the Lord,
> Let us, like them, without a word
> Rise up and follow Thee.
>
> O Sabbath rest by Galilee!
> O calm of hills above,
> Where Jesus knelt to share with Thee
> The silence of eternity
> Interpreted by love!
>
> With that deep hush subduing all
> Our words and works that drown
> The tender whisper of Thy call,
> As noiseless let Thy blessing fall
> As fell Thy manna down.
>
> Drop Thy still dews of quietness,
> Till all our strivings cease;
> Take from our souls the strain and stress,

And let our ordered lives confess
The beauty of Thy peace.

Breathe through the heats of our desire
Thy coolness and Thy balm;
Let sense be dumb, let flesh retire;
Speak through the earthquake, wind, and fire,
O still, small voice of calm.

As these words chimed with my spirit, God did indeed drop His still dews of quietness, removed from me any stress, and began five days of utter, beautiful, deep peace. And as I moved into the second exercise, of 'Praying with Pen in Hand', I had a whole series of images in my mind's eye. Firstly a picture of a long, windy path heading homewards. I was on a journey home. And I was falling in love with God's Church.

I reflected on my journey of faith thus far, from the time I became a Christian in 1994 until this moment on Christ Church Meadow in 2013. I felt God highlighting a number of key themes that have always been central to my faith journey, and always will be: ecumenical unity; a deep appreciation for the breadth, richness and depth of the Body of Christ worldwide; and the importance of people who have influenced me along the way, particularly in key ways, key places at key times. And then, as I continued reflectively along the path and drew towards the end of the first day of retreat, a sense of God saying simply and repeatedly: 'I am here.' On the path, now, there are two figures walking along, not one. Jesus is walking with me. As one of the descriptions of prayer in the *Catechism of the Catholic Church* puts it: 'The wonder of prayer is revealed beside the well where we come seeking water: there Christ meets every human being. It is he who first seeks us and asks us for a drink. Jesus thirsts; his asking arises from the depths of God's desire for us. Whether we realise it or not, prayer is the encounter of God's thirst with ours. God thirsts, that we may thirst for him.'[3]

On the second day, Fr Nicholas suggested I look at the First Principles of the Spiritual Exercises, and pray through them, and then contemplate the theme of 'journeys', through the story of Abram told in Genesis 12: 1–7 and through the disciples in Matthew 10: 1–10 and Jesus in Luke 9: 51–62. In keeping with this theme, I decided to try praying and walking, and so set off on a long walk along the canal in Oxford.

I must admit, this was not easy. My mind easily wandered; I was distracted by boats on the canal; I felt tired. But then I turned off the canal path after a while, and found myself in a part of Oxford which I had not been to before: Jericho. When I returned to my room, I turned to Joshua 5: 13–15 and Joshua 6. Fr Nicholas had referenced the old city walls just outside his room the previous day, and here was the story of the walls of Jericho coming 'tumbling down'. I wondered if God was saying something, perhaps about tearing down the walls that prevent me from drawing closer to Him and His Church.

Although I had found my prayer walk difficult in terms of concentration and contemplation, back in my room I saw an image of two figures walking along the canal. 'I was with you,' God said. 'I am still with you.' When two friends go out for a walk, they don't necessarily engage in ceaseless chatter. There may be periods of silence, as they admire the landscape or enjoy a sunset or listen to the birds. Fr Nicholas confirmed this, and likened it to walking a dog. You let the dog off its lead and it runs ahead of you, maybe even out of sight for a while, turns off here and there to explore: but now and then it returns, to check you are still there and to keep you company. If the dog owner told the dog: 'We did not go for a walk together', the dog would be quite upset. In the same way, walking with Jesus, sometimes we run ahead of Him, or we are diverted down some side-lane, but as long as we continue returning to him, He still walks with us.

Throughout that second day, while I cannot claim to have had a permanent sense of the presence of Christ, it was indeed as if He would come for a few moments, tap me on the shoulder, and say 'Come and look at this'.

As an evangelical Anglican, there were certainly some aspects of Catholic teaching, belief and tradition which were new to me and which required both intellectual and spiritual acceptance. These are, primarily, the doctrine of transubstantiation; the veneration of Mary; the intercessions of the Saints; and the infallibility of the pope. I will explore these in different ways throughout this book, but during this retreat I encountered two of them in a direct, personal way: the Real Presence, and Our Lady.

For the first time in my life, I spent some hours in the chapel at Campion Hall, praying in front of the Blessed Sacrament. Catholics believe in what we call the 'Real Presence' — that Christ is truly present in the Eucharist, which really is His body and blood under the form of bread and wine. For that reason, outside Mass the consecrated hosts are reserved in the tabernacle, and Catholics are encouraged to spend time in Eucharistic adoration: before the Lord, in His presence. As Pope Paul VI put it, as quoted in the Catechism, 'to visit the Blessed Sacrament is . . . a proof of gratitude, an expression of love, and a duty of adoration toward Christ our Lord.'[4]

I had already embraced the Real Presence as a teaching of the Catholic Church. I still did not fully grasp it, still struggled intellectually to see how the bread and the wine become flesh and blood, but I accepted it. Too often we are too willing to reject mystery as precisely that—mysterious—instead of entering into it and letting it draw us further in. But as I sat in the chapel one cold January afternoon, I encountered the Real Presence, in that form, for the first time. As I looked at the flickering lamp beside the tabernacle, indicating the presence of the Lord, I felt that a light was coming out from within it, drawing closer to me, and in so doing, Christ Himself was coming near. It may well have been a trick of light, but whatever it was, the meaning was profound. I was overcome with a profound sense—too profound to be adequately expressed—of the presence of Christ.

I focused on the Stations of the Cross[5] in the chapel, and felt in a new and deeper way the centrality of the Crucifixion and the Resurrection of Christ. Of course, that is—or should be—the case for every Christian, but in the type of work that I do, these pivotal events take on a particularly profound centrality. I prayed the Stations of the Cross, using Fr Nicholas King's superb little book by the same title. I had long been aware of the Stations of the Cross and had admired from a distance this aspect of Catholic spirituality. In East Timor on several occasions I had climbed the steps up to the 'Cristo Rei' (Christ the King) statue overlooking the sea, and had reflected on the Stations of the Cross which marked the journey up the hill. I witnessed the country's resurrection after it had undergone its Calvary. In Burma, I have witnessed the nation's many years on Golgotha, and now see perhaps just some fragile steps towards a new dawn; yet in North Korea, Pakistan and

West Papua, the dark night of crucifixion continues;
the Maldives is re-entering its darkness after a brief,
transitory resurrection of freedom; and in Indonesia,
while there is much to be hopeful about, for religious
minorities more dark nights seem to await as radical
Islamism and religious intolerance rise.

But this was really the first time I had prayed the
Stations earnestly. I sat in the chapel in Campion Hall,
reflecting on the passages which Fr Nicholas suggests,
starting with John 18: 28–38. The words of verse 37
struck me: 'Everyone who is of the Truth listens to
my voice.' Again, I felt an affirmation of my calling,
to 'bear witness' to the truth. In his book, Fr Nicholas
poses a series of questions for us to reflect on, one
of which is in response to Jesus's appearance before
Pilate: 'Whose side are you on?' In my heart, without
a flicker of doubt, I knew the answer: Jesus, and with
Him every dissident, every refugee, every prisoner of
conscience, every person around the world enduring
an unjust trial, every person striving for truth and for
freedom of conscience.

The Stations of the Cross spoke powerfully to me
about Jesus's call to speak out against injustice, and in
so doing, to deny ourselves and take up our cross and
follow Him (Mark 8: 31–6). I felt yet again confirmation of my vocation—not so much to carry the cross,
though that may come in some form, but to help others, my brothers and sisters under persecution, carry
theirs. I read Mark 14: 10–11, John 19: 25–7, Mark 15:
21–4, Matthew 27: 19, Mark 14: 66–72, Luke 23: 27–32,
Mark 14: 50–2, Mark 15: 23–6, Matthew 27: 33–44,
Mark 15: 33–7, Luke 2: 4–7 and Mark 15: 42–6 as I pondered the injustice, the agony, the pain, the weeping,
the betrayal, the courage, the weakness, which such
persecution always involves. And I reflected on the

amazing people I have known—some of whose stories will follow in this book—who have undergone horrific torture, loss, injustice and even in some cases death, or have risked so much to document these horrors in our modern world. They are walking their Stations of the Cross, and Christ walks with them. I know what a privilege it is to walk with them too, and to count them as my friends.

But in addition to speaking to me about the work I am called to in places of persecution and conflict, the Stations of the Cross have something to say for us as Christians, and particularly Catholics, today. This retreat took place during the final months of Benedict XVI's papacy, and therefore preceded the so-called 'Francis Effect,' but even today, it would be fair to say that in the western secular environment in which we live, one is not a Catholic because one seeks popularity. On a host of issues, from abortion to marriage and the family to contraception and euthanasia, the Church is at odds with much of the world. And so perhaps, through the Stations of the Cross, God was saying to me, in preparation for my reception into the Church: 'Take up your cross and follow me.' The words of Luke 10: 3 came to mind: 'I am sending you out as lambs in the midst of wolves.' That night, I had vivid dreams, which I recalled with surprising clarity the following morning. The first was encouraging and affirming; the second was filled with danger.

On the third day, I spent time with Mary. How Mary is viewed is one of the biggest areas of difference, and misunderstanding, between Catholics and Protestants. In my evangelical Anglican days, Mary almost never featured, except in the Nativity story at Christmas. And yet, she is the Mother of Christ. Why do Protestants ignore her?

There is a misperception among some Protestants that Catholics worship Mary. But this is absolutely and completely wrong. Catholics worship only God. We 'venerate' Mary. I looked up the word 'venerate', and it means simply to 'honour'. And I realised that if she is the mother of Christ, it is surely right to honour, respect, and 'hail' her. At school and university and even now, I like to take good friends to my parent's home, to introduce them to my mother and father. In a similar way, surely Christ wants us to know his mother? And it was then that it happened. He tapped me on the shoulder. 'Come, Ben, let me introduce you to my mother.'

For the first time, I understood the 'Hail Mary' prayer. And I discovered, to the surprise of my evangelical mind, that it is straight from the Bible. Read Luke 1: 26–8—where Mary travels to meet Elisabeth, whose unborn child, John the Baptist, 'leapt in her womb' at the sound of Mary's voice. 'Hail Mary, full of grace' is from verse 28; 'Blessed art thou among women, and blessed is the fruit of your womb'—from verse 42. I read Luke 2: 19 and Luke 2: 51, where twice Mary is said to have kept what she heard, 'pondering them in her heart'. I read the Magnificat in Luke 1: 46–56.

In his book *Credo for Today: What Christians Believe*, Pope Benedict XVI comments on this. He writes:

> 'Full of grace' therefore means, once again, that Mary is a wholly open human being, one who has opened herself entirely, one who has placed herself in God's hands boldly, limitlessly and without fear for her own fate. It means that she lives wholly by and in relation to God. She is a listener and a prayer, whose mind and soul are alive to the manifold ways in which the living God quietly calls her. She is one who prays and

stretches forth wholly to meet God; she is therefore a lover, who has the breadth and magnanimity of true love, but who also has its unerring powers of discernment and its readiness to suffer.[6]

Jean-Pierre de Caussade writes similarly in *Abandonment to Divine Providence*:

> Such were the hidden springs of Mary's conduct, for she was of all creation the most utterly submissive to God. Her reply to the angel when she said 'Let it be according to your word' (Luke 1: 38) contained all the mystical theology of our ancestors. Everything was reduced, as it is today, to complete and utter abandonment to God's will under whatever form it is manifested. His beautiful and lofty position of Mary's soul is admirably revealed in those simple words: 'Let it be.'[7]

And so isn't this woman, the mother of Christ and such a radiant example of obedience and devotion to Christ, someone we should honour, and indeed get to know?

I turned to the wedding at Cana in John 2: 1–11, which speaks to me more than Mary's encounter with the shepherds, because I enjoy wine (though I also love roast lamb!) What struck me reading this and reflecting on it was Mary's deference to Jesus—even though He tells her 'My hour has not yet come,' she still tells the servants: 'Do whatever he tells you.' Their interaction seems to be at two levels: a very human one, where he appears slightly irritated with her; and a divine one, where she knows his purposes and helps precipitate the birth of his public ministry. Turning water into wine was, as we read in verse 11, 'the first of Jesus's signs ... He revealed His glory, and His disciples believed in Him.'

This is a very different scene from the previous passage I had read, in Luke 2: 48–50, where Jesus is a young boy—and has gone missing. Mary and Joseph find him in the temple. Unlike Cana, where Mary tells others to do what He says, in the temple she appears to give him a maternal 'telling off,' asking: 'Why have you done this to us? See how worried your father and I have been.'

Watching these two scenes and the interaction between mother and Son, I was reminded of my own mother. Most of the time, she is my mother and exercises maternal instincts either to encourage and support me or, on occasion and where necessary, particularly when I was much younger, to reprimand or rebuke me, asking, with Mary: 'Why have you done this to us? See how worried your father and I have been.' But there is one arena where the dynamic has been different, and that is in Burma. As mentioned earlier, in 2006, my mother and sister came with me for the first time to visit refugees on the Thailand-Burma border, and it changed their lives. My mother returned home dedicated to helping Burma, raised funds, and established a small charity. She travelled to the Thailand-Burma border with me on two subsequent occasions, and once inside Burma. What is quite amusing though is that although she is now very knowledgeable about and committed to Burma, because it is my area of expertise and focus she defers to me, seeks advice and refers people seeking information to me. When we have travelled together, it has been the only time I have been in a position to tell my mother what to do and what not to do, and she has meekly concurred. 'Do whatever he tells you' are words which do not often come from my mother's lips, except in relation to Burma. It was therefore with great interest, and some amusement, that I observed the dynamics between Mary and Jesus.

In the final session of my third day, I pondered the Eucharist again, and reflected on John 6, Mark 14: 22–5 and Matthew 28: 11. I saw a picture of myself standing on the edge of a cliff, and being encouraged by God to jump—in other words, to take a leap of faith. I jumped, I fell, and then I started to fly. Then came the words of Isaiah 40: 31: 'You will fly on wings like eagles, you will run and not grow weary, you will walk and not faint.'[8]

Throughout the day, in between times of contemplative prayer and meditation, I read—a mixture of G. K. Chesterton, Jean-Pierre de Caussade, the Catechism and a book called *Glimpses of the Church Fathers*. On this third day, I read these words from the second century Church Father St Irenaeus's 'With one voice': 'The Church, which is spread throughout the whole world even to the ends of the earth, has received from the Apostles and their disciples that faith in one God, the Father Almighty who made heaven, earth, the sea and all that is in them, and in one Jesus Christ the Son of God, who became incarnate for our salvation, and in the Holy Spirit. Through the prophets, the Holy Spirit preached the designs of God and the advent, the birth from a virgin, the Passion, Resurrection from the dead and bodily Ascension into heaven of our beloved Lord Jesus Christ, as well as His coming in the glory of the Father.'[9] To such a God, how could I not say, with Mary, 'Let it be'[10] and 'Do whatever he tells you'?[11]

On the fourth day, temptation struck and concentration came unstuck. I found it particularly hard to get going in prayer, and I bumped into the world too much. I found myself thinking of various mundane things, such as new clothes that I needed to buy. I have never been keen on shopping, am not particularly materialistic, and have very little interest in my wardrobe. But my need for a new jumper, new shoes and new trousers, to replace the ones that by now had holes in, dominated my thoughts. Unwisely, I thought that perhaps one way to get rid of these thoughts was to pop out to the shops in Oxford, buy what I thought I needed, and then resume my retreat.

With hindsight, I don't think it is a good idea, on retreat, to go shopping. A retreat is precisely what it says—a retreat from the things of this world. Going shopping is an unnecessary distraction and an inappropriate interruption to one's time set aside with God, even if that time seems for a while slow and empty. The best that could be said for my diversion to the shops that morning was that it helped me realise how much I dislike consumerism and materialism. In one of my times of prayer later, I read John 17: 16, where Jesus says of his followers: 'They do not belong to the world any more than I belong to the world.'

I returned from the shops in time for the 12.30 Mass, followed by lunch. Here again, I encountered the world again, albeit in a much more pleasant and worthwhile way, when after Mass a young couple who were visiting were introduced to me. They were told I was on retreat. I was expecting to simply smile and perhaps say a greeting, and then resume my silence. But rather to my surprise, they asked: 'Are you on a silent retreat?' Yes, I told them, whereupon they said 'oh, how interesting' and engaged me in long conversation asking me what I do and how the retreat was going and discovering we had various mutual friends in common. I tried to extricate myself, but it was difficult without being discourteous. In a way, perhaps, this encounter, and my earlier shopping expedition, served a purpose: they helped 'get out of my system' any desire for human contact, and enabled me to return to silence and prayer with renewed vigour. At the same time, they reminded me that we are called to be 'in the world', but not 'of' it. My faith is meant to be engaged with the outside world. And if the morning had been a distraction, God and I made up for lost time in the afternoon.

The Catechism of the Catholic Church,[12] in Article 1 ('At the wellspring of prayer' of Chapter 2 ('The tradition of prayer') of Part 4 ('Christian prayer'), has this to say about prayer:

> The Holy Spirit is the living water 'welling up to eternal life' in the heart that prays. It is he who teaches us to accept it at its source: Christ. Indeed in the Christian life there are several wellsprings where Christ awaits us to enable us to drink of the Holy Spirit.[13]

It continues by emphasising the central importance of frequent reading of Scripture, but emphasises:

> Let them remember, however, that prayer should accompany the reading of Sacred Scripture, so that a dialogue takes place between God and man. For 'we speak to him when we pray; we listen to him when we read the divine oracles.'[14]

We sure do.

The Catechism continues:

> The spiritual writers, paraphrasing Matthew 7: 7, summarise in this way the dispositions of the heart nourished by the word of God in prayer: 'Seek in reading and you will find in meditating; knock in mental prayer and it will be opened to you by contemplation.'[15]

That afternoon, I found myself in the scene of Jesus's washing the disciples' feet, in John 13: 1–17. I recalled washing the feet of some wonderful sisters in East Timor in 2002, along with another young English Christian volunteer. It was a beautiful and humbling experience, of profound significance for us all—and it caught the sisters by surprise, perhaps just as our Lord caught his disciples by surprise.

I identified with Simon Peter, responding to the Lord's 'If I do not wash you, you can have no share in me' with 'well then, Lord, not only my feet, but my hands and my head as well'. Conscious of my need to be washed clean by Jesus, combined with a burning desire to have a share in Jesus, I could understand Simon Peter. Sometimes I was a bit like that in my journey into the Catholic Church—wanting to read, devour, explore everything all at once. Some cradle Catholic friends told me I had read far more widely than anyone who was born into a Catholic family. But I sensed Jesus saying: 'Bit by bit, Ben, piece by piece, step by step.'

I entered the washing of feet scene myself then. Jesus said: 'Ben, come here, I'll wash your feet.' He did, and I was acutely conscious not only of Him washing my feet, but the care He was taking over it, and the fact that he dried the feet with the towel he was wearing. Then someone—not me, though it easily could have been—knocked over the basin of dirty water by accident, and it spread across the floor. I sensed it represented the mess in parts of the Church, the mess we, humankind, have made of the Church, but then a sense of Jesus saying to the Church: 'I love you anyway.' The basin turned into a boat, and my mind turned to the passage of Jesus walking on water. 'Keep your eyes fixed on me, Ben, not on the water,' Jesus said. 'But to follow me, you have to get out of the boat.'

This then took me back to *The Life of Pi*, which I had just seen the night before coming on retreat. I pictured myself in the boat with the animals Pi travels with, on stormy seas: a tiger, a zebra, a hyena, an orang-utan and a rat. I found myself asking which of these I would choose as my companions, and which I would hope might die an early death. I chose the tiger, the zebra and the orang-utan as my companions. The tiger, despite the danger, for its strength and courage; the zebra, for its grace and beauty; the orang-utan, for humour and companionship—characteristics we all need to discover and develop and embrace in the course of a spiritual journey.

The boat arrived at an island. My animal companions faded out of the picture, and I asked the Lord: 'What do you want me to do with this?' Then came one of the most extraordinary moments of the day. The Lord's reply provoked a moment of irritability in me, because it was so ridiculous—and yet it affirmed everything I am already engaged in and therefore my vocation. His words were: 'Liberate it.' In my mind, I thought: 'Oh for goodness sake, Lord. As if Burma, North Korea and all the other places and issues on my plate are not enough, and as if I—little, frail, weak, immensely fallible me—can "liberate" anything. And with what, Lord?' His reply came fast and clear: 'With your voice, with your pen, with your prayers and with your broken heart.' Once again, confirmation of my vocation. I don't know exactly what the island represented, and of course no one would suggest that I alone am meant to, let alone able to, 'liberate' anything, but it was an affirmation of my calling: to do my bit towards helping people liberate themselves, using the few tools, gifts and weapons I have, and to call others to join me in the cause.

That took me into praying for the persecutors, which turned out to be the theme in CSW's Prayer Diary that week. I first recalled the mob of Islamists who had surrounded me as I stood amongst the congregation of a church in Indonesia in May 2012, shouting 'Christians get out, kill the Christians'. Then I pictured China's President Xi Jinping, Burma's President Thein Sein, and North Korea's Kim Jong-Un. What happened next was remarkable. I washed their feet; then they washed each others' feet; and then the feet of their own people, the people of Indonesia, China, Burma and North Korea. One day!

As if this was not exhausting or inspiring enough, I then turned to the 14th chapter of St John's Gospel. In the first verse, it says: 'Do not let your hearts be troubled. You trust in God, trust also in me.' This was followed by these words from the second verse: 'In my Father's house there are many places to live in; otherwise I would have told you. I am going now to prepare a place for you.' Finally, in verse 31: 'Come now, let us go.' Then in a vivid scene, two boys—Jesus and me—stood at the top of a hill. Jesus turned to me in a way a boy does and said: 'Race you.' We ran down the hill towards a huge mansion, a sort of heavenly Downton Abbey, and He got there first. 'Come, let us explore the nooks and crannies together, and see the secret ante-rooms,' He said. We entered the mansion, and went from room to room. Some rooms were bright, clean, well-furnished, comfortable; others were unused, dusty and cobwebbed. 'We have got some spring-cleaning to do,' said Jesus. He took a dustpan and brush and started working, and then handed me a dustpan and brush and said: 'Here, you do some.'

There are two possible interpretations for this spring-cleaning moment, and could be either or both.

Perhaps it represented the state of my heart and life, and Jesus was telling me that there are rooms in my heart which require some cleaning—or it could have represented the Church, which I was preparing to join, but which as Fr Nicholas and indeed Pope Francis confirmed has rooms that are in need of a good scrubbing.

Jesus then took me into the dining room, where there was a wonderful feast, a banquet with amazing food, a roaring fire, music, poetry, followed by dancing. 'Come, Ben, and dance,' he said. 'Lord, I cannot dance at all,' I protested. 'Come,' he beckoned. 'Dance with all your heart. Dance the dance of life.' It was Scottish dancing, and I joined in with gusto.

Then another tap on my shoulder and we were off again. 'Come, let us go'—in the words of John 14: 31—'I have more to show you later.' At that moment it was as if the television lost its signal, or somebody switched it off—the picture was lost, and there was no more in that session.

I turned then to chapters 15, 16 and 17 of the Gospel of St John, and was struck by Jesus's words in chapter 15, verses 12–13: 'This is my commandment: love one another, as I have loved you. No one can have greater love than to lay down his life for his friends.' Again and again the message is repeated, particularly in verse 17: 'My command to you is to love one another.' I found myself asking of the Church: 'So why do we not do this?'

Related to this message of love for one another are the words in John 17: 22–3: 'that they may be one'. If there is one single message, one overriding hope and prayer that should emerge from sharing my story and writing this book, it is that I long for Christians to unite. I have moved from one particular church tradition—an evangelical Anglican church background—into the

Catholic Church, but in so doing I have no desire at all
to further divide Christians. Indeed, my journey has
had the opposite effect: it is strengthened my yearning
for the Body of Christ to unite, to come together, to be
united in its diversity, to be one. I have always been
ecumenical in outlook, and that passion for ecumenical
unity has only deepened. I am Catholic with a capital
'C' now, but I am also deeply catholic in my belief in
the 'universal Church'.

Love is the key to unity: to love God, to love Jesus
Christ and to love one another. To recognise that what
we have in common—Jesus Christ—is far greater than
whatever might divide us. To come to appreciate—
even if not to embrace—that even those theological or
doctrinal teachings which for centuries have divided
Catholics and Protestants actually all come, even in
their divergence, from the same root: a profound love
of Christ. Catholics love Mary not as some heretical distraction from Christ, but precisely and solely because
we love Christ and if we do, we should surely love and
honour his mother. For Catholics, Mary points the way
to Christ—always. Similarly, the papacy and the apostolic succession—we believe in the pope's authority
because he is the successor of St Peter, on whom Christ
chose to build his Church. In the Eucharist, we believe
Christ himself is present. And for Evangelicals, whose
emphasis is particularly on Scripture—the 'Word'—
above all else, this arises from their love for the Word
made flesh, Jesus Christ. When evangelicals gather to
pray, they typically remember the words of Jesus in
Matthew 18: 20—'For when two or three are gathered
in my name, I am there among them.'

More of these thoughts later. But the key is love. And
so what does 'love' look like, I asked? I read the first
letter of St Paul to the Corinthians, chapter 13, verses

4–13. How often I fail, I thought. Patient, kind, never jealous, not boastful or conceited, never rude, never seeking my own advantage, does not take offence or store up grievances, does not rejoice in wrongdoing, finds joy in the truth, is always ready to make allowances, to trust, to hope, to endure, without end. I wish I could say, as Americans like to, 'check, check, check'. But I can't. On most of these criteria I fail miserably regularly, and all of them I have violated at one time or another.

'Our love must be not just words or mere talk, but something active and genuine,' says 1 John 2: 18. I turned then to 1 John 4: 7–21—I won't quote it here, but I urge you to look it up. Taken together with the words of 1 Corinthians 13, it is a description of love which we will never fulfil to perfection but for which we must surely strive.

And then I read John 18 and John 19. Once again, I was taken back to the persecutors. Pontius Pilate is alive and well today, in the form of many governments around the world. Not those such as the regimes in North Korea or Burma which are active persecutors—they are more akin to Herod massacring the innocent babes—but those which are faced with angry extremists shouting, as they did against Jesus, 'Crucify him'. In countries like Pakistan and Indonesia, where extremists use charges of blasphemy against Christians and others and in most cases it is not the State that is leading the charge. Often the State says, as Pilate said, 'I find no case against him'—but faced with an angry mob, they fear the zealots, the extremists, the religious police, and in the end they go along with them. I was struck by Pilate's decision to write 'Jesus the Nazarene, King of the Jews' on the cross, and the exchange with the chief priests who say, 'You should not write "King of the Jews", but that the man said "I am the King of the Jews"'. Pilate stood his ground: 'What I have written, I have written' (John 19: 19–22). Perhaps Pilate's one moment of courage?

I read through the rest of John 19. And at a certain point, I saw Mary, the mother of Jesus, standing near the cross. Then I found I was in the picture too, and Jesus looked down at me from his agony and said: 'Ben, are you prepared to come all the way with me?' Am I? Do I have my limits? How far would I go for Christ? For all of us, these are tough questions and ones which remain unanswered until the time when we are put to the test.

Then Jesus looked at me again and said: 'There is more that you can do, Ben.' It may be unlikely that I am ever called to suffer physical persecution, but I know that I am indeed called to help others carry their cross—and to take risks in the process. Being deported, missing a bomb by a few minutes, being surrounded by a mob of Islamists screaming 'Christians get out, kill the Christians', or fleeing the Chinese police are nothing compared to what many in the world today endure, but they amount to a small taste, a tiny sip, a droplet of wine from the same cup: and it is a privilege to be drawn into such moments. I thought of my friends who think I already work too much, who talk about 'work–life balance' and I then looked at Jesus who smiled and said: 'Remind them what I did.' I do not find the words 'work-life balance' in the Bible. Of course, Jesus went into the mountains to pray; Jesus took time out; and we should too. A balance needs to be struck between work, prayer and rest. The Benedictine motto of 'Ora et Labora'—pray and work—is absolutely right. But Jesus looked at me from the cross and said: 'There is more that you can do, Ben.'

At that point an image of ocean waves, rolling gently, came to mind and with the waves came three thoughts: a sense of deep, deep peace, of the sort that the calm sound of gentle waves often inspires; a sense of cleansing, being washed by the waves; and Jesus saying 'Take this message, this message of love, across the seas'. In John 15: 16 Jesus says: 'I commissioned you to go out and bear fruit, fruit that will last.'

This whole experience seemed like a divine power-point presentation, with a mix of photographs, audio and video. And in the power-point, there was real *power* to each *point* and a clear *point* to the *power*. To anyone who questions the merits of prayer, read Tertullian, who lived approximately from AD 155 to 240. He writes in 'The effectiveness of prayer':

> How much more is wrought by Christian prayer! It does not cause an angel of dew to appear in the midst of fire, nor does it stop the mouth of lions nor take the breakfast of country folk to the hungry; it does not destroy all sense of pain by the grace that is conferred. But by patient endurance it teaches those who suffer, those who are sensitive, and those who have sorrow. By virtue it increases grace that our faith may know what comes from the Lord and understand what it suffers for the name of God … The prayer of justice averts the wrath of God, is on the alert for enemies, and intercedes for persecutors … It likewise remits sins, repels temptations, stamps out persecution, consoles the fainthearted, delights the courageous, brings travellers safely home, calms the waves, stuns robbers, feeds the poor, directs the rich, raises up the fallen, sustains the falling, and supports those who are on their feet. Prayer is the wall of faith, our shield and weapons against the foe who studies us from all

sides. Hence, let us never set forth unarmed. Let
us be mindful of our guard-duty by day and our
vigil by night. Beneath the arms of prayer let us
guard the standard of our general, and let us pray
as we await the bugle call of the angel.[16]

Or as the Catechism, in paragraph 2658, puts it:

Love is the source of prayer; whoever draws from
it reaches the summit of prayer. In the words of
the Curé of Ars: 'I love you, O my God, and my
only desire is to love you until the last breath
of my life. I love you, O my infinitely lovable
God, and I would rather die loving you, than
live without loving you. I love you, Lord, and the
only grace I ask is to love you eternally ... My
God, if my tongue cannot say in every moment
that I love you, I want my heart to repeat it to
you as often as I draw breath.'

As I ended the fourth day of my retreat, a day in which
the theme was love—God's for us, ours for Him, and
ours for each other—there was no better image to sum
it all up than the picture which hangs on the wall of
the dining room in Cardinal Bo's residence in Rangoon: the image of the cross, with these words: 'I asked
Jesus "How much do you love me?" "This much," he
answered, then he stretched out his arms and died.'

The Catechism was instrumental in my journey into
the Church. I had been given a copy of the full Catechism by my friend James Mawdsley several years previously, long before I had even considered exploring
the possibility of becoming Catholic. Apart from very
occasional perusal, it had sat on a shelf gathering dust
for some years. But when I began my active journey
of exploration, I read it, from start to finish, through
the course of a year.

The Catechism's section on prayer is beautiful—and I don't think that it was any coincidence that I had reached the sections on prayer at exactly the time I was on retreat. Chapter Two of the final section of the Catechism, on 'Christian Prayer', is titled 'The Life of Prayer' and it begins:

> Prayer is the life of the new heart. It ought to animate us at every moment. But we tend to forget him who is our life and our all. This is why the Fathers of the spiritual life in the Deuteronomic and prophetic traditions insist that prayer is a remembrance of God often awakened by the memory of the heart: 'We must remember God more often than we draw breath.'[17]

It continues:

> Through his Word, God speaks to man. By words, mental or vocal, our prayer takes flesh. Yet it is most important that the heart should be present to him to whom we are speaking in prayer: 'Whether or not our prayer is heard depends not on the number of words, but on the fervour of our souls.'[18]

The Catechism provides a superb explanation of meditation and contemplative prayer which I would recommend reading in full.[19] Some lines that particularly struck me include:

> To meditate on what we read helps us to make it our own by confronting it with ourselves. Here, another book is opened: the book of life. We pass from thoughts to reality. To the extent that we are humble and faithful, we discover in meditation the movements that stir the heart and we are able to discern them. It is a question of acting

truthfully in order to come into the light: 'Lord, what do you want me to do?'[20]

Meditation, the Catechism says, 'engages thought, imagination, emotion, and desire' in order 'to deepen our convictions of faith, prompt the conversion of our heart, and strengthen our will to follow Christ'. Above all, it tries to 'meditate on the mysteries of Christ', with the aim of leading to 'the knowledge of the love of the Lord Jesus, to union with him'.[21]

Contemplative prayer, as described by St Teresa of Avila, is 'nothing else than a close sharing between friends; it means taking time frequently to be alone with him who we know loves us.' The Catechism says that 'we let our masks fall and turn our hearts back to the Lord who loves us, so as to hand ourselves over to him as an offering to be purified and transformed'.[22] It is 'a *gaze* of faith, fixed on Jesus. "I look at him and he looks at me": this is what a certain peasant of Ars in the time of his holy Curé used to say'.[23]

That is very much what happened during my retreat.

On the penultimate day of the retreat, I read about Mary Magdalene at the empty tomb, in John 20: 11–18. I identified with Mary Magdalene. After all the horrendous agony and excruciating pain and grief of Jesus's torture and death, now this: they have taken his body away. Of all the indignities, they couldn't even allow the decency of leaving his tomb undisturbed. I could imagine Mary's grief. I could imagine the grief of the families of dissidents, religious and political prisoners of conscience, who are executed or die as a result of torture or mistreatment in prison in China, Burma, North Korea ... and often the families are not told the truth, or they are not allowed to bury the body, or they have to pay for the bullet used to execute their loved one, or the body is 'disappeared' and the death denied or blamed on natural causes. Mary Magdalene understands how such families would be feeling.

I remember, as a teenager, going to visit some family friends when, halfway through lunch, a very scruffy old man ambled up to the table, with holes in his jumper and dirt on his trousers and looking exceptionally unkempt. It was summertime, we were eating outside, and he had appeared from somewhere in the large garden. I thought to myself at the time: 'How nice that they invite their gardener for lunch.' Luckily I didn't say anything, as 'the gardener' turned out to be the wife's elderly stepfather, a very wealthy man, certainly a millionaire, probably a multi-millionaire—just as Mary Magdalene mistakenly thought Jesus was the gardener near the empty tomb, but He turned out to be the man who contains the richness and truth of life.

Reflecting on that scene, suddenly Jesus said to me: 'Here I am.' Then he said: 'I am in fact the gardener. I am the gardener of your soul—planting, watering, growing, so that you may blossom.' Then he took me to another garden, the Garden of Eden, and said: 'Ben, if you keep following me, you will keep bearing fruit.'

Meditating on the Resurrection, I saw a bright sunrise slowly dawning, and the words of the song 'See what a morning' came to mind. If you don't know it, do find it on YouTube—it is well worth listening to. The final lines remind us: 'And we are raised with Him, death is dead, love has won, Christ has conquered. And we shall reign with Him, for He lives: Christ is risen from the dead.' I reflected on the birth of East Timor, and the words of Fr Fernandes, mentioned in the previous and the next chapter. I also reflected on the first glimmers of possible resurrection in Burma.

I then attended Mass, in the Oxford University Catholic Chaplaincy, and had a beautiful experience. In the homily, the priest referred to a text message he received from the Salesians, the religious order founded by St John Bosco, with a thought for the day: 'Give, without remembering; receive, without forgetting.' It is a good motto to live by. When we prayed 'Kyrie Eleison, Christe Eleison' ('Lord have mercy, Christ have mercy'), I felt something special, a tingle, the presence of the Holy Spirit. The words of the 'Kyrie Eleison' stayed with me for the rest of the day, often echoing in my head, as a prayer for the world. And when the Solemn Blessing for Epiphany was prayed at the end — 'May God, who has called you out of darkness into his wonderful light, pour out in kindness his blessing upon you and make your hearts firm in faith, hope and charity. Amen' — I saw a picture of a path or beam of light, a bit like that created by a spotlight or a torch in the darkness, and I was standing in that beam.

In the afternoon, I walked the road to Emmaus (Luke 24: 13–35). I walked from Campion Hall, along the Cherwell river, to Iffley Lock and on to Littlemore, where John Henry Newman lived for four years of his life and where he was received into the Catholic Church, having been an Anglican clergyman. I felt that my entire retreat had been my own road to Emmaus, and as I contemplated the passage, I was reminded of the number of times in the past few days that I had seen the image of a journey, two people walking along a path. I felt that, while I was by no means discovering Jesus for the first time, as I had been following Him, or trying to, for 19 years, I was discovering Him afresh. I had a picture of Him sitting down on the grass with me, beside the river. Jesus opened a book, which was the Scriptures, just as He explained the Scriptures to the two on the road to

Emmaus. But then He opened another book, and said it was the book of my life. And then, He said something which was both profound and amusing, and put me in my place, though lovingly, almost with a sense of fun: 'You think you're an author, eh Ben? Well, I'm the real author. Can you write a better book than me?'

As I approached Iffley Lock, I noticed that the river changed from being very slow and gentle, to being very very fast-flowing. I sensed God saying to me: 'Get ready to re-enter the world.' Later on, again He said: 'I am preparing you to re-enter the world.' On this, my last full day of retreat, I felt He was helping me to transition back into the rapid pace of the world, especially the world I live and work in, after several days of being still and silent in the gentle streams of the living water of His presence.

Visiting Littlemore was profoundly moving. I finally got there, and discovered to my disappointment that on Sundays at that time of year, one can only visit with an appointment. But I telephoned and a sister answered. I explained I was on retreat, had walked to Littlemore, and asked was there any chance I could visit? With a very kind and warm tone of understanding, she said: 'I will make an exception. Come to the main entrance and I will open the door.'

She was an Austrian sister, and she gave me a brief but beautiful tour of the library and the chapel. She told me the story of the night Fr Dominic Barberi came to Newman's home, heard his first confession, and received him into the Catholic Church. I saw the handwritten copy, framed on the wall, of his famous hymn, 'Lead, kindly Light'. She told me how painful his own conversion from the Church of England to the Catholic Church had been—how he had lost friends, even family, who never spoke to him again, and how many

Catholics had viewed him with suspicion and mistrust. I reflected on how fortunate I am, to have so many friends who have been so supportive and encouraging of my making a similar journey. Some wonderful Catholic friends who have helped me along the way; some wonderful friends from other Christian traditions, who have understood, and indeed even encouraged me, on this path; and even those friends who may have reservations or questions, or disagreed with my decision, but who would not abandon a friendship simply because of my becoming a Catholic.

I also thought how I have often had a sympathy for defectors — those who genuinely change because they see something true and beautiful that moves them. I think of some Burma Army defectors; former North Korean officials; former Islamists whom I have had the privilege of knowing: people who have the courage to follow their heart and their conscience in the direction it calls them, even if it means leaving a group they have been part of for a long time and been comfortable in, and even if it means entering something new, unknown or unfamiliar, they deserve my respect and support. And it is a journey, in some way, I was about to make myself.

I felt very blessed to visit Blessed John Henry Newman's home; very blessed that the sister opened it up for me, and gave up her time to show me around, to explain key parts of the story to me, and to engage for a few minutes of conversation about my own journey.

As I walked back some of the way, and then took a bus the rest of the way, happy and full of joy and peace, the words of a song came to mind: 'Be still and know that I am God; I am the Lord that leadeth thee; In thee O Lord do I put my trust.'

In the evening, I had the immense privilege of meeting Fr Gerard W. Hughes (Gerry Hughes), author of

God of Surprises, an amazing book which I had read some years ago. I had not known he was a member of the community at Campion Hall, until I happened to glance at the list of the community and saw his name. I asked Fr Nicholas, and he kindly introduced us, and after supper on my final evening, I had about half an hour talking to him in his room. He has worked very ecumenically over the years, with Christians of all denominations and with people of other religions and none, and said that what is most important for us as Christians is to focus on 'the essentials', not on what divides us. People are leaving the Church—of all denominations—because they perceive it as a body caught up in rules and regulations, or battles between people who want power and control, he said. That is the antithesis of Jesus's message, and so we need to return to living Jesus's message. He said that the amazing thing about the Gospel, if it is truly lived, is that 'it works'! He gave me a copy of another book he has written, called *Oh God Why?*

I spent the rest of my final evening finishing reading the Catechism. It seemed no coincidence that I should complete my reading of the entire Catechism on the final night of my retreat. It seemed no coincidence that I should do so in the 'Year of Faith'. And it was certainly no coincidence that I should do so in the year I would be received into the Catholic Church.

On the day when I visited Newman's home and after five days where I have been putting Newman's words 'Heart speaks unto Heart' into action, I read in the Catechism the wonderful words from Psalm 42:7—'Deep calls to deep'. During this five-day retreat, deep certainly called to deep and heart spoke unto heart. My soul leaped when I read the reflections on the Lord's Prayer in the Catechism, in particular these words:

in spite of the divisions among Christians, this prayer to 'our' Father remains our common patrimony and an urgent summons for all baptised. In communion by faith in Christ and by Baptism, they ought to join in Jesus's prayer for the unity of his disciples.[24]

It concludes that 'if we are to say' the Lord's Prayer 'truthfully, our divisions and oppositions have to be overcome'.[25]

Similarly, in the reflection on 'forgive us our trespasses', the Catechism notes:

Now—and this is daunting—this outpouring of mercy cannot penetrate our hearts as long as we have not forgiven those who have trespassed against us. Love, like the Body of Christ, is indivisible; we cannot love the God we cannot see if we do not love the brother or sister we do see. In refusing to forgive our brothers and sisters, our hearts are closed and their hardness makes them impervious to the Father's merciful love; but in confessing our sins, our hearts are opened to his grace.[26]

As I prepared to re-enter the world, I took with me the words attributed to St Ignatius of Loyola, the amazing man whose Spiritual Exercises and whose followers in the Society of Jesus which he founded have allowed Christ himself to speak to me: 'pray as if everything depended on God and work as if everything depended on you'. And Jesus looks on and says with a smile: 'There is more you can do, Ben. Get back to work, to the battlefield.'

I began my final morning by reading from Tobit and Ecclesiasticus, two of the books of the Old Testament which Catholic Bibles contain and Protestant versions do not. These—and the other five books of Wisdom, Judith, Baruch and 1 and 2 Maccabees—are wonderful. I once asked my parish priest why Catholics have seven extra books in the Old Testament, and he suggested the question could be put the other way round: why do Protestants have seven fewer? I thought that was a good point.

I then read, reflected and prayed. I read Origen's words on prayer from his *Treatise on Prayer*:[27]

> When speaking about praying, it is very useful to keep oneself in the presence of God and to speak with him as one converses with a friend who is physically present. Just as images which are stored in the memory give rise to thoughts when those figures are thought about in the mind, so too we believe that it is useful to recall God present in the soul. He controls all our movements, even the slightest ones, when we are willing to show gratitude to the one we know to be present with us, to this God who examines the heart and scrutinises the thoughts ... The person who in the fulfilment of his duties unites them to his prayer, and his prayer to his deeds, prays without ceasing; for virtuous actions and the fulfilment of the precepts become part of prayer. We then come to realise that the precept 'pray without ceasing' can only be fulfilled if we are able to say that the life of a person is a great continuous prayer.

That linkage between prayer and action was to come through strongly during the rest of the morning as I prepared to re-join the world. But I was also struck by these words of Origen: 'The one who tries to concentrate during the prayer and puts all his effort into listening ends up hearing: "I am here."' I was struck by this, because it was those words 'I am here' that came through regularly throughout the retreat.

The third and fourth verses of the Christmas carol 'It came upon the midnight clear' came to mind:

> Yet with the woes of sin and strife
> The world has suffered long;
> Beneath the angel-strain have rolled
> Two thousand years of wrong;
> And man at war with man hears not
> The love-song which they bring:
> O hush the noise, ye men of strife,
> And hear the angels sing.

> For lo! The days are hastening on
> By prophet bards foretold
> When, with the ever-circling years
> Comes round the age of gold.
> When peace shall over all the earth
> Its ancient splendours fling.
> And the whole world give back the song
> Which now the angels sing.

During these five days, I was blessed and privileged to be in a place where I could 'hush the noise,' or rather the noise was hushed for me, and I could hear the love song sung by the angels clearly and with striking beauty and harmony and even, with my own very poor and unharmonious voice, join in with them.

Then I moved into the final time of reflection which Fr Nicholas had suggested for me—reading the *Contemplation of Divine Love*, at the end of the fourth week of the Spiritual Exercises of St Ignatius. Fr Nicholas had said that as one leaves a retreat, having been through the Passion and the Resurrection of Christ, one ought to aim to re-enter the world with love. I was struck by Ignatius's words — 'Love ought to be put more in deeds than words' — once again that repeated message of linking prayer, love, and action. He also emphasises 'love consists in interchange between the two parties' — and that, I thought, is true both of the exchange between a person and God, and between people.

As I read and reflected and prayed and meditated, I felt immense and enormous gratitude. I had a picture of a beautiful waterfall, with a pool at the bottom in which I was swimming. I prayed St Ignatius's prayer: 'Take, Lord, and receive all my liberty, my memory, my intellect, and all my will — all that I have and possess. Thou gavest it to me: to Thee, Lord, I return it! All is Thine, dispose of it according to Thy will. Give me Thy love and grace, for this is enough for me.'

The hymn 'Love divine' came to mind. Then the words of Timothy Dudley-Smith's hymn 'Lord for the years', which were in the back of my Bible among a collection of other hymns and songs, and these verses in particular:

> Lord, for the years your love has kept and
>   guided
> Urged and inspired us, cheered us on our way;
> Sought us and saved us, pardoned and
>   provided;
> Lord of the years, we bring our thanks today.
>
> Lord, for ourselves, in living power re-make us,
> Self on the cross and Christ upon the throne
> Past put behind us, for the future take us:
> Lord of our lives, to live for Christ alone.

And finally, as I read the words of the following wonderful hymn, unexpectedly I began to weep. The tears came specifically during the third, fourth and fifth verses.

They were tears of gratitude, tears of commitment, tears of amazement, tears of love, tears of joy, as well as tears of commitment and grief for the world and for those I believe God has long called me to serve, a calling He has reaffirmed during this retreat:

> Brother, sister, let me serve you,
> Let me be as Christ to you;
> Pray that I may have the grace to
> Let you be my servant too.
>
> We are pilgrims on a journey
> And companions on the road;
> We are here to help each other
> Walk the mile and bear the load.
>
> I will hold the Christ-light for you
> In the night-time of your fear;
> I will hold my hand out to you,
> Speak the peace you long to hear.
>
> I will weep when you are weeping;
> When you laugh I'll laugh with you;
> I will share your joy and sorrow
> Till we've seen this journey through.
>
> When we sing to God in heaven
> We shall find such harmony
> Born of all we've known together
> Of Christ's love and agony.
>
> Brother, sister, let me serve you
> Let me be as Christ to you;
> Pray that I may have the grace to
> Let you be my servant too.

That emphasis on partnership—that we who try to stand alongside those who are suffering learn from them and receive so much more from them than we can give, as we seek to give—has always been at the centre of my experience in the work I do. As I continue to try to hold the Christ-light in dark places around the world, I am conscious that I do it together with the very brave, courageous and inspiring people who are risking their lives in those places day after day. And I am conscious of Mother Teresa's wonderful words: 'I can do things you cannot, you can do things I cannot; together we can do great things.' It was also interesting that once again, the imagery of a journey is in this hymn—'pilgrims on a journey, and companions on the road'. These five days were a journey in themselves, and a significant part of a longer journey, and I was privileged and blessed to have so much time with Jesus as my companion.

I ended my retreat with a few minutes' prayer in the old chapel. I understood the point of the holy water at the entrance to the chapel perhaps for the first time, and felt entirely comfortable dipping my finger into the font and then making the sign of the cross and genuflecting—it felt natural and normal to me; then as I looked at the Blessed Sacrament, I sensed Jesus saying to me: 'Go now. You are ready.' I prayed prayers of gratitude for the past few days; I prayed for my loved ones, including close friends who are sick; I prayed particularly for the Kachin people of Burma at this time, that I might be able to hold the Christ-light for them; I prayed for CSW and all our work; and I prayed a prayer dedicating myself to walk with Christ along the path He has for me in the world outside. And with that, I paid the bill, gathered my luggage and coat, and slipped out quietly to rejoin the world. To answer the question posed in that email from Colonel Chris Keeble, I had completed the retreat, and was ready to advance.

Notes

[1]   *Magnificat* is a monthly devotional, with prayers, hymns and the readings for each day, as well as the liturgy for Holy Mass.

[2]   Published by Alive Publishing.

[3]   *The Catechism of the Catholic Church*, paragraph 2560.

[4]   *The Catechism of the Catholic Church*, paragraph 1418.

[5]   A series of images depicting Jesus Christ on the day of his crucifixion, displayed in every Catholic church in the world, and a form of contemplative prayer.

[6]   Pope Benedict XVI, *Credo for Today: What Christians Believe* (San Francisco, Ignatius Press, 2009), p. 60.

[7]   Jean-Pierre de Caussade, *Abandonment to Divine Providence* (Notre Dame, Ave Maria Press, 2010), p. 3.

[8]   Isaiah 40: 31.

[9]   Claire Russell, *Glimpses of the Church Fathers*: St Irenaeus, 'With one voice' (London, Scepter, 1996), p. 1.

[10] Luke 1: 38.

[11] John 2: 5.

[12] *The Catechism of the Catholic Church* — http://www.vatican.va/ archive/ENG0015/_INDEX.HTM

[13] *Ibid.*, paragraph 2652.

[14] *Ibid.*, paragraph 2653.

[15] *Ibid.*, paragraph 2654.

[16] *Glimpses of the Church Fathers*: Tertullian, 'The effectiveness of prayer', p. 9.

[17] *The Catechism of the Catholic Church*, paragraph 2697.

[18] *Ibid.*, paragraph 2700.

[19] *Ibid.*, paragraphs 2705–19.

[20] *Ibid.*, paragraph 2706.

[21] *Ibid.*, paragraph 2708.

[22] *Ibid.*, paragraph 2711.

[23] *Ibid.*, paragraph 2715.

[24] *Ibid.*, paragraph 2791.

[25] *Ibid.*, paragraph 2792.

[26] *Ibid.*, paragraph 2840.

[27] *Glimpses of the Church Fathers*: Origen, 'When it's time to pray', pp. 9–82.

✢ 3 ✢

The Saints and Martyrs

Do not be afraid.

John Paul II

THE PREVIOUS TWO CHAPTERS, together with the final chapter and Epilogue, capture the most personal elements of my journey into the Catholic Church. Now it is time to shift focus, to what is really the heart of this book: the people who inspired me in this spiritual journey. Many of them are living saints, exuding an inspiring and infectious faith in action in some of the world's most dangerous and repressive places. Some of them have become martyrs. Two were people I never met but simply heard about: Cardinal Francis Xavier Nguyen Van Thuan of Vietnam, who spent many years in prison; and Seoul's Cardinal Stephen Kim Sou-hwan, who defied the military dictatorship at the time in South Korea and provided shelter in the Myeongdong Cathedral to student demonstrators in 1987. When the police and the army were on their way to the cathedral to arrest the students, the cardinal lined up the priests, and behind them the nuns, to protect the students. He stood in front of the rows of priests and nuns and told the security forces when they arrived: 'You can take the students, but first you have to take me, then you have to take all the priests, and then all the nuns, and

if you do that you can take the students.' The security
forces backed down, and not long afterwards the dictatorship ended and South Korea became the vibrant
democracy that it is today. Cardinal Kim is my kind of
cardinal, and I remembered this as I celebrated Easter
in the Myeongdong Cathedral in 2015.

But the heroes of faith whose stories are told in this
chapter are all people whom it has been my privilege
to know in person, to work with, to be able to call my
friends.

East Timor

Let us turn first to one of the world's newest, smallest
and poorest nations—East Timor or 'Timor-Leste' as
it is now officially known. For 24 years, East Timor—a
Portuguese colony for four hundred years—suffered
a brutal and repressive occupation by the Indonesian
military, which had invaded the tiny half-island on 7
December 1975. During the invasion and the subsequent
occupation, thousands were slaughtered, and thousands more raped and tortured. The bodies of many
victims were dumped into the sea. Tens of thousands
were displaced, and faced starvation. In total, at least a
quarter of the population died as a result of the Indonesian occupation. 'We are dying as a people and as a
nation,' wrote the Catholic bishop of Dili, Carlos Filipe
Ximenes Belo, in a letter to the UN Secretary-General
in 1989.[1] He never received a reply.

In 1999, however, the situation dramatically
changed. Following the fall of Indonesia's dictator
Suharto the previous year, in the wake of the Asian
financial crisis, his successor B. J. Habibie decided
to try to resolve the East Timor question once and

for all. Throughout the 24 years of occupation, the United Nations had refused to recognise Indonesian sovereignty in East Timor. Numerous UN resolutions called for Indonesia's withdrawal, though no action was taken to enforce these resolutions. In 1991, world opinion was galvanised by the slaughter in cold blood of over 200 peaceful, unarmed demonstrators who marched from the Motael Church in Dili to the Santa Cruz cemetery to lay flowers on the grave of a young man, Sebastião Gomes, who had been shot dead by the Indonesian army the previous week. In 1996, Bishop Belo and the exiled East Timorese spokesman José Ramos-Horta were awarded the Nobel Peace Prize. Faced with mounting diplomatic pressure, Indonesia's Foreign Minister Ali Alatas called East Timor a 'pebble in the shoe' of Indonesia. President Habibie wanted to be rid of the irritating stone, by resolving the question of sovereignty in a referendum.

I first became involved with East Timor while living in Hong Kong, where I got to know East Timorese refugees in Macau. The first East Timorese I ever met was Fr Francisco Maria Fernandes, or 'Padre Chico', who had been the first of his people to be exiled from his homeland in 1975. I have described my first encounter with Fr Chico in Chapter 1, but over the course of two years, between 1997 and 1999, I got to know him and other compatriots of his in Macau well, travelling from Hong Kong regularly to visit them and learn more about their struggle.

When President Habibie first announced the referendum, the world was stunned — and for a brief moment there was a sense of hope. However, the Indonesian military was determined once again to terrorise the people of East Timor into submission, and quickly formed militia gangs, armed, funded and controlled

by the Indonesians, to unleash a campaign of violence
and intimidation and create a climate of fear.

On 6 April 1999—four months before the referendum—Indonesian military and their militia surrounded the Catholic church in Liquiça, where hundreds of people from neighbouring villages had taken
refuge, having previously been driven out of their
homes. They had thought that the church would be
the one place of sanctuary.

I visited Liquiça nine months after the massacre. I
met the priest, Fr Rafael dos Santos. He described how
a soldier had tried to shoot at him, though mercifully
the gun had jammed and failed to fire. He also told
me how soldiers had thrown tear-gas into the church.
As the people came running out, they opened fire,
killing indiscriminately. People hiding in the roof of
Fr Rafael's house were also shot dead. The soldiers,
knowing people were in the roof, simply fired round
after round into the ceiling, until the blood dripped
through and the screaming stopped. Those who survived were forced to settle in the fields, under the menacing watchful eyes of the military and militia. It was
wet season, and the people had no shelter, no food
and no medicine.

Such violence continued right up until the referendum on 30 August. Despite this, 98 per cent of those
eligible to vote turned out to do so. When the result
was announced on 4 September, an overwhelming
78.5 per cent chose independence from Indonesia,
as opposed to the other option, special autonomy
within Indonesia.

For a few brief hours, there was euphoria. I spent
the day the results were announced with the East
Timorese in Macau, and I shared in their joy and
relief—and disbelief—that after 24 years of seem-

ingly impossible struggle and desperate suffering, their country was now free. A celebration dinner, to be hosted by the Governor of Macau, was planned for three days later.

The following day, the dinner was cancelled. It was no longer a time for celebration—indeed, it was now a time of deep tragedy and mourning. Within hours of the announcement of the results, the Indonesian military and the militia responded with an orgy of violence even more ferocious than the pre-referendum campaign of terror. Thousands were murdered, raped, maimed; 80 per cent of the buildings were looted, pillaged and burned, and the entire electricity grid was destroyed; women and children were slaughtered. Their attitude was that if Indonesia could not have East Timor any longer, they would destroy everything so that there would be nothing left for an independent nation. An Indonesian soldier scrawled graffiti on a wall with this message: 'You can have your independence, but you will eat stones.'

I watched these events through the media with increasing horror. I organised a demonstration in Hong Kong, joined by Fr Chico and the East Timorese from Macau as well as local churches and civil society. We delivered a letter to the Indonesian consulate protesting at the violence. We held a press conference in the Foreign Correspondents Club. We held prayer vigils. But the crisis seemed unstoppable. The international community was not willing to intervene unless Indonesia would accept an international peace-keeping force—something that, given Indonesia's track record up to this point, seemed impossible.

After eight days of killing, rape and destruction, I was on my knees in prayer on Sunday, 12 September 1999, when my telephone rang. Slowly I rose from my knees and answered it. 'Ben,' said a friend. 'I just thought you might like to know that the Indonesian President Habibie has agreed to allow an international peace-keeping force into East Timor. It is on the news now.'

Within seconds, joy and relief replaced the despera-tion and despair I had been feeling. Within seconds, the East Timorese people who had been facing carnage on a genocidal scale were given a breath of life. President Habibie had come under sustained pressure from the United States, Australia, the European Union, the UN and others, with the threat of financial sanctions and the cancellation of loans, and in the end he overruled his military and conceded. On 15 September, the UN Security Council authorised an international peace-keeping force, to be led by Australia, and five days later the International Force for East Timor (INTERFET) began its deployment. Indonesia withdrew, a United Nations transitional government was established, and three years later, on 20 May 2002, East Timor became an independent nation.

Just over three months after the arrival of INTERFET, I visited East Timor for the first time. Within half an hour of my arrival in Dili, I heard first-hand the horrors of what had gone before.

'My mother — dead,' said the 15-year-old street boy standing before me. His name was Amil. He drew his index finger down his stomach and demonstrated the action of pulling out his intestines. 'My mother with baby — both dead,' he said in broken English, as his eyes filled with tears.

'My father dead too,' he continued, indicating a thrusting movement of a spear going through his stomach. 'And my big brother too,' he explained. His brother's attackers had burned both sides of his face with cigarette butts and hacked off his arms and legs with machetes. Amil had witnessed these atrocities with his own eyes. And he was not unusual.

At the heart of East Timor's struggle, during the occupation and in the bloodbath in 1999, was the Catholic Church. Catholicism was brought to East Timor by the Portuguese, but in fact it was the Indonesian brutality that drove many East Timorese into the Church. Prior to the invasion in 1975, only 30 per cent of the population was Catholic. But Indonesia's dictator Suharto required the population to abide by Indonesia's philosophy of 'Pancasila,' which compels all citizens to adopt one of the recognised religions — Islam, Buddhism, Hinduism, Confucianism, Protestantism and Catholicism. The East Timorese were never going to accept Islam, the majority religion of their invader, and so they opted for Catholicism as a symbol of resistance.

Throughout the struggle, there were many Catholic priests, nuns and lay people whose faith inspired them to extraordinarily heroic deeds. One such person was Fr Domingos Soares, known as 'Father Maubere,' who served on the Commission for Reception, Truth and Reconciliation during East Timor's transition.

I met Fr Domingos in his beautiful parish in the mountains, in a village called Lete-foho. He spoke of reconciliation, forgiveness and peace. But he added that reconciliation cannot happen without the perpetrators of violence acknowledging their crimes. 'There is no way for reconciliation without justice,' he said. 'Even with the Cross, there is justice — Jesus paid the price. There must be confession, apology, dialogue.'

Another priest, Fr Jovito Araujo, who chaired the truth and reconciliation commission, agreed that justice and reconciliation go hand in hand. 'Some people say forget the past, yet it is something which sounds beautiful but is not easy to do,' he said. The Church must instead help victims forgive their attackers. 'If we talk about reconciliation, it is a theological expression, it is the language of the Church. The whole pastoral care of the Church is about reconciliation—how to live in peace, live in harmony, how to bring them to a better way to understand the Christian faith.'

Fr Domingos, who received the Pax Christi award in 1997, told me that in the months leading up to the referendum, the Indonesian military warned people: 'If you choose autonomy, there will be a little blood; if you choose independence, blood will run like rivers.' Others told me that the militia had said: 'You can have your land, but it will be a land of widows.' In Ermera district alone, there were believed to be 3,000 widows. Still others recalled being told that if they voted for independence, 'only the birds will sing'.

According to Fr Domingos, the militia had been recruited by the Indonesian army from among criminal elements in East Timor, paid 100,000 rupiah a day (approximately £5 at today's exchange rate), and were often supplied with ecstasy and other drugs, and alcohol. The military also went to many villages and forced village leaders to provide a certain number of young men to join the militia.

But like many in East Timor, Fr Domingos also displays remarkable grace. 'If we have not got hope, we cannot do anything. This is the land God gave us.'

The Church's robust commitment to seeking justice for its people in East Timor was led most visibly by Bishop Belo. Appointed as apostolic administrator and bishop of Dili in 1983, Carlos Filipe Ximenes Belo was at first believed to be more conciliatory towards Indonesian rule. His predecessor, Dom Martinho da Costa Lopes, who became the first East Timorese bishop in

1977, had made the Church realise it could not stay silent in the face of the barbaric violations of human rights by the Indonesian military. He began to make appeals to the international community, and became so troublesome that Indonesia requested the Vatican to remove him. Unfortunately the Vatican, concerned about the interests of Catholics in Indonesia, played *realpolitik* and complied. Bishop da Costa Lopes went into exile in Portugal, and was replaced by Carlos Belo. But Bishop Belo, suspected by his own priests of being Jakarta's plant in Dili, found he too could not remain silent.

According to the Australian Bishop Hilton Deakin, a long-time activist for East Timor, the turning point for Bishop Belo was a visit to an area of the country that had just experienced a dreadful massacre. 'When he went there, there were no villages where there were villages, there were no people where there had been hundreds of people,' Bishop Deakin told me. 'He suddenly started walking up a hill and saw a foot sticking out of the ground. He saw pieces of people strewn around. He said he became quite ill. While he wanted to concede as much goodwill as he could to the Indonesians, this was when it changed.'

Six years after becoming bishop, Carlos Belo wrote the letter to the UN Secretary-General mentioned earlier. Bishop Deakin believes that letter was the making of Bishop Belo. 'It put him on a different level. After a great deal of cold shouldering and rejection even from church bodies, people began then to listen to him in different ways.' His leadership of the Church became 'extraordinarily significant' in the cause of justice. 'All the years I have seen him, his door was always open to people who had problems,' Bishop Deakin observes.

Under Indonesian rule, the use of Portuguese and the native language, Tetun, were banned in schools and work places. East Timorese were required to speak Bahasa Indonesia. But one of Bishop Belo's most important contributions to the struggle was his decision to hold all Masses and other religious and liturgical occasions in Tetun. 'That preserved a cultural place for the things the Indonesians wanted to destroy—they had banned it in the schools and everywhere else, and so he said they would not ban it in the churches,' notes Bishop Deakin. 'Tetun then began to be seen not just as a garbage-guts language, but people began to take it seriously as a cultural artefact. Various groups wrote books and grammars and translated church books and the Bible. That was the beginning of the Church identifying itself with the culture that was being destroyed.'

During the bloodshed in 1999, Bishop Belo's own life was endangered. Hundreds of people had found refuge in the grounds of his sea-front residence, but just outside the gates the militia roared around on motorbikes and in trucks, terrorising the neighbourhood. Then, on 6 September, two days after the referendum result, the militia went in and began their slaughter. They set the house alight.

Bishop Belo faced a terrible choice—to stay with his people and probably be killed, or to flee and have the opportunity to tell the world what was happening. He chose the latter course, but with reluctance. When he arrived in Darwin, Australia, he received a telephone call from Bishop Deakin. 'Bishop Belo was basically pushed out of East Timor,' Bishop Deakin recalls. 'He was advised to go because he was a danger to anybody who was found to be in his company: they were out to get him. It was traumatic.' But while devastated, Bishop Belo stayed strong. 'He had got to Darwin, and

I rang him up there. I thought I was going to ring a broken man but I didn't—he was not broken. He was shattered but he still had it in him.'

The attack on Bishop Belo's house was not a surprise. One week before the attack, Bishop Deakin was with Bishop Belo in Dili, and he says the bishop knew what might come. 'He showed me a document which was a report from senior military commanders to the army headquarters in Denpasar, Bali, of what to do not 'if' but 'when' the withdrawal took place after the referendum,' says Bishop Deakin. 'The people who wrote the document were convinced that the Indonesians were going to be rejected at the referendum and rejected mightily. They talked about 75 per cent. It was 78.5 per cent, so they were pretty close. The document described exactly every step that was to be taken, including the burning of this house. He had actually shown it to the Australian Foreign Minister—but he had just pushed it back.'

I had the privilege of meeting Bishop Belo in East Timor several times during the transition. His courage and robust defence of human rights inspired me deeply. And interestingly, he had one other thing in common with two other bishops who later proved to be my inspiration—Cardinal Zen in Hong Kong and Cardinal Bo in Burma: they were all Salesians, the religious order founded by St John Bosco in 1859.

In awarding the Nobel Peace Prize to Bishop Belo and José Ramos-Horta in 1996, the Chairman of the Norwegian Nobel Committee, Francis Sejersted, said this of the bishop: 'Again and again, in the midst of everyday terror and suffering, he has intervened, trying to reconcile and mediate and lessen confrontation, and in doing so he has saved many lives. Intervening in a violent conflict entails a risk of being crushed between the antagonists. "Pray for me, please," he said in one such situation, "because now I have to defend myself on both sides." But Bishop Belo has become much more than a mediator: this man of peace has also become a rallying point for his sorely tried people, a representative of their hope for a better future. The love his people feel for this mediator springs from certain fundamental principles he has adhered to. Show the people respect. Give them freedom to develop their humanity to the full. Then ask them whether they want to be Indonesians, Portuguese, or independent. Bishop Belo shares with his people the insight of the oppressed, an insight deeper than that of generals or oppressors. Why all this brutality? It does not even serve its purpose. You do not gain respect if you do not show respect.'[2]

In his acceptance speech, Bishop Belo said:

> What reasons brought the Catholic bishop of East Timor to be here in the presence of this assembly? ... Taking the words from Terentius: 'Homo sum; humani nihil a me alienum puto' —(Terentius 1, 1,25). As a man, as a human being, I cannot stay indifferent in front of what concerns man. As a member of a people, I have to share the destiny of the people, taking upon myself completely this mandate, knowing the risks that such an attitude will involve. Striving for the defence of the rights of all people is not only the privilege of those guiding the destiny of the people or those enjoying lofty positions in society, but it is the duty of everyone whatever rank or status.
>
> The Catholic bishop is a pastor of a part of God's people. His specific mission is spiritual. Such a mission is incumbent upon him basically as a dispenser of spiritual resources for the salvation of persons and consolidating them in

faith in Jesus Christ. But mankind is not limited to a spiritual dimension, one should be saved as a whole, human and spiritual. In this aspect, any Catholic bishop shall never be indifferent when a people's possibilities for human realisation, in all dimensions, are not respected.

So the Nobel Peace Prize, attributed to a Catholic bishop, is not a homage for one person but also basically the gratitude for the encouragement that the Catholic Church has developed over the centuries in defence and promotion of the rights of human beings.

It is known to your excellencies, the efforts of the Church concerning the suffering of the people of East Timor over the last twenty-one years. As bishop of this people, I regard the Nobel Peace Prize not as something to merely esteem one person but as the rightful homage for the work done by the Catholic Church in East Timor, defending the inalienable rights of her people.

I do believe for sure that among us we have something in common, that is we affirm that the human being is the subject of all concept and human activities. We declare that one's value and dignity does not depend on the individual's belief, religion, politics, philosophy, race or colour of skin.

Man is a being for freedom. It means that one's realisation is complete when capable to decide about one's options and taking responsibility for his or her actions without any kind of intimidation. Man is a being realised in a community. It means that the social and ethnic group one belongs to is the background for his or her fulfilment. Man is a being realised when there is a reciprocity of respect. It means that wherever human beings are not respected in their elementary rights by those in charge or by those responsible in society, as a consequence, we have oppression, slavery, arrogance, arbitrariness, death of individuals and death of a people. I am profoundly honoured to be before you today to receive the Nobel prize for peace. But whatever personal compliment I may receive, I believe that I have received this high tribute not because of who I am or what I have done. I firmly believe that I am here essentially as the voice of the voiceless people of East Timor who are with me today in spirit, if not in person. And what the people want is peace, an end to violence and the respect for their human rights. It is my fervent hope that the 1996 Nobel prize for peace will advance these goals.[3]

Interestingly, he also referred to Burma's struggle:

I salute the strength and grace of Aung San Suu Kyi, and pray that a better day may soon arrive for her and all her people. May the beauty of music from her piano soften the hearts of armies and nations. In Burma and throughout the world in places known and not well known, let us apply the words in the fifth chapter of Amos of the Old Testament: 'Let Justice roll down like waters.'

The faith of lay Catholic activists during the struggle was also profoundly significant. Gregório da Cunha Saldanha and Francisco Miranda Branco spent years in prison for their involvement in planning and leading the Santa Cruz demonstration in 1991. In a letter to a CSW supporter in the United Kingdom, sent from his prison cell, Francisco shared his faith. 'I beg you to pray for me and my family, in order that God the Almighty [will] always ... grant me spiritual and phys-ical health in the prosecution of this long walk, and embrace with deep love the Cross of Hope ... We are all one in Christ ... I feel the force which upholds me,

it is this: the prayers of my people and the words of
the Lord in the sacred scriptures ... My brother, God
is very kind and just, and he loves us, you and me who
believe in Him ... My brother, we can never feel angry
and upset at God when we suffer, because behind all
the suffering He has a beautiful surprise for us.' To be
able to write such words from the darkness of a prison
cell is remarkable.

In the late 1980s and early 1990s, several democracy
uprisings occurred in Asia: in 1987 in South Korea,
1988 in Burma, 1989 in China and 1991 in East Timor.
Only South Korea's demonstrations led to a transition
to democracy; in the other three, the protests were
violently suppressed. Santa Cruz was for East Timor
what Tiananmen Square was for China.

It all started with a Portuguese parliamentary delegation which was due to visit East Timor. Students were
preparing to meet them, to demonstrate with banners
and present petitions urging them to do something to
stop the human rights violations in their land. It was
a unique opportunity, the first of its kind since 1975.

The Portuguese, however, cancelled the visit, after
the Indonesians blacklisted some of the journalists
accompanying the delegation, and left the students
dangerously exposed. The students took refuge in the
Motael Church, on the seafront in Dili. But late at night
on 28 October 1991 military vehicles circled the church
and when one young man, Sebastião Gomes, came out
onto the steps of the church he was shot dead. A week
later, hundreds gathered at the church for his funeral,
and then marched to the cemetery to lay flowers on his
grave. As they walked, they unfurled banners calling
for independence, peace, an end to oppression. When
they reached the Santa Cruz cemetery, they were surrounded, hemmed in by units of the Indonesian army,

who opened fire. Constancio Pinto, who was present at the scene, estimates that at least 271 people were killed.

Gregorio was shot and rushed to hospital. But in the hospital, the police caught up with him and he was arrested. During his interrogation, he was subjected to various forms of torture. Police took a chair and repeatedly thrust it down on his feet, crushing his toes.

Gregorio was sentenced to life imprisonment, and Francisco to 15 years. The sentences had been pre-determined. After sentencing Gregorio for life, the judge — an East Timorese — came down from his seat, weeping. 'You are a Christian, I am a Christian. I did not want to do this, but I had no choice,' he told Gregorio.

Like Francisco, Gregorio's faith sustained him in jail. 'I trusted God. No one else could help me except God,' he said. He and Francisco prayed together and studied the Bible regularly.

Sister Maria Lourdes Martins da Cruz, or 'Mana Lou' as she is known, made perhaps the most profound impression on me. She could be described as East Timor's Mother Teresa.

Born in 1962, Sister Lourdes's personal faith began when she was just four years old. Her father, a coffee farmer, told her the story of the birth of Christ, of how there had been no room for Mary and Joseph at the inn in Bethlehem, of how Jesus had been born in a stable. When she heard the story, the little girl was outraged at such injustice, and went to prepare her own bedroom to receive the Son of God.

From that moment on, Mana Lou knew Christ's presence in her life. At school many of her friends had boyfriends and girlfriends, but she told them that Jesus was her lover. They laughed at her. 'Jesus does not come and kiss you, or visit you,' they scoffed. 'Of course He does,' she replied. 'He is with me all the time.' Their love was temporal, she said, but the love she received from Him is eternal.

As a teenager, Mana Lou discovered her vocation to religious life, and spent her school holidays accompanying priests in their work. At the age of 13 she entered a Canossian convent, with the intention of joining the order. Two years later, she befriended some foreign missionaries and began working with them. When she was 17, she worked with the parish priest in Liquiça, and helped prepare 10,000 people to receive the sacraments in Liquiça, Maubara and Bazartete. This attracted the attention of the then bishop, Dom Martinho da Costa Lopes, who could see she was a very special person.

In pursuing her vocation, Mana Lou spent time in more than ten different convents, including Dominican and Canossian congregations, but found it very difficult to discern which order she should join. She could not settle in one. The bishop encouraged her to study at a Jesuit Institute in Yogyakarta, Java, and it was there that her specific calling became clear. She studied catechism and pastoral care, as well as social and political issues, which provided the theory to complement the practical experiences she had had. Mana Lou's passion for integrating faith with life was shaped by this period of study, and she wrote her master's thesis on community development.

It was one day in 1985, when Mana Lou was 23, that her specific vision became clear. The suffering of her people in East Timor had upset her profoundly, and she was praying almost all the time. At a retreat with 78 other students, the priest showed some slides. One of the pictures was an image of Jesus Christ on the cross, the crown of thorns on His head. Then she heard a voice: 'I am suffering, What will you do for me? Why do you spend all your time inside the convent? I do not live only in the convent, I live out there with the poor, with the people in the mountains far from the town, especially in places where there are no priests, no pastoral companionship. I need you to follow me there. I need your help.'

Mana Lou fell down, unconscious. When she came round, she shared the vision with the priest, who told her that she must do what God had commanded. She returned to Dili, and gave Bishop Belo a copy of her thesis. He was delighted, telling her that most people talk about the problems, but she had focused on solutions. He told her he was on her side, but warned she would face criticism from some people. He suggested she go to Baucau, the country's second major town on the north coast, for three years to put her ideas into practice and so in 1989 she moved there, where she led retreats and started her outreach to the poor. But within a year, she decided it was time to return to Dili, the capital further along the north coast.

In August 1989, Mana Lou gathered together a group of 13 girls in a house belonging to her family in Bairro-Pite, a neighbourhood of Dili. The following year, after returning from Baucau, she and her friends established the 'Simpatissantes Instituto Secular', otherwise known as 'Poor People Together'. Three years later, the name was changed to 'the Secular Institute of Brothers and Sisters in Christ' to reflect their explicitly Christian calling. In the Catholic Church, a 'secular institute' is an organisation of individuals who are consecrated and live in community – professing the vows of chastity, poverty and obedience – but focus on working in the wider, secular world, unlike members of a religious institute.

In 1992, Mana Lou's father gave her some land in his coffee plantation in the hills above Dare, 45 minutes' drive out of Dili, and she and 16 other women excavated the land to construct the Institute's Centre of Formation, or Mother House. Just as Bishop Belo had warned, the new Institute attracted criticism. The members wear secular clothes, which provoked grumblings from some clergy. The construction at Dare was criticised by some local civil society groups, who told her she was irresponsible to be leading a group of young women with no money. Mana Lou, however, was confident of her calling, and would not be distracted. As the fruits of her ministry became known, her critics fell silent, and in 1998 the Church formally recognised the Institute. Today she is regularly invited to teach in seminaries, lead retreats, prepare catechists, teach liturgy, and share her principles in parishes around the country. In Hatu-Beilico, at the base of Mount Ramelau, for example, the Institute's sisters lead the church because there is no parish priest. A priest comes occasionally to consecrate the Eucharist, but otherwise the sisters lead the regular liturgies and provide pastoral care for the parishioners.

The Secular Institute of Brothers and Sisters in Christ is founded on four simple principles: 'solidarity, fraternity, simplicity and happiness'. Much like any religious congregation, the Institute has a constitution, and a process for becoming a member. Before someone is accepted as a candidate, Mana Lou interviews them and then sends them out to work in the districts with the Institute's members for a month, to test their heart for the poor. Then they return to the mother house in Dare for a year, doing basic work in the kitchens to test their humility. After the first year, each subsequent year is divided into three-month periods: three months in

Dare studying, followed by three months in one of the Institute's other nine houses, which include a centre for non-formal education for local people in Aileu, an educational centre for children in Viqueque, a school in Loes, an educational centre in Betano, a retreat centre in the mountains in Hatu-Beilico, a sick house in Kuluhun in Dili, modelled on Mother Teresa's principles of care for the terminally ill, and a house in Bairro Pite in Dili associated with the Bairro Pite Clinic. After four years, candidates take their perpetual vows of poverty, chastity and obedience.

Mana Lou's teaching focuses on a combination of spirituality, based on sacred scripture, reflection and contemplative prayer, with practical skills: community development, child care, primary healthcare, handicrafts, construction, agriculture, psychology, church leadership, organising prayer groups, teaching the liturgy and catechism. Mana Lou adapts and develops the curriculum as she goes along, and it is flexible and responsive to the needs and the political, social and economic climate in East Timor. The timetable is also flexible, enabling members to change plans to respond to an urgent need. She encourages members to find their specific calling for the poor, whether it is working with the sick, the elderly, children or youth, and to develop their individual gifts within the community. The Institute also focuses on women's empowerment, and advocacy for the poor.

In addition to members, there are also what Mana Lou calls 'animators', who live with the community and share in the life and work of the Institute but do not take vows and are free to marry. And there are 'collaborators', people who continue with their own lives and jobs but support and help Mana Lou and the Institute when they can.

The impact which Mana Lou and her Institute have had on East Timor has been extraordinary. During the Indonesian occupation and the violence in 1999, they played a crucial role. For many years, the Indonesian military stationed a watch-post outside the Mother House in Dare, believing Mana Lou was a dangerous subversive who needed to be kept under surveillance. She was followed wherever she went.

Mana Lou, however, has a remarkable gift to touch hearts and change attitudes, and the Indonesian soldiers assigned to monitor her were moved by what they saw. She befriended them, and they started to help: they built a road to her house, provided tables and chairs for the classroom of the orphanage that she runs, and even started to teach the children, though she insisted they remove their military uniforms to do so. Whenever she had a party, the Indonesian soldiers did the cooking, and when they left East Timor they told her if she ever wanted to start a work for the poor in Java, they would help her. While deeply committed to her people, she did not work for one side or the other during the Indonesian occupation—she saw the brokenness and hurt in all people, Timorese and Indonesian, and wanted to show Christ's love to them.

She did, however, experience occasional difficulties with the soldiers. There was one soldier who regularly wandered into the Institute naked, making lewd remarks and threatening the sisters. On one occasion Mana Lou was having an afternoon nap, when the sisters came to wake her for help. She came out to face a completely naked soldier.

'Can I help you?', she asked calmly but firmly.

'Why do your girls not marry? Why do they not have sex?', he asked.

Mana Lou explained to this soldier, a Muslim, that the sisters had chosen a celibate life in order to serve Christ and the poor. He failed to comprehend. 'How can you survive without sex?', he asked. Her response was typical of her sharp mind. 'Are you married?', she asked. He said he was. 'Then why are you so worried about sex? It seems that you who are married are more concerned about missing sex than we who have chosen to be celibate.' She then took the naked man back to his unit, and shared the Gospel with him. A male villager saw the scene and was horrified. 'How dare you sit naked in front of Mana Lou,' he shouted. Poised for a fight, Mana Lou had to restrain him. 'We are just having a little chat,' she assured the villager. 'It is okay. Everything is in order.'

On occasions, Mana Lou witnessed the brutality of military discipline: beatings and water torture. She suggested to the officers that if they had to discipline their men, why not send them to her Institute, where they could help dig the land, excavate the garden and build the road.

But she knew only too well how the military treated her own people too. At the time of the invasion in 1975, her family had to flee into the forest, where they lived for several months. She recalled a time when, as a teenager, Indonesian soldiers came to her family home and demanded that she be given as a 'wife' for the troops. Indonesian soldiers came on one occasion and stole her father's whole harvest of coffee. And she knew many stories of torture. One man who had been captured by the military, she told me, was tied to a tree by his genitals, tortured and beaten, made to dig his own grave and shot dead.

In 1999, Mana Lou put her life on the line every day to try to help people displaced by the violence. After the Liquiça massacre, Fr Rafael and other village leaders fled, traumatised, but when she heard about the crisis, Mana Lou decided to go to help. She arranged food to be distributed, and went to pray with and comfort the people.

The militia allowed her to stay in Liquiça for several months, but they always accompanied her and monitored her to ensure she did not distribute pro-independence propaganda. She restricted her speech to spiritual and religious topics. According to Dr Daniel Murphy, an American doctor who works closely with her, her ability to soften the hearts of the militia was extraordinary. At militia roadblocks she would get out of her car to speak to the armed men, who would often be pointing their weapons directly at her. 'Within minutes, she would have them laughing with her, then crying with her, and then on their knees praying with her,' he recalls.

But there came a day when the militia decided to kill Mana Lou. When she heard of this, she confronted them directly. 'I know you want to kill me. Why?', she asked. They told her they believed she worked with the United Nations Assistance Mission to East Timor (UNAMET), which was organising the referendum. The following day, the militia launched an attack on UNAMET personnel, surrounding them on a beach.

Miraculous interventions were commonplace in Mana Lou's work. Just as the militia had the UNAMET staff surrounded, the skies opened and it began to pour with rain. The militia dispersed. Mana Lou believes that if there had been no rain, the UNAMET staff would have been killed.

When the violence escalated after the referendum result was announced, and Dili was on fire, an estimated 15,000 people fled the capital into the hills and

forests around Mana Lou's Institute near Dare. When
I first met Mana Lou just over three months later, she
told me that she and the members of the Institute
fed and cared for them. 'All 15,000?', I asked incred-
ulously. She nodded. 'How did you feed them?', I
asked naively.

Mana Lou laughed and looked as if I had asked a
silly question. 'God worked a miracle,' she explained.
'Of course we did not have enough food for 15,000,
but each morning I woke up very early, I prayed, and I
started cooking rice. The barrel of rice was not enough
to feed many, but as I cooked and prayed, the rice just
kept coming out of the barrel. The rice never ran out.
The day the rice ran out was the day INTERFET came.'

Despite the violence, and the threats to her own
life, Mana Lou saw the militia as victims too. One day,
independence supporters captured some militia men
and brought them to the Institute. There they proposed
to kill them, but Mana Lou intervened. She told them
she would take the militia in, and keep them with her
until they could be brought to justice through proper
means. The hot-headed youths said if she would
not let them kill the militia, they would kill her. She
simply laughed, took the militia in and held them until
INTERFET arrived.

In the post-referendum carnage, the Indonesian military and militia forced thousands of Timorese across
the border into Indonesian-controlled West Timor.
Many were still there for several years after the referendum, held in desperate conditions in camps. In spring
2001, Mana Lou travelled to Atambua, West Timor, to
provide humanitarian help and spiritual support, and
encourage those who wanted to return to East Timor.

The camps were still controlled by the militia, who
wanted to kill her. Each time she held a meeting with

the refugees, bare-chested aggressive tough-looking militia would ride their motorbikes right into the room, and sit inches from her, revving their engines and looking menacing. She decided to confront them—but to confront them not with hatred or fear, but with faith.

'Will you come home?', she asked them. 'Will you come home to the Father's house—to God?'

At that moment, she recalls, many of these militia-men—thugs guilty of horrific crimes—broke down in tears and converted. Those who converted then joined her in her work encouraging the refugees to return to East Timor—the very refugees they had been holding hostage.

I had the great privilege of working with Mana Lou for three months in 2002, and visiting her many times in previous and subsequent years. More than a decade before I became a Catholic, I believe that through my relationship with her and the members of her Institute, God was already sowing seeds in my heart. Her vision is summed up in the words of the message she sent in 1997, when she won the Pax Christi Peace Award together with Fr Domingos Soares. She said:

> As servants of Christ, we have ideals and dreams. We would like to work with all our strength to build a new world where there will be sisterly and brotherly relations among people. In the spirit of being daughter, sister, initiator, and animator, we would like to help people love one another as true sisters and brothers in Christ ... How can we help to lift up the people to human dignity? ... If we could succeed in this, we would be sure that peace, love, justice, truth, freedom, forgiveness, and unity will be born. Peace begins with solidarity.

There were, of course, many other sisters and priests in East Timor who courageously served their suffering people. The Carmelite Sisters in Maubara, just beyond Liquiça, ran clinics and an orphanage. Many of the children under their care were the children of the East Timorese resistance fighters, making them prime targets for the militia. Their clinic in Dili was the only place victims of militia violence felt safe to go—they did not dare seek treatment at government hospitals. By treating them, the nuns were taking a risk.

In September 1999, the militia attacked the orphanage and Carmelite retreat house in Maubara. I visited a few months later. It is in a picturesque location, overlooking the sea. When they attacked, the militia did not burn down the buildings, but they looted the place and scrawled obscene graffiti on the walls.

The nuns, however, had been wise. Just a day or two before, they decided it was time to escape. They gathered up the 15 children, aged between 5 and 15, and bundled them all into a car. They buried their valuables under ground, and set off for Kupang, West Timor, where they found refuge not in the militia-run camps but in the home of a Catholic priest.

Just before East Timor's independence, I stayed overnight with the Sisters of Charity of the Precious Blood in their convent in a beautiful wood just outside Lospalos. Sister Julia recalled the events of 1999. The slaughter was going on all around them. At the height of the violence, Indonesian soldiers knocked on the door of the convent. One brave sister opened the door, and the army commander ordered her to gather all the other sisters and leave for Kupang with the army convoy. The sister refused. These nuns were in fact Indonesian, but they believed their place was with the dying and injured East Timorese.

'Don't you know who I am?' replied the soldier, shocked that a nun—especially an Indonesian nun—should disobey him. 'I am military.'

The sister nodded. 'Yes,' she replied. 'I know. I am military too. Military for Christ.'

When I left the convent, I asked Sister Julia if they had email so we could keep in touch. She laughed and shook her head. 'No,' she said. 'We don't have email. But we have Emmanuel.'

And it is that faith in Emmanuel—'God with us'—that sustained the people of East Timor through years of appalling suffering. On the day of the attack on Bishop Belo's residence, East Timor's resistance leader Xanana Gusmão, who had been released from prison and placed under house arrest in February 1999 and then into the sanctuary of the British Embassy in Jakarta hours after the referendum, received yet more terrible news. A British diplomat who was with him at the time recounted the scene to me. The telephone rang and the receiver was passed to Xanana. The caller told him he was sheltering, along with many others, in a church in Suai.

'We have been told that the militia are coming here tonight,' he said. 'We believe we will be killed. But we wanted to tell you that although we may die tonight, we will die free men.'

Some 200 people died in Suai that night. They paid the ultimate price, so that their country could be free. The parish priest, Fr Rene Manubag, wrote soon after the massacre that 'the history of East Timor was really written in an ink of blood. Now is the time when we are free to write it with an ink of love, an ink of freedom, an ink of love and peace.'

Hong Kong

In 1997, just two months after the handover of Hong Kong from British colonial rule to China, I moved to the territory to begin my first job after graduation, as a journalist. I lived in Hong Kong for five years, the first five years of Chinese sovereignty. I got to know a number of Hong Kong's leading voices for democracy and human rights, including Catholics Martin Lee, whose story features in the next chapter, Christine Loh, and Cardinal Joseph Zen.

Cardinal Zen—or Bishop Zen as he was when I first knew him—became a great inspiration to me. Like Bishop Belo and Cardinal Bo, he has been a passionate voice for justice. Thoughtful, prayerful, gentle and gracious, this diminutive and humble Salesian does not look like a rabble-rouser. But he has been one of Beijing's fiercest opponents.

Born in Shanghai in 1932 to first-generation Catholics, his family fled to Hong Kong to escape Communist rule when he was 16. He describes his parents as 'fervent' in their faith, having been baptised while in college, and they worshipped in a parish in the French concession of Shanghai. Previously wealthy, the family fell into poverty during the Japanese occupation.

Schooled by Salesians, Zen decided when he reached Hong Kong to join the order. He began his novitiate, and was ordained to the priesthood in 1961. He studied at the Salesian Pontifical University in Rome, where he was particularly influenced by the encyclicals of Pope John XXIII on social ethics and by the Second Vatican Council which took place while he was there. He was also inspired by his professor, Joseph Mattai.

In 1996, Zen was appointed coadjutor bishop of Hong Kong, after many years teaching at the Holy

Spirit Seminary and the Salesian School in Macau, and serving as Provincial Superior of the Salesians, responsible for mainland China, Hong Kong, Macau and Taiwan. He had also lectured in State-approved seminaries in China.

In 2002, he was appointed bishop of Hong Kong, and almost immediately led the Diocese in protesting against proposed anti-subversion laws. In subsequent years he participated in demonstrations, led prayer vigils and spoke out in the media on a range of issues relating to the erosion of freedoms in Hong Kong and the violation of human rights, particularly religious freedom, in China. He urged the Chinese government to 'tell the truth' about the crackdown on demonstrations in Tiananmen Square in 1989. On 4 June 2006, soon after he had been appointed cardinal, he urged Hong Kong people not to forget the massacre. 'The young people who fought and died for democracy in Tiananmen Square were their brothers and sisters,' he said. 'After June 4, we can no longer fight selfishly just to win the most rights for Hong Kong.'[4] He later said that it was Tiananmen Square which had motivated him to devote seven years to teaching in seminaries in mainland China. 'This force supported me from 1989 to 1996 to spend half of my life in China nurturing people who can work for the Church and become shepherds of the Church in China.' Liu Bainian, general secretary of China's state-run Catholic Patriotic Association, described his elevation to cardinal as 'a hostile act'.[5]

Upon his appointment as cardinal, Zen showed little sign of softening his approach. 'We should learn from the Holy Father's example of clearly voicing the truth without being afraid of the opposing currents,' he said.[6] If anything, he became more outspoken and active. In October 2011, he went on a three-day hunger strike as part of his campaign for freedom for Hong Kong's Catholic schools. In 2014, Cardinal Zen—who retired as bishop of Hong Kong in 2009—took a leading role in the protests which became known as the 'Occupy' movement. Demonstrating for full democracy by 2017, Cardinal Zen—aged 82 at the time—took to the streets, marching 84 kilometres over seven days and telling protestors: 'It's high time we really showed that we want to be free and not to be slaves ... We must unite together.'[7]

In January 2015, I spoke to Cardinal Zen by telephone, about the Occupy movement. He had surrendered himself to the police in December 2014. 'We planned to be there occupying, getting arrested and jailed. That was our purpose. We wanted to tell people that we are a law-abiding people, but we want to show the problem with the whole system. We hoped people would then pay attention,' he said. 'We wanted to be arrested. We informed the police that we had illegally occupied a place and acted against the law. The police registered a report and then told us to go home.'

The striking fact about the Occupy movement in Hong Kong, Cardinal Zen told me, was that it was completely peaceful. 'The Church has always been engaged in education, and perhaps one reason the protests were peaceful is because of education,' he said. 'Half a million people protested, yet there were no disturbances, no windows broken, no tyres burned. On 28 September 2014, police fired 87 canisters of tear-gas—and people just regrouped and made no action against the police.'

Pope Francis described Cardinal Zen as 'the one who fights with a "sling"', a comparison with David and Goliath.[8] It is clear that he has been held in high regard by both Pope Francis and Pope Benedict XVI, if not always by Vatican diplomats. In 2008, Cardinal Zen was requested by Benedict XVI to write the meditations for the traditional Stations of the Cross led by the pope at the Colisseum on Good Friday.

Cardinal Zen, whose motto is 'Ipsa cura est' from 1 Peter 5: 7—'Cast all your anxieties on him, for he cares about you'—is particularly keen to emphasise the importance of non-violence. 'For Catholics, we encourage people to persevere in a strategy of peace. When we engage in the important work of social justice, human rights and democracy, we must really believe that the peaceful way is the most efficacious,' he told me. 'We must resist the temptation of violence. Sometimes we may encounter violence—then we must be very careful. In extreme cases, violence may be necessary but only ever as a last resort. We must keep our hearts calm and full of love for everybody, including the enemy.'

Pakistan

In my work at CSW, I had the privilege of working on Pakistan for five years. Our closest partners in Pakistan were two of the most inspirational people it is possible to find. Both were devout Catholics and courageous men who devoted their lives to the cause of human rights, particularly religious freedom: Cecil Chaudhry and Shahbaz Bhatti.

Group Captain Cecil Chaudhry was a highly decorated fighter pilot who had served in the Pakistani Air Force for almost 30 years. Regarded as a national hero, he shot down several Indian aircraft in the 1965 India–Pakistan war and in the 1971 war flew an incredible mission behind enemy lines. Most of his fellow pilots did not believe he would come back alive. He was shot down and forced to bail out in no man's land. After landing, he folded up his parachute, looked around and ran some distance to take cover. As he approached some trees, a group of soldiers stood up, pointing their guns at him. He raised his arms in surrender, and they questioned him. Neither Cecil nor the soldiers knew whose side the other was on because Indian and Pakistani uniforms were similar, but it turned out the soldiers were part of a Pakistani patrol. 'But you have just run through several hundred metres of landmines— one of the most heavily mined stretches of land in the area,' they exclaimed. Later in life, Cecil—a keen mathematician—worked out the odds of survival in such a minefield and concluded that it was nothing short of a miracle.

Cecil's distinguished air force career continued, with him serving as defence attaché in Iraq from 1979 to 1983 and head of the Pakistan Military Mission in Iraq in 1980. He should have risen to the very top of the Air Force but, despite being one of Pakistan's most highly decorated war heroes, he was denied further promotion by the ruling dictator at the time, General Zia ul-Haq, for one reason: because Cecil was a Christian. That was the turning point in his life.

Cecil resigned in protest, and became one of Pakistan's leading human rights campaigners. Describing his birth into human rights activism as 'a baptism of fire,' Cecil launched a legal challenge in the Supreme Court against an extremist Islamic party's election manifesto—and succeeded in getting the party to change its policies. He faced constant death threats, as well as threats that his daughters would be kidnapped, but he never gave in.

Over the years Cecil organised street protests, hunger strikes and press conferences in protest at persecution of Christians and other religious minorities. He led the successful campaign for the restoration of the Joint Electorate System, seeking to abolish the system which required voters to vote for candidates of their own religion, which he described as 'religious apartheid'. He told me once that the system of separate electorates meant no political interaction among religious communities. 'It resulted in a close marriage between politics and religion, because candidates were elected on religious grounds. It fragmented the entire population of Pakistan, violated basic political human rights and totally disrupted the social harmony of the country,' he said. 'It created sectarianism, which is tearing this country apart.'

Cecil also led the campaign for the abolition or reform of the notorious blasphemy laws and the Hudood Ordinance, and was at the forefront of the struggle against bonded labour. He once spent a week incognito working in a brick kiln in order to find out what life as a bonded labourer was like—and became determined to break that unjust system.

He also became a peace activist, working to promote reconciliation between India and Pakistan, and a leading educationalist, as Principal of Lahore's prestigious Catholic school, St Anthony's College and St Mary's Academy in Rawalpindi.

In his work for religious freedom, Cecil founded several organisations, including the National Christian Action Forum, the Christian Organisation for Social Action in Pakistan and the All Pakistan Minorities Alliance. He worked closely with the Human Rights Commission of Pakistan and the Catholic Bishops Conference's National Commission for Justice and Peace.

But it was his personal devotion which was particularly inspiring. He looked after numerous Christians facing charges of blasphemy, at huge personal risk.

Cecil was born on 27 August 1941, in a small village called Dalwal, in Punjab. His family were the only Christian family in the village. His father was an acclaimed photo-journalist, his mother a school teacher.

His maternal grandfather, Raja Shakir Mehdi, converted to Christianity after exploring various religions, but he had been born into a conservative Muslim family, which reacted to his conversion with fury. He ran away to Lahore where he was baptised in the Catholic Church, and lived with the priests until he could find a place of his own. In 1900, Raja Shakir Mehdi established Mission High School in Dalwal, which became a prestigious educational institution run by the Church.

Cecil was devout in his faith, but was reluctant to make too public a display of it. Quietly, however, he had particular devotion to the Virgin Mary, and carried a rosary with him in his wallet wherever he went. 'There was always a rosary in the pocket of his Coverall flying suit,' recalls his daughter Michelle. 'He truly believed that it was the Virgin Mary who protected him on some of the most dangerous flying missions. Whenever we faced any difficulties, he would just say three Hail Marys.'

One of his closest friends was Bishop John Joseph, the bishop of Faisalabad who in 1998 shot himself dead in protest at Pakistan's blasphemy laws after a Christian, Ayub Masih, was sentenced to death. In a fax message to the Vatican, Bishop Joseph wrote: 'I only hope and pray that God accepts the sacrifice of my blood for his people.' According to Cecil, what he did was 'premeditated and pre-planned.' The bishop had warned some months previously that if the blasphemy laws were not repealed, 'We will launch a protest which will stun the whole world'. After seven days of fasting and prayer, Bishop Joseph came to Lahore and, dressed in his white cassock, shot himself on the steps of the Sessions Court in Sahiwal.

'My father was very close to Bishop John Joseph,' says Cecil's daughter Michelle. 'They were not only good friends but together they worked for the rights of the marginalised, especially victims of blasphemy laws and the religiously persecuted. They were a team, and provided the strongest ever leadership to the community. Both of them were extremely bold and courageous, and Bishop John Joseph was like family to us.' The night before he sacrificed his life, he had dinner with the Chaudhry family. 'He was worried and a little quiet,' Michelle recalls. 'On the way to Sahiwal (where he shot himself), which was a few hours after he left our home, he called my father and said "if anything happened to me, you take care of things".'

I had the privilege of working closely with Cecil for five years. I stayed in his home in Lahore, and got to know his family as well. He was always wonderfully supported by his loyal wife, Iris. He was the most wonderful blend of distinction and warmth, stature and humour, integrity, faith and wisdom. We travelled together several times, to advocacy meetings in London, Brussels and Washington, DC, and when I visited Pakistan. He commanded unbounded respect, but also genuine love. Major (Rtd) Justin Sharaf sums him up well in these words: 'Cecil would walk into a room and without ever saying a word, every head would turn to look at his buoyant and eternal smile, beneath a thick moustache, with prayerful admiration. The ensuing silence would be an enduring testament that words were inadequate and unnecessary to express the boundless feelings of love and gratitude ... With his gallantry, valour and dedication, Cecil Chaudhry had given Pakistani Christians an identity ... Every Pakistani Christian needs to know and teach his children for generations to come the wonderful gift of God in the person of Cecil Chaudhry ... What a difference one man can make.'

Major Sharaf continues by noting that 'the defining moment' of Cecil Chaudhry's life, even above his epic war hero moments, was 'when he stood up to the wrong; when he spoke up for the oppressed; and when he lent a helping hand.' As I type these words my eyes fill with tears, because this was absolutely the Cecil Chaudhry I knew and loved, the Cecil Chaudhry I turned to several times a week for advice and wisdom on how to advocate, how to respond to urgent needs in Pakistan. There was never a step I took in CSW's advocacy on Pakistan without first seeking Cecil's advice. And Cecil was an inspiration to me in my faith too. I looked at the way he wove together faith, courage, wisdom and humour, with a shoulder of responsibility, a depth of spirit but also a lightness of touch, and I thought: if Catholics are like that, I like them.

Cecil was known for his courage. 'I have fought two wars for this country, but am willing to fight 100 wars against extremism,' he used to say. But his humanity, and his commitment not simply to his own Christian community, but to the values of humanity and the cause of freedom and justice for all was inspiring. 'By faith, I'm a Christian, but my religion is humanity,' he often said. 'I have never talked in terms of only my community being persecuted. I consider all of the 170 million people of this country as my community, and believe that 90 per cent of them are being persecuted at the hands of the powerful. As such, I am involved in the struggle for everyone's rights.' That was precisely why I felt such deep respect and love for Cecil Chaudhry.

At the end of a long day of briefing Parliamentarians in London or Brussels or Congressman in Washington, DC, or speaking in churches, or in Pakistan interviewing victims of religious persecution, Cecil and I would sit down for a glass or two of whisky and exchange jokes. Sometimes we would e-mail each other jokes too. Not all of Cecil's jokes are repeatable in a book like this, but there are two that I love that I will share here.

The first involves an ultra-conservative evangelical church that has very robust views on alcohol. Opposite the church, an entrepreneur buys a plot of land and builds a pub. The leaders of the church object to having a pub opposite the church, and they plead with the pub owner not to proceed. The construction continues, however, and the congregation prays. Suddenly one night, there is a storm. Thunder rolls and lightning flashes. The pub is then struck by lightning, and collapses. Some days later, the pub landlord sues the church, and the case comes to court. The pub owner sets out his case, convinced that the church congregation is responsible. The church leaders stand in the witness box and deny any involvement. They did nothing, they declare. In his summing up, the judge concludes: 'This is the strangest case I have ever dealt with. We seem to have a situation where there is a pub owner who believes profoundly in the power of prayer—and a church that clearly does not!'

The second is a little more risqué, and involves a nun. Sister Mary grew up in a rough part of town, and one evening, after dark, she goes to the mother superior with a request to visit her parents that very night. 'But

Sister Mary, it is after dark and your parents live in a very rough part of town. It is not safe to go there at this hour,' she responds. 'But Mother,' Sister Mary replies, 'I know the area so well and I know exactly how to look after myself.' 'No,' the mother superior retorts, 'if you are down a dark alley and a man approaches you, it is very dangerous.' 'Mother,' says Sister Mary, 'if that happens, I know precisely what I would do.' 'What would you do?', enquires the mother superior. 'First, I would ask the man to pull his trousers down,' says the sister. The mother superior's face turns white with shock. 'Sister Mary, what has come over you? What are you thinking?' The sister continues: 'Then I will pull my habit up.' By this point the mother superior is almost fainting. 'Sister, sister, I don't know what is wrong with you. Don't you know what could happen?' Calmly, Sister Mary replies: 'Mother, it's simple. He can't run with his trousers down, I can run with my habit up.'

It was jokes like these, alongside his courage, integrity, and faith that so drew me—and everyone who met him—to Cecil Chaudhry. Often when he spoke, and was asked how he coped with the threats to his life, the agony of seeing such injustice, the stresses and demands on him, he replied serenely by reciting a little poem called 'It all depends on whose hands it is in'. It goes like this:

> A basketball in my hands is worth about $19.
> A basketball in Michael Jordan's hands is worth
>   about $33 million.
> It all depends on whose hands it is in.
>
> A golf club in my hands is useless.
> A golf club in Tiger Woods' hands is four major
>   golf championships.
> It all depends on whose hands it is in.

A rod in my hands will keep away a wild
   animal.
A rod in Moses' hands will part the mighty sea.
It all depends on whose hands it is in.

A sling shot in my hands is a kid's toy.
A sling shot in David's hands is a mighty
   weapon.
It all depends on whose hands it is in.

Two fish and five loaves of bread in my hands
   is a couple of fish sandwiches.
Two fish and five loaves in Jesus' hands will
   feed thousands.
It all depends on whose hands it is in.

Nails in my hands might produce a birdhouse.
Nails in Jesus Christ's hands produced
   salvation for the entire world.
It all depends on whose hands it is in.

So we in Pakistan put our concerns, our fears,
our hopes, our families, and our work in God's
hands because . . . it all depends on whose hands
they are in.

Cecil's final battle in life was with lung cancer. As with
all his previous battles, Cecil fought this one with
courage and dignity. Michelle recalls: 'Throughout
his illness he always managed to sit up and pray, read
the Bible and say his daily prayers. Whenever anyone
asked him how he was feeling he would say: "My
Jesus is making me well everyday."' Cecil died on 13
April 2012. Major Sharaf's conclusion is beautiful and
makes me wipe away my tears: 'Then one day, with
loved ones by his side, he bid us farewell. He flew
on "wings of angels" to his next assignment: Heaven
needed a hero too!' His children, Michelle and Cecil
Jr, have continued his work, both through the Cecil

and Iris Chaudhry Foundation and through the Justice and Peace Commission of the Catholic Church in Pakistan. Michelle says, in introducing the Foundation, that it 'dedicates itself to the services of humanity and humanitarian causes with emphasis on the uplift, welfare and equality of rights of all religious minorities in Pakistan' and that 'as the daughter of a man who gave his all to Pakistan, I have pledged to carry forward my father's legacy. I fearlessly fight for a just and tolerant Pakistan.'

Cecil worked very closely with another of Pakistan's heroes, Shahbaz Bhatti. Indeed, Cecil was Shahbaz's mentor. Together they founded the All Pakistan Minorities Alliance (APMA) and were at the forefront of campaigning for the rights of minorities of all religious backgrounds, and for women.

Shahbaz was a young student when he met Cecil, in 1992. Their partnership, combining Cecil's wisdom with Shahbaz's idealism, made them an inspiring duo. At just 17 Shahbaz had formed the Christian Liberation Front with fellow students in 1985, after experiencing first-hand discrimination and at the same time a spiritual awakening. He was like a son to Cecil, who praised his friend's commitment, saying 'he never faltered from his goal, not for one minute, not even when he became a minister'.

On the morning of 2 March 2011 I woke up, opened my emails and turned on the radio to hear the news that my close friend Shahbaz Bhatti had been assassinated. His car had been sprayed with bullets, and his security protection team were nowhere to be seen. I was shocked, deeply saddened, but not surprised. He had been receiving daily death threats for years. I always thought it was probably only a matter of time.

Shahbaz and I used to speak by telephone at least once a week. I travelled in Pakistan with him. On one occasion, we missed a bomb together by five minutes. We had been meeting for dinner with others in the Marriot Hotel in Islamabad, and had left the premises just minutes before a bomb explosion. On another occasion, Shahbaz took me to meet a little seven-year-old girl, Sharee Komal, who had been brutally raped and tortured because she came from a Christian family. Shahbaz was helping her and her family, because no one else would.

I remember many times between 2004 and 2009 when Shahbaz was placed on Pakistan's 'exit control list', prohibited from leaving the country, and when he was arrested or threatened with arrest. I remember speaking to him by phone almost daily during certain crisis points, and being constantly impressed by his calmness and courage. Of course at times he was fearful, and with very good reason—but the mark of courage is not an absence of fear, but a matter of how one handles it. Shahbaz never allowed fear to paralyse or overcome him.

In the time I worked with Shahbaz, I was amazed by his devotion to the cause he had made his own. I remember he once told me that he had never taken a holiday, and he worked extraordinary hours. He said he was in a battle, in the trenches, and when you're a soldier in a war you don't get holidays. He was one of the most selfless people I have ever known.

In 2007, for example, a Christian community in Charsadda, in the North-West Frontier Province, received threats from extremists, giving them an ultimatum: convert to Islam or face the consequences. The night the deadline expired, I telephoned Shahbaz to ask for an update, and to my surprise he told me he was in Charsadda. The community were terrified, he said, and they expected an attack at any moment, so he had gone to be with them. That was typical of Shahbaz. But he also told me that the community had been praying. They felt alone, they felt that the rest of the world didn't know, or didn't care. 'The fact that you have telephoned means I can tell them that someone does know, does care, is praying for them and is speaking for them.'

He was a man of enormous humility, but with a good sense of humour too. He never wanted to grandstand or to receive credit—his only interest was in making a difference for the persecuted, oppressed and marginalised. The various international prizes he received, as well as his audience with Pope Benedict XVI, a meeting with the archbishop of Canterbury, encounters with influential US Congressmen were all viewed in the same way by Shahbaz—as valuable opportunities for advancing the cause, never as moments of personal aggrandisement. Even when he became Federal Minister, he maintained a simple lifestyle. After taking the oath of office, he told the media: 'I, as a humble servant of Jesus Christ, will continue to serve the suffering, victimised and persecuted communities and am ready to even sacrifice my life to defend the principles of religious freedom, human equality and the rights of minorities.'

He lived each day with the knowledge that he might one day pay the ultimate price, but never once did I see him morbid or depressed. He had the serenity and humour of someone who knew that his fate, and the cause for which he was fighting, were in the hands of his Maker. When he came to London as Minister not long before his murder, he was keen to have photographs taken of him smiling, because—he joked—there were too many 'serious pictures' of him.

But Shahbaz was also deeply devout in his Catholic faith. Whenever I spoke to him, his first request was always for prayer. Not once did he ask for money. According to his friend Michelle Chaudhry, Cecil's daughter, who worked closely with him, he would pray twice a day and for long hours into the night. His office and home were blessed with holy water on a regular basis. 'He would not leave home without praying, and would often call on priests and nuns to pray for his work,' recalls Michelle. 'He always carried a rosary with him; he read the Bible regularly.' Shahbaz's personal Bible is now placed on the altar in San Bartolomeo all'Isola in Rome as a relic of a twenty-first-century martyr, and on 13 February 2015—the day before Archbishop Charles Maung Bo of Burma, who had received me into the Church two years previously, was to become cardinal—I spent some time in prayer and reflection and remembrance in that basilica, joining my heart and my spirit once more with Shahbaz, in front of his Bible.

In 2008, Shahbaz became a member of Parliament. He was a strong supporter and close confidante of former prime minister Benazir Bhutto, who was herself assassinated the year before. He had been at the rally where she was killed. After her party, the Pakistan People's Party (PPP), formed a government, Shahbaz was appointed Federal Minister for Minorities Affairs—the first time a Christian activist of his calibre and conviction had held the post. There had been token Christian ministers before, but he was the first Minister who one knew would really fight to make a difference.

As Minister, Shahbaz lived up to his promise to continue to serve the suffering. When eight people were killed and more than 100 houses destroyed in Gojra in 2009, he immediately visited the scene and refused to leave the police station until the crimes were registered. When Asia Bibi was sentenced to death on blasphemy charges, he said: 'I will knock on every door for the release of Asia Bibi.'

He also built bridges with Muslims and promoted inter-faith dialogue and reconciliation. He spoke at large mosques at the invitation of senior imams and secured a groundbreaking statement from religious leaders denouncing terrorism. He launched a network of 'district interfaith harmony committees' to encourage dialogue and unite communities through common concerns.

And he constantly emphasised his patriotism. 'Minorities are sons of the soil,' he said. 'Pakistan belongs to them and they belong to Pakistan. They have made sacrifices and shed their blood for the creation and development of Pakistan.'

In October 2009, Shahbaz came to London to address the annual conference of Christian Solidarity Worldwide. As usual, his first request was for prayer. He summed up his life's vocation in these words:

> I live for religious freedom, and I am ready to die for this cause. We have a commitment to bring a change in the lives of people. We will bring a change in the life of those who are living in darkness, we will bring a change in the lives of those who don't have a hope, and we will bring a smile on the faces of those living under severe harassment and victimisation ... This is the key objective of my life—to live for those who are voiceless, who are suffering. We need to change the plight of those who are living in the darkness of persecution, victimisation, and that is the commitment we made, to bring justice for those who are denied justice.

He challenged head-on the 'forces of intolerance,' pledging that, in unity with others, 'we will not allow you to capture our country.' He called on his audience to join with him in this struggle. 'Let's pledge that we will work together to promote harmony and tolerance. We will bridge the gaps among different faiths. We will strengthen this world with the message of peace and tolerance.'[9]

At the heart of Shahbaz's work, particularly as a minister, was an effort to reform, or repeal, Pakistan's notorious blasphemy laws which have been so widely misused with such disastrous consequences for many. But it was this very campaign that in the end cost Shahbaz his own life. As he proposed reforms to the laws, the death threats increased in number and intensity. He knew he was in grave danger, but repeated requests, by him and by many of his influential, international friends, for a bullet-proof car were ignored by the Pakistani government. Four months before his assassination, he recorded an interview with the BBC, for broadcast in the event of his death. He said: 'These Taliban threaten me. But I want to share that I believe in Jesus Christ, who has given his own life for us. I know what is the meaning of the cross and I am following the cross. I am ready to die for a cause. I am living for my community and suffering people and I will die to defend their rights.'[10] Those words encapsulate the essence of Shahbaz Bhatti, and should stand as his epitaph.

Burma

Sister Lourdes, Fr Domingos Soares, Fr Francisco Fernandes, Gregorio da Cunha Saldanha, Francisco Miranda Branco, Bishop Belo, Cardinal Zen, Cecil

Chaudhry and Shahbaz Bhatti all influenced me over the years preceding my decision to become Catholic, but it was Cardinal Charles Maung Bo of Burma who opened the door.

I first met Archishop Charles Bo in 2007, as described in the Introduction to this book. In 2015, two years after receiving me into the Church, Archbishop Bo was appointed Burma's first ever cardinal, and I had the privilege of travelling to Rome for the occasion.

Charles Maung Bo was born in Monhla village, near Shwebo in Sagaing Division, just beyond Mandalay, in 1948 to a deeply Catholic family with ten children. Monhla was one of nine settlements the Portuguese established precisely four hundred years ago, and it was a mixed Catholic and Buddhist village. His ancestors were among Burma's first Catholics, converted by the Portuguese. 'We are very grateful to our great grandparents who brought faith to our land. Faith is a gift,' says Cardinal Bo. Shwebo was the birthplace of U Aung Zeya, a Burmese king who united Burma in the eighteenth century.

Charles Bo's upbringing was, he recalls, 'a Catholic environment' in which he was able to grow in faith. 'There were no problems of materialism and secularism. It was so calm and there was a religious atmosphere. The whole village was very religious, with special love and respect for what was sacred and holy. There was a God-minded orientation.'

His father was a farmer, who died when Charles Bo was just two. Five of his siblings also died while very young. 'But my childhood memories are photographic,' he claims. 'I can still see the scene of my father's funeral. My mother was a tailor with a remarkable character, well-known in the village for her meekness. She never quarrelled with neighbours.'

Charles Bo first felt called to the priesthood through his mother's inspiration. 'She inspired me every night, when she told stories of saints and priests before going to bed. Another person who inspired me to the priesthood was my parish priest, Don Luwi. He loved my father and mother, and he loved me too. He taught me catechism when I was between five and seven years old. I wanted to be like him.'

At the age of eight, he was taken in by a Salesian-run boarding house in Mandalay. 'We were a poor family, and my parish priest had a special sympathy for the family.' With the Salesians, Charles Bo became inspired by their style and life and the example of Don Bosco, which he describes as 'active, caring and out for the young and poor'. That lifestyle, he says, 'influenced my bearing'.

His faith was also inspired by his teachers at the Lafon School, and especially the rector, Fr Giacomin Fortunato, who later taught Charles Bo philosophy and theology and became his novice master. Italian missionaries from the Pontifical Institute for Foreign Missions (known as 'PIME'), founded in 1850, and the French priests from the Society of Foreign Missions of Paris (known as 'MEP') also encouraged him. 'I wanted to be a missionary and a parish priest like them,' he says.

Charles Bo is unusual in the Christian population in Burma, in that he is from the majority Bamar or Burman population. The Burmans are predominantly Buddhist, and there is a sense of religious nationalism that for many concludes that to be Burman is to be Buddhist. In contrast, most Christians come from the other ethnic groups, particularly the Chin, Kachin, Karen and Karenni. So Charles Bo is in a minority in every sense—a minority Burman among the Christian population dominated by other ethnic groups, and a minority Christian among his own Burman race. But throughout his life, from his schooling at Lafon's to his time as a priest and then bishop in Lashio, Pathein and other ethnic areas, he has displayed a deep connection with the ethnic nationalities. At the Lafon School, he recalls, the boys came from a variety of different ethnic groups. 'I could live with them with love and I liked all the different ethnic groups—Kachin, Karen, Chin, Wa, Shan, Chinese, Karenni and also many Anglo-Burmese,' he says. 'I did not feel different from them. Later in the Salesian seminary the candidates also came from all the different ethnic groups. This training of living and loving together gave me a good formation.'

Indeed, Cardinal Bo says that it was only much later in life, as bishop of Lashio in Shan State, and then as bishop of Pathein, that he encountered an 'attitude of racism' among some clergy towards him as a Burman. 'I do not blame them, because of the history of the conflict between the Burmans or Bamar and the Karens and the civil war between the Burmese military and different ethnic minorities from the time of independence in 1948 until today.'

Charles Bo was born in the very year that Burma became independent, and was 14 years old when General Ne Win seized power in a coup d'etat in 1962. For his entire adult life and his life as a priest, he has lived under military-dominated dictatorship. 'Ne Win kept the whole nation under his military boots,' he recalls. 'Soon after the coup I saw a photo of Ne Win in a newspaper. I didn't know anything about him, but some of the boys I was with were praising him because he began to repair the roads. But when he started nationalising the shops and banks, and arresting military officials and business people, and then especially when he nationalised the Church mission schools, a real aversion, even hatred, and fear grew in me towards him. Worse was when he expelled all the missionaries who had arrived after the Second World War. One man destroyed the nation with an iron first. A great nation became the poorest in the world. How could one man destroy a nation, one maniac do such harm?' Ne Win, he added, is 'on the same level as Hitler and Pol Pot'.

From 1962 to 1976, Charles Bo studied at the Nazareth Aspirantate, a Salesian seminary, in Anisakan village, near Maymyo (now Pyin Oo Lwin), and was ordained a Salesian priest on 9 April 1976. Until his appointment as archbishop of Rangoon or Yangon in 2003, Charles Bo spent most of his years as a priest in the ethnic areas, which gave him a direct knowledge of the consequences of ethnic conflict. As parish priest in Loihkam, near Lashio, an area which was a base for the Kachin Independence Army (KIA), he won the people's hearts by learning the local language, Maru, a Kachin dialect. 'After one week, I was giving a homily in Maru,' he explains. 'Most of the five years I spent in Loihkam I was living among the KIA. Once or twice a year, the Burma Army soldiers would come, and there would be shooting. Politically I could do little as an individual, but I was able to negotiate with both the KIA and the Burma Army to persuade them not to engage in shooting and confrontration, but to try to avoid each other,' he recalls. 'To be the parish priest in Loihkam with all the insurgent groups—the KIA, Wa, Kukant, Shan, Palaung, Loimaw and Communists—wasn't so comfortable. But we went from day to day and adjusted to the situation from moment to moment.'

In 1990, he became bishop of Lashio, and in the same year he founded a new religious order, the Congregation of St Paul's Brothers and Sisters. The congregation has, he says, 'one vision of sharing the Good News of Jesus with those who have not heard of Him'. Initially, the religious brothers and sisters were sent to the remote Wa people in Shan State, to assist with education, health and evangelisation. Today, there are about one hundred sisters and about 30 brothers and priests, working in six dioceses. 'Their charism is to go where there are no churches and Christians, and to go to the most abandoned places and remotest areas,' Cardinal Bo explains. 'They face challenges: no proper shelter, no decent food, no security and protection. It is not an international congregation, so there is no proper support from anywhere. There is no assurance for their livelihood and daily food. Yet, they risk themselves and are often wounded and bruised — yet at the same time they offer good news and consolation to the lost and the last.'

After six years in Lashio, Bishop Bo as he was then was translated to Pathein. There he encountered the Karen people and their sentiment after decades of war. 'When I arrived in Pathein, and even before that, I was hearing of the real hatred that Karens felt for the Burmans. This was very evident,' he notes. 'The Karens could not forget and forgive the Burmans. The decades of war and massacres and oppression meant, sadly, that the Karens would foster hatred against the Burmans. For the seven years I spent in Pathein, I was insistent in preaching homilies on reconciliation, forgiveness and unity among the different ethnic groups. Jubilee, I said, means to forgive one's enemy.'

Charles Bo was the first bishop in the Church in Burma to be translated from one diocese to another, before becoming archbishop of Rangoon in 2003. 'The people and especially the clergy were not used to that. Coming to Pathein and Yangon Dioceses was difficult for some priests to accept. But I accepted it as coming from the Lord through the guidance of the Holy Father, Pope John Paul II,' he recalls. 'Catholics in general were happy and excited, and so too were the religious sisters and brothers. Some priests were not excited but were indifferent, and some resisted, but I took up the challenge.'

Cardinal Bo recalls that 'indifference' or 'resistance' from clergy took various forms, but it was generally a reaction to his warm and charismatic personal style. 'Many commented that I was exaggerating when I expressed good wishes to them whenever I saw them, or when I sent them birthday or feast day cards. Some would say I was lobbying for something when I sent them postcards from abroad, though lobbying for what I do not know.' Some contrasted Charles Bo's loving, compassionate style with the stern, more traditional approach of his predecessor; others were hostile because they had been marked as Episcopabiles (appointment as bishops) by his predecessor and they felt he had invaded their territory. 'But gradually and with kindness we managed to gather together for decisions and plans for the future.'

Central to Cardinal Bo's leadership of the Rangoon Archdiocese has been his personal commitment to social justice. 'Our vision and mission,' he says, 'is to reach out to the poor: the lost, the last and the least. "Go to the sheep and return with the smell of the sheep," says Pope Francis.'

Several tragic events in Burma's recent history occurred since Cardinal Bo became archbishop of Rangoon, notably the pro-democracy uprising led by Buddhist monks in 2007, which became known as the 'Saffron Revolution', and the worst natural disaster to hit Burma in recent times, Cyclone Nargis in 2008.

Cardinal Bo has always been clear where he stands. 'I try to follow the Social Teaching of the Catholic Church, which emphasises that we are for the whole of humanity, and for the country. At the same time, as a religious leader I am not supposed to get involved in political matters directly, or favour any one particular political party. But we must fight for justice, human rights, human dignity and freedom, and we must fight to free our people from oppression. We should be on the side of the poor and marginalised.'

In the pro-democracy demonstrations in 1988, Cardinal Bo was bishop of Lashio in northern Shan State. 'My stance was clear. I guided the people to choose freedom, rights and justice, without myself going onto the streets,' he explains. 'So again in 2007 during the Saffron Revolution, I followed the same principle. The Catholic community and some religious sisters were demanding that priests and sisters and bishops should go onto the streets, together with the Buddhist monks. I said no for the clergy, but yes for the laity.'

When Cyclone Nargis hit Burma in 2008, Cardinal Bo was in Nepal. He returned to Rangoon the following day. 'There was no one who would take up the challenge of responding to this crisis. The disaster was too much,' he recalls. 'Over 150,000 deaths and millions displaced. I arrived at the archbishop's house, which looked like a swimming pool. All the roofs were gone.' Cardinal Bo, together with an Indian Jesuit, Fr Amal, decided to lead the Church's response. With the help of Caritas International, a disaster relief service was established by the Church. A total of $11 million was sent to Burma through the Church. 'It was wonderful—such a response raised the quality of our people, built capacity, transparency, disaster preparedness. Just due to one firm decision at a critical time.'

Despite the aftermath of Cyclone Nargis, the regime in Burma went ahead with a referendum on a new constitution within days of the disaster. Two years later, in 2010, elections were held, but with widespread harassment and vote rigging, and with Burma's democracy leader Aung San Suu Kyi still under house arrest and her party, the National League for Democracy (NLD), boycotting the election, the winners were the military-backed Union Solidarity and Development Party (USDP). In effect, the same people were in charge, but they changed out of their military uniforms and put on civilian suits.

'The elections and the referendum were all a sham,' says Cardinal Bo with characteristic forthrightness. 'The same old generals are still in power. We need to be optimistic but at the same time realistic. As a people we are often too gentle, too patient, and too easily cowed into obedience. This means the military is able to take advantage of the goodness of our people.' He calls for genuine change. 'The time has come for all the old generals to get off the scene. No more U Thein Sein, no more Thura Shwe Man. Let us give the chance to Aung San Suu Kyi and others.' He draws a parallel with the Israelites in the Old Testament. 'We have had military regimes for [over 50] years. The Israelites were wandering in the wilderness for only 40 years. We are going beyond that.'

Cardinal Bo is a close friend of Aung San Suu Kyi, and has made no secret of his respect for her. When he visited the United Kingdom for the first time in October 1993, as bishop of Lashio, he met Aung San Suu Kyi's British husband, Michael Aris. Two sisters from the Congregation of St Paul's Brothers and Sisters were living in a religious house in Oxford, to study English. 'Michael found out that they had some difficulties to continue staying there in that community, and he asked me whether I could allow them to stay at his house, take care of the house, and at the same time look after his son Kim. He would take care of all their expenses and arrange for their studies,' recalls Cardinal Bo. 'It was a big risk, I knew, to stay in the family home of the opposition leader Aung San Suu Kyi. Yet despite knowing the risks, I gave Michael Aris the green light. I just wanted to assist those in need.'

Burmese intelligence, however, were monitoring the house in Oxford, and had noticed the sisters coming in and out of the house in their religious habits. When they returned to Burma the following year, they were arrested at the airport. They eventually escaped again and have lived to this day in exile in Britain.

Ever since 1988, Cardinal Bo has been one of the few Christian leaders in Burma to speak out courageously about human rights and democracy. Until Burma began to open up in 2011, his messages were subtle, careful but nevertheless still surprisingly bold. In his homilies he wove in clear messages, but in a way that kept him just the right side of the line as far as the authorities were concerned. 'I spoke without attacking anyone personally,' he says. But since 2011, he has become even more outspoken.

'My personal vision and mission for myself and for the nation is to see people be free to love and serve others. To achieve this, we need to get rid of the evil forces: sin, addiction, anything that controls our life, and human injustice, discrimination and military force,' he reflects. 'As Jesus said, "The truth will set you free" (John 8: 32). In order to enjoy full freedom there must be truth in everything. No lies, no cheating, no bullying, no discrimination. One needs to speak out for the truth. There must be truth in our love and truth in our service. It is urgent that we see truth in those who rule the nation, truth in the non-governmental organisations, and truth in the churches. Then we could be authentically free as God's sons and daughters. All these past years the nation was under a big lie.' His personal motto as a priest and later as a bishop is 'Omnia possum in Eo' — 'I can do all things in Him', from Philippians 4: 13. 'At least one can serve as a thin voice in the wilderness,' he adds. 'And often this thin voice is taken up by the international community and it can become a stronger voice.'

That 'thin' voice of Cardinal Bo's has become stronger and stronger in recent years, and particularly on the theme of inter-religious harmony, religious intolerance and religious freedom. In 2012, horrific violence against the Muslim Rohingya people erupted in Arakan State, and wider anti-Muslim violence occurred in 2013 and 2014 across the country, in places such as Meikhtila, Lashio and Oakkan. Cardinal Bo issued several personal statements, and he and I co-authored two articles, on the English-language Burma-focused news website *Mizzima*[11] and in the weekly newspaper *The Myanmar Times*. We argued that 'true peace and real freedom hinge on respect for Burma's ethnic and religious diversity ... Real peace will be achieved only when the guns fall silent and are put away across the whole nation; when people can return to their homes without fear; and the people of Burma enter into a dialogue with each other and with the government in an atmosphere of mutual respect.' We emphasised that 'no society can be truly democratic, free and peaceful if it does not respect political, racial and religious diversity ... Freedom of thought, conscience, religion or belief, as detailed in Article 18 of the Universal Declaration of Human Rights, is perhaps the most precious and most basic freedom of all. Without the freedom to choose, practise, share and change your beliefs, there is no freedom ... We call on everyone who has a position of influence—in politics, in religion, in the media, in education and in civil society—to use their voice to speak out against religious hatred and intolerance.'[12]

In June 2014, Cardinal Bo wrote a powerful article in *The Washington Post*, in which he said that 'Burma stands on a knife-edge of hope and fear'. He welcomed the political reforms that have occurred, but highlighted the plight of ethnic and religious minorities, as well as other injustices, and appealed to people of all faiths and ethnicities to work for 'unity in diversity.' He warned against 'premature euphoria', saying:

> Concern fills our hearts as we see darkness compete with hope. We pray this is not a false dawn. For five decades Burma endured crucifixion on a cross of injustice bearing five nails: dictatorship, war, displacement, poverty and oppression. Today, a new crucifixion threatens the country, with five new nails: landgrabbing, corruption, economic injustice, ethnic conflict and displacement and religious hatred and violence ... Burma's future hangs in the balance.[13]

In almost every homily, Cardinal Bo finds a way to engage with the social and political challenges the country faces. In his Easter homily in 2014, he said:

> The task of Christians is to move fences, to tear down walls. God was in Christ reconciling the world to Himself, and has given us the ministry of reconciliation ... We went through our way of the cross for the last five decades. A nation was crucified and left to hang on the cross of inhumanity. We were a Good Friday people;

Easter was a distant dream. But there are streaks of hope today ... We are an Easter people. And when are we most like Christ? We are most like Christ when we are doing what he did in his extravagant gift of love on Calvary—forgiving. Hatred has no place in this nation.

In his Christmas homily in 2014, his message was equally clear:

Do not be afraid. Do not be afraid to seek your rights to dignity. Do not be afraid of resisting injustice. Do not be afraid to dream, to imagine a new Burma where justice and righteousness flow like a river ... The Christian community is at the service of the nation and its people. Empowering the vulnerable will be a major task for the Church in a new Burma.

And in his Easter message in 2015, he repeated this call:

This nation was buried in the tomb of oppression and exploitation for six decades. We call for a new resurrection in peace and prosperity for all people ... Christians are the Easter people. We refuse to submit ourselves to the power of darkness ... Our task is unfinished. This is a wounded nation, a bleeding nation. We need to work proactively for peace. 'Injustice anywhere is injustice everywhere,' said Dr Martin Luther King Jr. Our conflicts are rooted in injustice ... Stand for the truth ... We fear no one. We love all. So we will continue to work for peace and justice in this land, bringing mercy and promoting reconciliation.

He highlighted the ethnic conflicts, drugs, human trafficking and poverty, and referred to the role of the Church in Burma, having celebrated the 500th anniversary of its establishment in the country just the previous year. 'We have taught the devil two or three lessons,' said Cardinal Bo. 'Those who thought the Church in Burma was buried in the 1960s were rudely woken up during the 500 years' jubilee. Ours is a resurrected Church. We were buried, but we were risen in faith. And we were the angels of mercy—reaching out to thousands of poor through education, health and human development. We saw God in our suffering brothers and sisters.'

In 1511, the first traders arrived in Burma, together with Portuguese Catholic missionaries, although as early as 1287 evidence of the presence of Christianity was found, in the form of frescos containing crosses and Latin and Greek words in Bagan. The great Jesuit missionary St Francis Xavier had written to his Jesuits in Europe suggesting Pegu, alongside the Moluccas, China or Japan, as a destination to consider. Cardinal Bo decided to hold the 500th Jubilee Celebration in 2014, because the situation had opened in a way that made such a celebration possible. The main message of the Jubilee was, he explains, to 'tell the nation that Catholicism did not just arrive recently. It has permeated this nation, and we are part of the nation.' Over the course of five hundred years, the Church has contributed to education, health and nation-building. In his Jubilee sermon on 22 November 2014, Cardinal Bo described the occasion as 'a day of Epiphany' and 'a Pentecost' for the Church in Burma. The Church is, he said, 'the one institution in the country' that 'can boast of membership from every known ethnic tribe and language group.' It is, he concluded, 'a truly colourful rainbow church'.

Like so many of his sermons, the Jubilee sermon was another cry for justice. 'Our clarion call is to total freedom as St Paul tells the Galatians—"For you were

all called to freedom—love one another". A freedom
from hatred, a freedom from want, a freedom from all
kinds of oppression,' he declared.

The Church in Burma is, according to Cardinal Bo,
'a church of initiative', 'a crucified church', 'a church
of exodus' with hundreds of thousands having fled
war, oppression and poverty in Burma over the past
six decades, and 'a wounded healer'. He challenged the
church to 'reach out' to others and to work for justice
and peace. 'The Church has never flinched from her
social mission, even when it had no support,' he noted.

On Sunday, 4 January 2015, the Vatican announced
the appointment of 20 new cardinals. I returned home
from Mass to hear the news that Archbishop Charles
Maung Bo, my friend, the person who inspired me to
explore becoming a Catholic and then received me
into the Church, was to become Burma's first-ever
cardinal.[14]

Over the subsequent month, Cardinal-elect Bo
gave numerous media interviews, including to the
BBC, *The Wall Street Journal*, Radio Free Asia, Voice of
America and a multitude of other broadcast and print
news organisations. His key priority theme? Religious
freedom, inter-religious harmony, justice and human
rights—repeatedly emphasised in every single interview. 'I want to be a voice for the voiceless,' he said.[15]

Just over a month later, on 14 February—St Val-
entine's Day, as we know it, and the Feast of Saints
Cyril and Methodius, Patrons of Europe, according
to the current Universal Calendar—I had the privilege of being in Rome for the occasion, and attending
Holy Mass the next day with the Holy Father and all
the cardinals. It was a most joyous occasion. At least
three hundred Burmese people came to Rome to be
with their new cardinal. I learned later that when Pope

Francis placed the red biretta on Cardinal Bo's head, he whispered: 'Be strong! Courage! Burma is a little flock, yet God is with you! Go ahead!' In his public homily at the ceremony, Pope Francis explained that the word 'cardinal' comes from the word 'cardo', a hinge. 'As such it is not a kind of accessory, a decoration, like an honorary title,' said the Holy Father. 'Rather, it is a pivot, a point of support and movement essential for the life of the community. You are 'hinges' and are 'incardinated' in the Church of Rome … In the Church, all 'presiding' flows from charity, must be exercised in charity, and is ordered towards charity … It means being able to love without limits.'[16] For Burma, as well as for me personally, Cardinal Bo has long been a 'hinge' who exudes love—and now he is shared with the universal Church.

At Holy Mass in St Peter's the next day, the Holy Father's homily seemed to reflect exactly the ethos by which Cardinal Bo has always lived. Pope Francis said:

> I urge you to serve Jesus crucified in every person who is emarginated, for whatever reason; to see the Lord in every excluded person who is hungry, thirsty, naked; to see the Lord present even in those who have lost their faith, or turned away from the practice of their faith; to see the Lord who is imprisoned, sick, unemployed, persecuted; to see the Lord in the leper—whether in body or soul—who encounters discrimination! We will not find the Lord unless we truly accept the marginalised. May we always have before us the image of Saint Francis, who was unafraid to embrace the leper and to accept every kind of outcast. Truly the Gospel of the marginalised is where our credibility is found and revealed.[17]

On 28 February 2015, just two weeks after he had been created cardinal, 100,000 pilgrims at the 113th celebration of Our Lady of Lourdes at the Marian shrine at Nyaunglebin in Bago province heard Cardinal Bo's homily—which, true to form, focused yet again on the themes of justice, speaking for the poor and oppressed, working for peace and reconciliation. 'Let us not live with indifference,' he said. 'Let us not challenge God, like Cain, the murderer, "Am I my brother's keeper?" God will reply: "Yes, you are your brother's keeper! You have the duty to take care of him!"' In a gesture designed to symbolise a call for peace, Cardinal Bo then released a flock of doves, and called on the Burma Army to initiate a peace process with the ethnic nationalities. 'People are suffering because of the war,' he said, 'and it is up to Tatmadaw (the Armed Forces), as parents [of the nation], to lead the negotiations.'[18]

I was privileged to be received into the Church in Burma at an exciting time for the Church. I became a Catholic in Burma in 2013, a year before the celebration of the 500th anniversary of the arrival of Catholicism in Burma and two years before the appointment of Burma's first-ever cardinal. Towards the end of 2013, there was another exciting development—the announcement that Isodore Ngei Ko Lat, a lay catechist who was killed by Burmese rebels in 1950, was on course to become Burma's first saint.[19] According to Cardinal Bo, in the early stages of the conflict between the Karenni ethnic people and the Burma Army, Italian missionaries and Catholic laity in Karenni State were 'falsely accused of being on the side of the government.' The ethnic armed resistance were predominantly Baptists, and they distrusted the Catholics. A catechist, Zakomo Saw Le-i, and a missionary known as Luigi were killed, and so the priest, Fr Mario Vegara, went to meet the leader of the ethnic armed group in Shadaw. Fr Vegara and his assistant, Fr Peter Galastri, were arrested and brought to Ta-ta-maw village near the Than Lwin river. Catechist Isodore Ngei Ko Lat followed them up to Sa-long village, where the priests' captors asked him to go home. He refused, saying he could not leave his priests. He was shot dead on the spot, and the two missionary priests were killed on the banks of the Than Lwin river.

'Isodore is an example of a faithful follower and a boy of gratitude towards the missionaries and to his cause,' reflects Cardinal Bo. 'But there are many like him who died for the faith and for the Church around the country.' Men such as Fr Stephen Wong, who was martyred in Kengtung Diocese on 7 April 1961, by a Shan Buddhist monk. According to Cardinal Bo, Fr Wong was the sixth priest from the Pontifical Institute for Foreign Missions (PIME) to meet a violent death in the space of ten years. Baptised at the age of seven, Stephen Wong asked his father what he should do with his life. His father, not a Catholic, answered: 'If you want to make money, become a merchant; if you want to acquire merits, become a monk.' He became a priest, and travelled extensively in mountainous areas, on foot or on horseback. He baptised thousands of people, particularly the Akhas, and was particularly active in trying to counter the opium trade. He built 36 opium-free villages for his Christian flock. It was his successful evangelism that angered a Shan Buddhist monk who had been unable to convert the Akhas to Buddhism. The monk concluded that if he could eliminate Fr Wong, the Akhas would convert to Buddhism out of fear. Just before Easter, on route to Meung Chong to hear confessions and baptise a number of people, he was ambushed, shot and beheaded. 'His companions fled and alerted the nearby Catholic Akha village and the Buddhist Shan village,' Cardinal Bo recounts. 'When the people arrived, they found Stephen lying in a pool of his own blood. The Shans made a coffin and the body was transported to the cathedral in Kengtung. It became as dark as night for several hours—even though it was daytime. All knew that a new martyr had laid down his life for them. Thousands came for his funeral, including many Buddhist monks, ashamed that he should be killed by one of them.'[20]

Strengthened by the Jubilee, the possibility of a Burmese saint being recognised and the appointment of the first cardinal, the Church in Burma—with approximately 800,000 followers—is devout, traditional and enthusiastic, according to Cardinal Bo. 'At the same time, we need to upgrade the intellectual and spiritual formation of seminarians and priests. Many priests feel inadequate compared to other Christian pastors,' he says. 'Our hope would be that the Church would be a strong agent in building the nation, in the fields of education, health, peace-building and harmony in the nation. It is not by proselytizing that the Church grows, but it is by attraction. The Church must strive to bring reconciliation and peace. No peace, no progress. No justice, no peace.'

As this chapter shows, there were a number of courageous Catholics who played an important part in my journey into the Church, but of them all, Cardinal Bo was the most instrumental. When I used that word—'instrumental'—in conversation with the cardinal, asking his thoughts on evangelisation, he immediately latched on to its correct meaning. 'As you rightly said, we are just the instruments. The whole process of accepting Christ and coming into the Church is the entire work of the Spirit,' he said. 'The Spirit proceeds to the person and to the places before the arrival of the instruments. Faith is a gift, but it demands a response. Before sharing one's faith, it is necessary that we become acquainted with each other. We are all human beings. The first technique for social and evangelical need is that we take an interest in others, especially their language and culture. I always remind myself that to win the hearts of the people, speaking their dialect and being interested in their culture is the key. Once you speak a language or know the culture, speaking about Jesus becomes easy.'

It is hard to know Cardinal Bo and not love him; and indeed hard to love Cardinal Bo and not be attracted to the Church he serves. At least that is my experience. And according to him, I am the only foreigner to have been received into the Church in Burma during his time as a bishop. When I asked him, several years later, why he first invited me to be the first to receive this honour, he said simply: 'I made the proposal to receive you in St Mary's Cathedral, Rangoon, simply because you love Burma and you have sacrificed so much for the truth, especially for Christians and other minorities.' And when I asked what he felt when I accepted his invitation to be received into the Church, he said with typical humility, grace and generosity: 'You yourself were and are a gift to me. You are more a treasure to us than I to you. When you were baptised into the Catholic Church at St Mary's Cathedral in Rangoon, I just simply thanked God for his great and wonderful ways, which I did not understand. I do not take any credit, except I thank God for you. You are a gift for the Church and for the nation of Burma. It is not that we gave something to you, it is you who brought a gift for the Church and the nation.' I beg to differ with His Eminence. I contend that I have received infinitely more from him and from the people of Burma than I can ever possibly give.

Notes

1   Arnold S. Kohen, *From the Place of the Dead: The Epic Struggles of Bishop Belo of East Timor* (New York, St Martin's Press, 1999), p. 37.

2   Francis Sejersted, Chairman of the Norwegian Nobel Committee, Award Ceremony Speech, 10 December 1996.

3   Bishop Carlos Filipe Ximenes Belo, Nobel Peace Prize Lecture, 10 December 1996.

4   Keith Bradsher, 'Gentle cleric's stature grows as he risks ire of China', *The New York Times*, 8 July 2006.

5   *Ibid.*

6   BBC News, Profile: Cardinal Zen

7   James Pomfret and Yimou Lee, 'Hong Kong clashes, arrests kick-start plans to blockade city', Reuters, 27 September 2014.

8   Asia News, 'Pope Francis encourages Cardinal Zen, "the one who fights with a sling"', 24 October 2014.

9   See youtube video — https://www.youtube.com/watch?v=aYhPP3VNymk.

10 BBC, 'Pakistan Minorities Minister Shahbaz Bhatti shot dead', 2 March 2011.

11 Archbishop Charles Maung Bo and Benedict Rogers, 'Religious violence threatens to tear Myanmar apart', *Mizzima*, 3 May 2013.

12 Archbishop Charles Maung Bo and Benedict Rogers, 'Myanmar's religious diversity: dialogue trumps violence', *The Myanmar Times*, 23 August 2013.

13 Archbishop Charles Bo, 'Burma needs tolerance to reach its potential', *The Washington Post*, 13 June 2014.

14 Stuart Alan Becker, 'Myanmar's first cardinal strives to be a "voice for the voiceless"', *The Myanmar Times*, 1 April 2015.

15 Shibani Mahtani, 'Myanmar Cardinal Charles Maung Bo to work toward religious tolerance', *The Wall Street Journal*, 7 January 2014.

16 Pope Francis, address to new cardinals: 'Presiding flows from charity', 14 February 2015.

17 Pope Francis: 'Cardinals are servants of the Church', 15 February 2015.

18   Asia News, 'Yangon cardinal calls for dialogue between military and ethnic militias to end conflict in Myanmar', 2 March 2015.

19   Simon Roughneen, 'With Burma's first Catholic saint possible, archbishop hopes for papal visit', *The Irrawaddy*, 19 December 2013.

20   Fr Edward P. Evans, *The History of the Catholic Church in Burma 1856–1966.*

✣ 4 ✣

The Politicians, the Soldier
and the Activist

Trust in God and tether your camel.

An Arabic proverb

POLITICS AND ACTIVISM have been inter-twined with my journey of faith since the very beginning. For me, the words of James 2: 14–26 strike a chord—'Faith without deeds is dead'. How faith impacts society is a question that has been at the heart of my spiritual life.

My interest in politics, human rights and international affairs predated my conscious journey of faith, but it came alive once I encountered Christ. As a consequence, I have had the privilege of knowing and working closely with several politicians and public figures who have exemplified faith in action. Several are Christians from Protestant traditions, and they inspire me just as much as those who are Catholic. Indeed, as previously mentioned, the fuse for my passion for human rights advocacy was lit by Baroness Caroline Cox, a practising Anglican, and I have had the privilege of travelling and working very closely with her. US Congressman Frank Wolf, with whom I travelled, together with Baroness Cox, to Armenia and war-torn Nagorno Karabakh in 1994, just a few months after coming to faith in Christ, is a hero of mine. No one has done more than Frank Wolf, a Presbyterian, to highlight religious persecution and human rights in the American political arena. Several Evangelical Christian Members of Parliament in Britain—notably Gary Streeter and more recently David Burrowes and Fiona Bruce, among others—stand out as champions on the issues about which I care. And in history, I am constantly inspired by the examples of William Wilberforce, Dietrich Bonhoeffer, Martin Luther King and Archbishop Desmond Tutu—all Protestants, and in several instances Evangelicals. Similarly among authors, evangelical writers such as C. S. Lewis, John Stott, Os Guinness, Tom Wright, Charles Colson, John Eldredge, Nicky Gumbel, Jim Wallis and Philip Yancey are among my favourite Christian writers.

So, there are Christians of all traditions who have inspired and influenced me. Nevertheless, this book focuses primarily on my journey into the Catholic Church, and no one has done more to encourage me than Lord Alton of Liverpool, a long-standing parliamentarian.

Lord Alton of Liverpool

David Alton's story is worth a book of its own. Born on a housing estate in the east end of London in 1951, he was educated at the Jesuit-run Campion School in Hornchurch which, he told me, encouraged young Catholics to apply their faith to the world. His interest in politics was first aroused by the Soviet occupation of Czechoslovakia, apartheid in South Africa and the assassinations of Martin Luther King Jr and Robert Kennedy. Racial or religious discrimination aroused his passionate opposition. But it was the passage of the 1967 Abortion Act which most engaged him. 'I collected petitions against it,' he told me in an interview for a Catholic magazine called *Crisis*. 'The die was being cast for the future.'[1]

At 17, David joined the Liberal Party, which at the time had just six members of Parliament and was at 3 per cent in the opinion polls. A year later, he went to Liverpool to study history and divinity at a Catholic college and 'was shocked by the extent of the poverty and deprivation'. Like many young Catholic boys he thought about religious life—and at the age of 12, he wrote to an African missionary society—but soon realised that his vocation was in 'lay ministry through public and political life'.

The Liberal Party was, at the time, very different from today's Liberal Democrats. 'It had a non-corporatist, non-state approach to industry and ownership, as opposed to the nationalising tendencies of the Labour Party,' David recalls. 'The Liberals emphasised liberty, but also the importance of the strength of community.' It was the party of Gladstone, G. K. Chesterton and Hilaire Belloc.

There followed a meteoric rise through the ranks. Upon graduation, David became a special-needs teacher and at age 21 was elected the youngest city councillor in Britain, going on to become the council's deputy leader and housing chairman. Aged 23 he contested the two general elections of 1974 and then, in 1979, the Labour member of Parliament for Liverpool Edge Hill died and a by-election was called. At the age of just 28 David stood as the Liberal candidate, won the seat and became the youngest MP at the time. It was at the height of the 'Winter of Discontent', with the country in economic turmoil and the Labour government held to ransom by the trade unions. 'The country was in anarchy,' he recalls. 'The dead were not being buried.' The by-election took place amidst what David describes as 'the most bizarre few weeks of my life'.

Winning the seat was an extraordinary moment. 'From nowhere I got what was then the biggest ever political swing — a 38 per cent swing. But I was also the shortest-lived MP ever. The night before I was elected, the Labour government was defeated by Margaret Thatcher in a vote of confidence, and a general election was called. I thought I would become an after-dinner joke for the rest of my life.'

Taking his seat the next day, David chose to focus in his maiden speech on 'terrorism, Ireland, the lessons of Liverpool where sectarianism had been overcome by Christian cooperation, by the outstanding leadership of the Anglican bishop and the Catholic archbishop who healed so many of the strains of the past'. Such a theme could not have been more apposite, because on the day after the Edge Hill by-election one of Margaret Thatcher's closest allies, Airey Neave, was blown up by a car bomb as he was leaving Parliament. The Irish National Liberation Army (INLA), an off-shoot of the Irish Republican Army (IRA) terrorist organisation, claimed responsibility. Four hours after David's maiden speech, Parliament was prorogued and the general election campaign began.

To his surprise, David was re-elected. Most by-election victories by Liberals tend to be protest votes against the two major parties, and so he had feared that the Liverpool electorate would return to Labour in the general election. Instead, they stuck with him and he served for the next 18 years in the House of Commons. He became his party's chief whip, and was talked of as a future leader.

The year 1987 brought the moment for which David is perhaps best known. Winning a place in the private members' ballot, 20 years to the day since the introduction of the Abortion Act, he decided to put forward a bill to reduce the time in which abortions could take place, from 28 weeks' gestation down to 18 weeks. He told his party leader David Steel, who had introduced the original abortion legislation, that he planned 'to do everything I can to mitigate your legislation' — and yet, with typical graciousness, he emphasised that their disagreement was not personal. 'We fundamentally disagree about the right to life, and I hope that like Jane Roe he will one day change his mind, but you don't have to hate someone because they take a contrary view to you. In David Steel's favour, he never believed that his legislation would lead to some of its outcomes, such as multiple abortions and gender abortions, and he adamantly opposed Paddy Ashdown's support for abortion becoming a party policy — he understood that this is a fundamental issue of conscience.'

Not everyone was as gracious. His home was picketed, his constituency offices burned down, and his public meetings around the country were met with demonstrations. 'There were police cordons everywhere,' he says. At a party conference one delegate spat at him. 'I had been a member since I was 17, and if I did not have the right to hold my own views about abortion, then the party no longer had a right to call itself Liberal,' he says. But this was not the first time he endured such abuse. As a councillor and then an MP earlier in the 1980s, he was Liverpool's only non-Socialist representative at a time when Trotskyite militant forces had taken control of the city. Riots fomented by the Workers Revolutionary Party left streets on fire. 'I had a brick in my face and had 12 stitches, and I had a chair thrown at me,' he recalls. 'On one occasion, the council was suspended when a man had his hands round my throat and had to be pulled off by the police. As an MP, my weekly advice centres were regularly picketed. But the nastier they got, the bigger my majority got. Ordinary people could see these people for what they were. It was important to be robust and to see them off democratically.'

His bill to reduce the time in which abortions could take place won every round of voting in the House of Commons, and secured the biggest turnout for a private member's bill since the Second World War. 'It never lost a vote at any stage, and won on second reading by a majority of 45,' he says.

A key aspect of his campaign on abortion was building cross-party, ecumenical and indeed inter-religious support. 'I have always enjoyed working with people of different political colours. I've learned far more doing that than by digging into a partisan hole and thinking "my party, right or wrong",' he says. Evangelical Christians and Jews became major allies, with a Jewish entrepreneur sponsoring a million copies of a photograph of a baby at 18 weeks' gestation. David persuaded a major national newspaper to run it on the front page. 'When a Catholic and an Orthodox Jew get together, it's a powerful combination,' he notes. The image began to transform the debate. 'A million of these cards arrived in Parliament. Every day I could see them arriving at every MP's office. Colleagues started coming to me and asking what it was all about.' An opinion poll in *The Guardian* showed that 67 per cent of women and 54 per cent of men supported the bill.

Despite all this success, the bill never made it into law. It was 'talked out' by opponents in the chamber.

'I managed the extraordinary feat of uniting all four political leaders, who could agree about nothing else, but were all agreed in their opposition to my Bill,' he notes. 'There have been nearly eight million abortions since 1967. One in five pregnancies ends in abortion. There are 184,000 abortions a year. If my bill had passed, it would have saved 8,000 lives a year.'

The bill sought to place limits on abortion, not to ban it altogether, though David is unflinching in his pro-life stand: 'Apart from where a mother's life is at risk, I am opposed to abortion at any stage. Life begins at fertilisation and it deserves our protection from the outset.' He says 'the slogan "my right to choose" has "me", "my", "I" at the heart of the equation. It distorts the argument by emphasising rights shorn of responsibilities. It's worth unpicking the slogan. "Choice" comes from the same Greek word as the word "heresy". The modern heresy is to imagine that you can exercise choice without consequences. It is clap-trap to say "I've got my values, you've got yours, I can make my choice, you can make yours". This leads to a neutrality which implies that there is nothing right or wrong, nothing absolute. The right to stop someone from having the opportunity to be born? This profoundly mistaken view has had disastrous consequences.' In his view, for Christians the position is non-negotiable. 'If every one of us is made in the image of God, then this is not an issue on which we can be neutral.' To Catholic politicians who have supported abortion — including recent votes on the abortion of girls on the grounds of their gender — David says simply: 'We need to reflect on Jesus's words "You do it to the least of my brethren, you do it to me". Any politician voting in favour of killing or experimenting on unborn children should read Psalm 138.'

The fact that his bill did not attempt to completely reverse the 1967 Abortion Act, but instead place limits, was therefore not a reflection of David's opinion but a question of tactics. 'If you look back at Wilberforce's struggles against slavery, he hacked away year after year, chipping away at the legislation, sometimes winning, sometimes being defeated, but incrementally building up opposition to slavery.' In the same way, by challenging the upper time limits for abortion and illustrating the humanity of the child, his bill helped clear the way for further debates, which continue to this day. He has always made it clear that he is pro-life rather than 'anti-abortion'—for the woman and the child—and in saying that 'life begins at conception but it doesn't end at birth' he says human rights, human life, and human dignity stand together.

Out of this episode came several unexpected blessings.

Firstly, David met his wife, Elizabeth, daughter of an Anglican vicar, who volunteered to help in the campaign.

Secondly, a new ecumenical organisation, the Epiphany Group, was born. 'My bill was the first time evangelicals came alongside Catholics to oppose abortion. Cardinal Hume spoke at a rally alongside the head of the Evangelical Alliance. I thought it would be a pity to lose this, and so I drew together a group of Catholics and evangelicals to see if there were other things we had in common,' explains David. 'We met at a Catholic monastery over the Epiphany weekend of 1989. Those who met founded the Epiphany Group because, like the Epiphanarians—the Magi—we knew what our gifts were, we knew who we followed, but we weren't sure where we were going or how long it would take to get there!'

This led to a rally of 2,000 people at which the Westminster Declaration was launched, establishing six principles for Christian engagement in politics: social justice, respect for life, active compassion, empowerment, reconciliation and good stewardship. This then gave rise to the Movement for Christian Democracy, with three objectives: to engage Christians in political life, to develop as a think-tank for policy ideas and ultimately, if people wished, to evolve into a political party modelled on Christian Democrat traditions in Europe. 'It was a transitional point for people going into the political parties,' says David. 'No party in this country is Christian, even those that call themselves such, because all of us fall short of what Jesus would wish of us.'

The third blessing was a number of life-long cross-party friendships. Three Conservatives became very active in support of David's bill, the most prominent of whom was Ann Widdecombe. Describing her as 'a doughty, formidable ally' and one of the Catholic Church's greatest assets, David became her sponsor when she left the Church of England to become Catholic, and she became godmother to one of his children.

David's pro-life battles have continued throughout his political career. In 1992, the Liberal Democrats passed a party conference motion adopting a pro-abortion policy. Traditionally, abortion—along with euthanasia, capital punishment and other ethical questions—has been regarded as a matter of conscience and therefore left to a free vote in Parliament, with the political parties not adopting an official position. The Liberal Democrats' 1992 decision changed that, and David realised he could not in good conscience run for election on such a ticket. On the same day as the adoption of a pro-abortion motion, the party voted for a motion which included a ban on the use of goldfish as prizes at fairs. David went on national television that night, announcing he would not seek re-election and would be leaving the party at the general election. 'A party that votes for the killing of the unborn in the afternoon, after voting to protect goldfish in the morning, is a party which has forfeited my intellectual and emotional support,' he said.

A decision based on integrity and conscience which might well have led to the end of his political career was instead rewarded with a new phase of political life. In 1997, having just lost the general election, the outgoing prime minister, John Major, as one of his last acts, offered David a seat in the House of Lords. David made it clear that although he was leaving the Liberal Democrats he was not ready to join another party, to which John Major responded with extraordinary political generosity by saying that where David sat in the House of Lords was his own decision. David became an independent crossbencher, free of party affiliation, and continues two decades later to make a much-respected contribution to political life.

Pro-life work remains central to David's political activities, as does his other major passion: international human rights, and particularly religious freedom. It is through these issues that I have come to know him and be inspired by him, working closely with him on North Korea and Burma and following with interest his work in other parts of the world: Sudan, the Democratic Republic of Congo, Brazil, Vietnam and China, to name just a few.

From the very start of his parliamentary career, David became a champion for human rights and democracy. He co-founded the Christian advocacy group Jubilee Campaign in 1987, and campaigned for the release of seven Siberian Pentecostals sheltered in the American Embassy in Moscow. At the height of the Cold War, he travelled to the Soviet Union to deliver a printing machine to the Russian dissident, Alexander Ogorodnikov, and on a visit to Ukraine he was arrested at midnight, carrying 200 Ukrainian prayer books and a television camera. 'But when the guards opened my bags, all they took were a biography of Cardinal Hume that I had for personal reading, and a copy of my local newspaper, *The Liverpool Echo*! The Soviets weren't ready for the Scouse Mouse cartoon,' he recalls.

In 2010, I travelled with David, and Baroness Cox, to Pyongyang, to try to talk to the North Korean regime about their horrific human rights record. No one has done more than David to highlight the crimes against humanity that the ruling Kim dynasty has perpetrated in North Korea, and yet at the same time he has managed, uniquely, to open up channels of communication with the regime. He has visited North Korea four times, and written a superb book—*Building Bridges: Is there Hope for North Korea?* I helped draft the report which David and Baroness Cox published following our visit, with a title reflective of the same theme— *Building Bridges, not Walls: The Case for Constructive, Critical Engagement with North Korea.*[2]

That visit to North Korea was not only a profoundly significant experience in my human rights work—it was like walking into the pages of George Orwell's *Nineteen Eighty-Four*—but it was also, with hindsight, an important staging post on my journey into the Catholic Church. Firstly, while at the time I was not actively considering Catholicism, I had decided out of curiosity to read Pope Benedict XVI's encyclicals, and took them with me on the journey. My in-flight reading was *Caritas in veritate, Spe salvi* and *Deus caritas est*. As I have written earlier and as I will later discuss, the writings of Benedict XVI had a profound impact on me. But equally significant was what David introduced me to. On the flight from Beijing to Pyongyang, he pulled out a DVD. It was a documentary film about Saint Pope John Paul II's first visit to Poland after he became pope. Made by Newt Gingrich, it is called *Nine Days that Changed the World*.[3] A powerful film wherever it is viewed, its impact was made all the more significant by the fact that we watched it, the three of us, in our Pyongyang hotel room, conscious that just as St John Paul II's visit to Poland challenged the very foundations of the Communist regime with life-changing repercussions across Europe, there we were trying to shine a very small flickering light in the darkest corner of the earth today. North Korea must rank as the world's most repressive regime, its most closed society, where alternative ideas or external sources of information are regarded as treasonous. I have re-watched that documentary countless times, and without doubt the story of St John Paul II sowed seeds in my own spirit that later bore fruit in my journey of faith.

Five years earlier, I stood as a parliamentary candidate myself, in the City of Durham. In the run-up to the 2005 general election, David offered to come and support me in my campaign. However, he said there was one condition: I was the Conservative Party candidate, and as an independent he would not come on a party platform. He would, however, come on a pro-life platform.

I had not particularly focused on pro-life issues, but I knew instinctively that I was pro-life and so I gladly organised a pro-life public meeting, which David would address. Chaired by Dr Robert Song, a specialist in bio-ethics at Durham University and—

conveniently—a Labour Party member, the packed meeting heard from my friend James Mawdsley, at the time the Conservative candidate in Hyndburn, a representative of LIFE North-East, and from me, briefly, before David gave the keynote speech.

David had no text, just a few bullet point notes. Halfway through his speech, he told the story of a student from Oxford University who, almost 20 years previously, had launched a legal challenge against his ex-girlfriend who was pregnant with his child and planned to have an abortion. So impressed with the courage of his convictions, his ex-girlfriend agreed to proceed with the pregnancy and abandon her intention to have an abortion, on one condition: that he raise the child himself, and that she would have nothing more to do with either of them. He agreed, and the child was born. It became known as the 'Oxford Student Case'.

David told me afterwards that he had had no intention of telling this particular story when he had prepared his remarks, that he had not told it for many years, and that it came to him as he was speaking. What he could not possibly have known was that anyone connected with the case would be in that Durham meeting hall that night.

At the end of the meeting, a middle-aged man approached us. His name was Robert Carver. 'I was the Oxford student,' he told us. A few days later, I went to have tea with Robert, his wife and his daughter who was preparing to go off to university. She was the daughter who, if he had not acted, would not be alive today.

Another surprise occurred as we were leaving the event. The president of the Students' Union approached us. He was, as it happened, a Conservative, and a sensible middle-of-the-road person, not a radical liberal, but nevertheless he admitted that abortion and other pro-life issues were not topics he had previously given much thought to. Having heard David, however, he said that it was 'the most important speech' he had ever heard, and that the evidence and arguments David had laid out had 'blown' his mind.

A few days previously, a student who had been helping in my election campaign approached me, saying she was 'very worried'. I asked why. She asked whether the meeting planned with David was to be 'an anti-abortion meeting'. I told her it was 'a pro-life meeting'. She asked whether it would include discussion of abortion, and I said of course—but also euthanasia and bio-ethics. She told me that because of my background as a human rights activist and the interesting campaign I had fought, I had attracted quite a lot of student support. However, she was concerned that if I was associated with an anti-abortion gathering, I would lose support. She suggested it would be better if I keep my views on this topic to myself, until such a time as I am elected to Parliament and then I can speak up. I told her that I did not want to succeed in politics by hiding my views, and that I'd rather be honest about what I believe and lose, than win by deception. The fact that the room was packed, with standing room only; that I had a number of people telling me that for the first time in their lives they would vote Conservative because of the stand I had taken; that the Student Union president had been so influenced by what he heard; and that we met the Oxford Student all made it worthwhile. And it made me appreciate, once again, David Alton's courage, conviction and integrity.

In an interview I did with David for *Crisis* magazine, he summed up his view that life needs to be measured by 'human ecology'.[4] In Britain today, he claimed, 43 per cent of marriages end in divorce; hundreds of thousands of children have no contact with their fathers; a million elderly people do not see a friend, relative or neighbour during an average week; and one in five pregnancies ends in abortion. Add to this genocide, crimes against humanity, torture, sexual violence, slavery, trafficking and religious persecution, all causes David has highlighted in debates in Parliament and by travelling to gather first-hand evidence.

'If we measure the happiness of society in these terms rather than the Dow Jones Index or the value of the pound to the dollar, we come to a rather different conclusion about the health of our society. Wilberforce campaigned against the evil of slavery but he also had a second objective—"the reformation of manners". He believed that a religious renewal would transform the person and that subsequently this would change the nature and direction of society,' said David.[5]

When he chaired a meeting at Westminster for Dr Alveda King, the niece of Martin Luther King, who, having had three abortions has, along with Jane Roe (Roe *v.* Wade), become a leading prolife activist, David Alton argued that the prolife battle could draw on the experience of Wilberforce and the abolitionists. Dr King said it is the civil rights campaign of our time and they both looked forward to the day when, from the next generation, a Wilberforce emerges to successfully change hearts, minds and laws.

In 2011, after I had had that significant conversation with Archbishop Bo in Rangoon and begun actively to explore the Catholic faith, one of the first people to whom I turned was David. In personal discussions and by e-mail, he introduced me to a range of literary works which fuelled my journey. He was a source of good counsel and encouragement. And he then travelled with me to Burma, as my sponsor into the Church. I owe him a great debt of gratitude both for the causes he champions, and for the personal mentoring and inspiration he has given to me.

Ann Widdecombe

David's close friend and ally, Ann Widdecombe, is another Catholic politician whom I admire. I first met her with David on Shrove Tuesday 2003. I had been meeting David to discuss Burma, and had only recently moved back to London after five years in Hong Kong. David and I were in the bar in the House of Lords. Suddenly, he looked at his watch and exclaimed: 'Oh dear, Ann will kill me!' He asked me to wait, while he went to collect her from the Peer's Lobby.

I knew very well which 'Ann' he was referring to. At that time I knew her only from her media persona, and I felt a little intimidated. I had not been planning an evening with Ann Widdecombe. However, when she joined us she could not have been warmer. She put me at ease immediately, and when we finished drinks in the House of Lords, and she and David were discussing where to go on for dinner, she insisted I join them. I had not wanted to intrude on an evening that was established as a tradition for them, in preparation for giving up alcohol for Lent. But she encouraged me to come along, and we ended up drinking retsina at a Greek restaurant in Pimlico. At one point she fixed me with a beady eye across the table and asked: 'Are *you* giving up drinking for Lent?' Before I could answer, David gave me a wink and said 'You are now!'

That evening Ann promised that if I was selected as a parliamentary candidate, she would come and campaign for me. She was as good as her word, and spent an evening and a morning with me in Durham in the 2005 campaign.

What struck me at the time was how ordinary people in Durham responded to her. They loved her. In the city's Market Place, as we did a walk-about, people kept coming up to shake her hand. At a public meeting, people found her down-to-earth common sense answers refreshing. And when we went to visit a deprived housing estate, she took off like an exocet missile, careering from one side of the street to the other, handing out leaflets and waving at people. This was not long after she had left the frontbench and begun her television career, and so people were hanging out of upstairs windows shouting 'Ann, Ann, we've seen you on *Celebrity Fit Club*. We love you!' It was a struggle for me to keep up with her.

As we drove around the constituency, I gave Ann the loud-hailer. She had a very clever knack of deliberately not speaking in complete sentences—because, as she explained, if a pedestrian is to hear anything from a passing vehicle, it has to be instant words or they will have lost the thread by the time the sentence has been completed and the car will have disappeared into the distance. So her mantra involved throwing out the following words in quick succession: 'Vote Conservative. Vote Rogers. Ben Rogers. May 5th.' But every few moments she would throw in the phrase: 'Be Positive. Vote Conservative.' The speed of the word machine increased as we went along so it became: 'Conservative. Rogers. May 5th. Be Positive. Rogers. Ben Rogers. Be Positive. May 5th. Conservative.' Her energy and tenacity were phenomenal. At one point we pulled up alongside a bus at a traffic lights and I thought she would give it a rest, but not a bit of it.

'Hello bus. Be positive,' she trilled. I got the giggles and unfortunately swerved into the next lane without concentrating, narrowly missing a road accident but causing a stream of car horns to beep. They were not beeping in support of my campaign, I was sure.

At one point, overcome with the wonder of the occasion, I completely forgot where I had parked the car. I knew what street it was in, but could not find it. Ann and I walked up and down repeatedly trying to find it. In her wonderful matronly way, she tried to help by saying repeatedly: 'Now come on Ben, think. Think. *Think.* Think where you parked it. *Think*, Ben. *Think. Think!*' I was trying to think but Ann encouraging me to do so without leaving me much time in between to give my thoughts a chance did not help. We did eventually find the car, however, and she was remarkably understanding and gracious.

I have always admired Ann as one of a very rare breed: a politician who speaks her mind regardless of what people think. Whether one agrees with her or not, one has to respect her integrity, the courage of her convictions. In her Craigmyle Lecture to the Catholic Union in 2014 she cited Pope St John Paul II's encyclical *Veritatis splendor*, noting that 'one may not determine good by what is popular or popularly accepted but only by reference to absolute truth. Something may be widely accepted as right but can still be wrong and vice versa.'

Yet contrary to her public image, in addition to being a person of very firm convictions, she is a remarkably generous, warm and fun person. The City of Durham was hardly a seat which the Conservatives were ever going to win, and as a former Shadow Home Secretary she could quite understandably have concluded it was not worth her time. But on the contrary, perhaps conscious of the commitment she had made in that Greek restaurant in Pimlico two years previously, she came to support and encourage me—and has continued to do so ever since.

Interviewing Ann for this book, I asked her—somewhat foolishly—how she lived out her faith post-politics. Typically, I received a very straight, sensible answer: 'Faith governs everything you do.'

Ann was, like me, a convert to the Catholic Church from the Church of England. 'I had very deep Anglican roots,' she told me. Her brother, nephew and uncle were Anglican vicars, and her ancestors had Anglican clergy among them for several generations. 'But I very gradually became disillusioned with the Church of England. There was Hugh Montefiore [bishop of Birmingham] suggesting that Christ was gay; David Jenkins [bishop of Durham] questioning the Virgin birth. The Church never seemed to know what it believed, and it was sacrificing faith to fashion and creed to compromise.'

Her disillusion led at one stage to despair, and she went through a period of agnosticism. She returned to the Church, but continued to struggle with its departure from orthodoxy. 'The last straw was the debate about the ordination of women. The debate was not asking "Is this theologically right?" I left the Church of England within five minutes of the ordination of women [in November 1992], and the following March I was received into the Catholic Church,' she recalls.

As she said in an interview with *The New Statesman*, 'the Catholic Church doesn't care if something is unpopular. As far as the Catholic Church is concerned if it's true it's true, and if it's false it's false. The issue over women priests was not only that I think it's theologically impossible to ordain women, it was the nature of the debate that was the damaging thing, because instead of the debate being "Is this theologically possible?" the debate was "If we don't do this we won't be acceptable to the outside world". To me, that was an abdication of the Church's role, which is to lead, not to follow.'[6]

Like many converts, including myself, she did have doctrinal reservations about Catholicism — particularly purgatory, and transubstantiation. But today, she says she has no regrets. 'I certainly have feelings of nostalgia, but not regret. Nostalgia for things such as church bells peeling, pews and polish. I went on Easter Sunday with relatives to an Anglican 1662 Prayer Book service recently, and I love the old language.' Unlike me, she admits that 'there was a large push factor — I can't deny that', but there was a 'pull factor' towards Catholicism as well. 'I could have gone to a number of places, and in the end I was drawn to the Catholic Church.' Catholics who inspired her included Cardinal Basil Hume, Pope St John Paul II, Mother Theresa and Blessed John Henry Newman. William Wilberforce, an evangelical, is also among her heroes, as he is among mine — 'not just', as she says, 'because of the abolition of slavery, but because he stuck at it when everything else was against him. So, if you like, what I respect in Wilberforce is the sheer moral resolution.'[7]

Her pro-life campaigning preceded her Catholic faith. 'I am pro-life not because I am Catholic — I was a pro-life Anglican and a pro-life agnostic before I became a Catholic. I could say though that I am Catholic because I am pro-life.'

As described earlier, she joined forces with David Alton and they have been close friends ever since. She shares David's mix of conviction and pragmatism — a firm set of beliefs rooted in Catholic principles, yet some canny political skills too. In regard to David's private member's bill, 'the challenge was around where to compromise and where not to compromise,' she told me. 'Should there, for example, be exemption for the severely handicapped? Ninety-two per cent of children are aborted not because of handicap—so if there is a shipwreck, would you try to get the ninety-two off, or would you focus on the eight?'

And her common sense, no nonsense approach has led her to challenge some of the Church's practices. In 2010—pre-Pope Francis—she criticised the Church's poor public relations skills in an article in *The Guardian*.

> One of the biggest propaganda coups against the Catholic church in recent years has been to portray it as riddled with paedophiles whose vile activities it sought to cover up. Apart from the occasional defensive flash when a senior churchman is wrongly accused of inaction, the Church has merely apologised and asked for forgiveness. Well, so it should. One child abused would be one too many; but it is frustrating that the church does so little to put its role in proportion. Meek and mild may be good, but leaving the ordinary members of the flock bleating in bewilderment as the wolves of Fleet Street snarl around them, jaws foaming with allegations, is not good. For those of us who do both God and PR, that will be as frustrating as it is heartbreaking.[8]

As well as being known as a devout Catholic convert, Ann emphasised to me the importance of Christian unity. 'We should not become too preoccupied with our differences. We read the same Scriptures, believe the same Creed, say the same Lord's prayer. What's the issue? We need to be more outward-looking. We need to see our common ground—and we need common sense.' Even the fiery Northern Ireland Protestant preacher and politician Ian Paisley, who was as anti-Catholic as they come, joined Catholics 'on things like abortion,' she points out. Once again, that firm conviction mixed with common sense is what I, and many others, love about Ann Widdecombe. Her straight-talking is imbued with St Paul's words in 2 Corinthians 4: 13—'I believed, and so I spoke.'

Jim Dobbin

Another Catholic member of Parliament with whom I had the privilege of working occasionally was Jim Dobbin, a Labour politician who died tragically in 2014 while on a parliamentary visit to Poland. According to an obituary by Chris Whitehouse in *The Tablet*, Jim—who chaired the All-Party Parliamentary Pro-Life Group—'often said that promoting the pro-life cause was the primary reason he wanted to be an MP'.[9]

I worked closely with Jim on issues of international human rights, particularly religious freedom. He took an especially close interest in North Korea.

Jim was also a leading light in the Catholic Legislators Network, supporting its convenor Rob Flello—another Labour MP who had a remarkable conversion to Catholicism—in his efforts to strengthen the Catholic community in Parliament. Every Wednesday, Mass is celebrated in the Crypt Chapel known as St Mary Undercroft, which lies underneath Westminster Hall, the scene of many historic events in parliamentary history over 900 years including the trial of King Charles I in 1649.

US Catholic legislators

Across the Atlantic, two American politicians who have long inspired me because of the way their Catholic faith is lived out in their commitment to international human rights, humanitarian needs and the pro-life cause are Congressman Christopher Smith of New Jersey, and Sam Brownback, former Senator and now Governor of Kansas who ran for president in 2008.

Governor Brownback went through a similar spiritual journey to my own, from evangelical to Catholic. And like me, he has a deep desire to build Christian unity across the traditions, and rejects the use of the word 'conversion.' Indeed, he described his journey from Methodist upbringing through evangelicalism to Catholicism as not so much a change of faith as a return to its roots. 'A conversion is if I became a Buddhist,' he says. 'Joining the Catholic Church was joining the early Church. This is the mother Church. This is the Church out of which orthodoxy and Protestantism came.'[10]

During his years in the United States Senate, Sam Brownback championed a variety of international human rights and humanitarian causes, joining forces with political rivals to help victims of human trafficking, women's rights in Afghanistan, the people of Sudan, North Korea, Burma and beyond. He talks of the need to 'convert the culture' by spreading God's love, and speaks of grace and mercy—not typical themes for a politician. He once apologised to Hillary Clinton for what he had thought about her and her husband; he washed the feet of one of his staff at a farewell party. According to *The Washington Post*, 'when he feels his staffers need guidance, he gives them index cards with Scripture encouraging them to follow Christ's model of servant leadership, or reminding them that "pride goes before destruction".'[11] He admits to struggling 'to be really fully committed to the faith—to die to self', to 'pick up His cross daily and carry it'.

In 2010, I travelled to Washington, DC, with a representative of one of the most marginalised and persecuted people on earth, Burma's Muslim Rohingyas. One of the meetings we were fortunate to secure was with Congressman Christopher Smith. I had long been an admirer of Chris Smith—but from that meeting on he became a real inspiration to me.

I had told my Rohingya friend that it was very unusual to secure a meeting with a Congressman—usually one meets with their staff. Most likely, I said, we would have 10 or 15 minutes, and so would need to get across the key points concisely and clearly, take a photograph, make one request for action, and leave.

My Rohingya friend was superb, and did precisely as instructed. But after he had given a very brief introduction to the situation, and Mr Smith heard the appalling dehumanisation of the Rohingyas, he kept asking questions. He got out a map to see where the Rohingyas are located. He asked to see photographs. He asked what he could do. We discussed various ideas, including a Congressional resolution. Over an hour later, we emerged from his office, elated that someone in his position had shown such concern.

But that, I discovered, is Chris Smith. He is in politics for the right reasons, and he wants to make a difference. Motivated deeply by his Catholic faith, he has become a champion for international human rights and religious freedom—particularly in places like China—and issues such as human trafficking. 'If we're silent on human rights, the bad guys look at that and say, 'All they care about is trade and making money. They don't care if we put our people in prison,' he says. For that reason, he has made a point of meeting with dissidents from a range of countries, and speaking out robustly.[12] He is also the leading pro-life campaigner in Congress.

Elected in 1981 at the age of just 27 as a Republican in a Democrat seat in New Jersey, Congressman Smith had previously worked as executive director of the New Jersey Right to Life Committee. His passion for the pro-life cause began at college, several years before the landmark case of Roe *v*. Wade, when New York's governor Nelson Rockefeller legalised abortion and New Jersey was poised to do the same.

'My involvement began when I took an assignment on the topic for one of my classes,' he said in an interview. 'While doing the reading, I encountered a number of facts and stories, including one story about a child in New York who survived a late-term abortion. The abortionist and so-called advocates were upset, seeing it as a complication. And it just struck me: thank the Lord that this baby survived. Where were this little child's human rights?'[13]

From there, Chris Smith formed a pro-life committee in college, and then decided to run for office. 'If it weren't for my work in the pro-life movement, I probably wouldn't have run for Congress. I majored in business and thought I'd have a business career. But the sheer human need was a magnet, and it coincided with the maturing of my faith as a Catholic.'

Since 1981, Congressman Smith has authored numerous pieces of legislation—he ranks as the fourth most active author of laws in the House of Representatives. Most relate to human rights, humanitarian and pro-life causes. He sees pro-life, human rights and humanitarian issues as 'all inter-related'. The Church and government, he argues, 'need to stand side by side with those who are weak and vulnerable'.

Born and raised in a devout Catholic family, and educated at Catholic schools, Chris Smith's personal faith was particularly influenced by the writings of Archbishop Fulton Sheen. 'I began to realise that there really is no other institution on earth that is more comprehensive and consistent than the Catholic Church. Unfortunately, our culture buys into euphemisms and shallow bumper sticker slogans. But for the Church, it's all about truth.'

Sacred Scripture then deepened his faith. 'What stood out above all else was the verse in Matthew 25, where the Lord said, "Whatever you do to the least of these, you do likewise to me". The unborn child is the ultimate "least of these". Others are similarly disenfranchised and vulnerable, but the child has no say, no voice — and if we don't rise to their defence, the culture of death will claim even more victims.'

In 2011, I appeared before the United States Congress Foreign Affairs Committee's Subcommittee on Africa, Global Health, Global Human Rights, and International Organisations, chaired by Congressman Smith. I gave evidence at a hearing on international religious freedom. In 2014, I was invited again to testify before Mr Smith's committee. On both occasions, I had no doubt in my mind: the person in the chair, Mr Smith, was not there because he was marking up a slot on his political resumé; he was not there because he was fascinated by procedure; he was not there because he wanted to catch me out. He was there because he genuinely cared passionately about these issues and he was generous in giving me time to testify, uninterrupted, because he wanted to hear the evidence I could present. What was even more remarkable was that on both occasions, at the end of the hearing, he invited me back to his office for further conversation. He did not have to. He could easily have gone on to another appointment and I would have perfectly well understood. But he invited me back, he pulled out some cans of Coca-Cola, and we discussed a whole range of mutual interests from human rights, justice and religious freedom to faith and politics. 'I look at politics as a kind of ministry,' he says, 'to defend and advance the Gospel of Life. Like many ministries, it is very challenging.'[14]

His wife Marie, his faith, and the inspiration of others keep him going. 'It's been my faith and my family,' he told *The Catholic World Report*.[15] 'What I like so much about our faith, beside it being true and the revelation of God's will for us on earth, is the heavy emphasis on selflessly caring for others—Matthew 25—and especially caring for the disenfranchised and the weakest and the most vulnerable. The Catholic Church radiates Christ to the poor and forgotten. For me, that means human rights, and that means humanitarian issues. And the definition of human rights absolutely has to include the unborn child and his or her mother, who are co-victims of every abortion.' He describes his political philosophy as 'very pro-human rights, pro-humanitarian, pro-growth.' When asked what he would like his legacy to be, Chris Smith says, with typical faith and humility, very simply: 'To have served God. And if someone were to mention that I worked on Matthew 25 issues, that would say it all.'[16]

Hong Kong

The man who is known as the 'father' of Hong Kong's democracy movement, and founding Chairman of Hong Kong's first political party, the Democratic Party, is a devout Catholic. Martin Lee, who became a Queen's Counsel (referred to as Senior Counsel after the handover) in 1979, was baptised when he was 12 while being educated at a Jesuit school. Interestingly though, neither of his parents were Catholic at the time — though they both entered the Church much later in life. His father wanted to be a Catholic at the age of 80, three days after the death of Lee's best friend whom Lee believes to be responsible for converting his father from Heaven. In what was perhaps a hereditary trait, Lee's father 'had a tendency to go against the rules'. Lee and his sisters and brother would observe the Friday abstinence, along with Catholics around the world, by avoiding eating meat. But not his father. In an illustration of the principle of following the spirit rather than the letter of the law, Lee recalls: 'My father liked fish very much, and ate it every night *except* Fridays.'

Lee had been influenced by religious classes at school, and his two sisters had also chosen to be baptised at a young age. 'I believed all the things I was taught,' he told me. 'Faith is a gift, and faith has been with me all the time.'

In the early 1980s, Hong Kong people began to consider the future of the territory, knowing that its return to Chinese sovereignty was approaching. Many of his friends were thinking of emigrating, but Lee decided not to. He had just become Chairman of the Hong Kong Bar Association, and decided to stay and help fight for Hong Kong's future. 'I thought I could help Hong Kong maintain the rule of law, so that freedom could be preserved,' he said. He was an elected member of the Legislative Council from 1985 to 2008, and served from 1985 to 1989 as a member of the Basic Law Drafting Committee, the body appointed by Beijing to draft Hong Kong's post-1997 constitution, until his expulsion following the 1989 Tiananmen crackdown. Throughout the past 30 years, Lee has led Hong Kong's struggle for democracy. He says his faith has always been a source of strength in that struggle. 'Sometimes I would feel very despondent, and didn't know what to do, and I would just go into a church, and recall a passage from the Bible which talks about birds being cheap but not a single one falls to the ground without the Father knowing about it (Matthew 10: 29). I don't know about the future, and where to go, but God knows, so I will just carry on and God will guide me along.'

In 2014, aged 76, Lee came out on the streets with the Occupy Central movement to call for the democratic election of the Chief Executive. At one rally he criticised Beijing's proposal that there would be universal suffrage in 2017, but that all the candidates must be chosen by Beijing. If all the candidates are handpicked, he asked rhetorically, 'What's the difference between a rotten orange, a rotten apple and a rotten banana?'[17]

What struck Lee—as it did the world—was the fact that the student-led protests, and the 'Umbrella' movement, were so peaceful. 'I thought it might be negative, but in fact it won the hearts of so many people around the world,' he told me. 'It was conducted with love and peace. It was the most peaceful movement I have seen. I feel God's hand is in it.'

Despite the peaceful nature of the protests, Beijing launched a crackdown. In an article in *The New York Times* Lee wrote: 'At 76 years old, I never expected to be tear-gassed in Hong Kong, my once peaceful home.'[18] The protests were, he noted, the 'last stand in defence of Hong Kong's core values, the values that have long set us apart from China: the rule of law, press freedom, good governance, judicial independence and protection for basic human rights. Beijing's heavy-handed response earlier this week made it clearer than ever that our future as a free society is at stake.' Hong Kong, he added, deserves 'more vigorous backing from Washington and London', which, 'in their failure to come out strongly in favour of the peaceful democracy protesters, have effectively sided with Beijing in a disgraceful display of power politics'.

He told me that Hong Kong is now ruled 'by Communist Party cadres'. Even judges, at all levels, are described by Beijing as 'administrators' under the supervision of the Central People's Government. 'This is a departure from the Joint Declaration which provides for an independent judiciary,' he said. 'The rule of law is now under attack.'

I have known Martin Lee for 18 years, ever since I lived in Hong Kong. He was supportive of Christian Solidarity Worldwide, and served on our Hong Kong Board of Reference. I have always admired his courage and conviction, and the way his political struggle is strengthened by his quiet faith. When asked which saints or well-known Catholics most inspired him, he answered immediately: St John Paul II and Mother Teresa. It is not difficult to work out why.

Colonel Chris Keeble

In September 2012, the staff and board of Christian Solidarity Worldwide gathered for one of our periodic weekend retreats. After dinner on the Saturday evening, we had a guest speaker. I had little idea beforehand how much his story would inspire me, and encourage me along my journey. I was already actively exploring the Catholic faith, and indeed was approaching a decision. His story, and his reflections on Catholic Social Teaching, were yet another nudge along the path.

Colonel Chris Keeble was born in Quetta, in what was then British India and is now Pakistan, in 1941 and then raised in Calcutta until the end of the Second World War. His father fought against the Japanese in Burma with the Royal Signals, while his future father-in-law fought as a Chindit in two of Orde Wingate's campaigns. 'So Burma is on the backdrop of both our lives,' he notes. 'It was the first country I ever learned about.'

Chris was raised in a Catholic family, his father a convert, and educated at a Catholic prep school, Ditcham Park on the South Downs, and then Douai Abbey near Reading. But he attributes his personal Catholic faith to two sources: his grandmother, and the Benedictines at Douai Abbey.

'My grandmother was a very pious, almost saintly, ascetic woman whose husband had died before I was born. She was Irish, and lived in a nice house in Wimbledon, full of Irish Catholic iconography including a little flickering light that was on all night because she had a host in a ciborium—which is unusual outside the Mass. Every morning she would get up and put on her fox fur stole and coat, and walk to Sacred Heart, Edge Hill, for Mass,' he recalls. 'She was holy. She was a gentle woman. I found that very attractive.'

Chris also found the Benedictines 'immensely attractive.' There was, he recalls, 'an awareness of Christ's presence, which has never really left me. Real presence.

I picked it up quite early on—even to the extent that I thought I was a bit odd, a bit weird, because nobody else seemed to understand what I was talking about. It was obvious to me and yet it isn't to many others, which I find puzzling—but maybe that is what faith is about: a gift. I think I was given that gift very, very early on.'

From Douai Abbey Chris went to Sandhurst to join the army, where the principles of discipline, order, obedience were 'easy' for him to adopt. In 1963 he was commissioned into the Royal Leicestershire Regiment, but joined the Parachute Regiment in 1971. Military life 'fitted in to the Benedictine rule: stability, obedience, *conversatio morum*: constantly turning to God, constantly trying to make progress. It is a wonderful foundation for faith and for communal effort, which is exactly what the military is—a communal endeavour.'

Christianity is well accepted into the fabric and culture of the military, Chris believes, because the established Church, the Church of England is 'prominent' and 'religious faith is encouraged.' Church-going on Sundays was 'not unusual' in the army. 'On operations, there is always a willing group of people who are happy to attend a service, either in a church or in the field, and there is something poignant about a bunch of soldiers with their head-dress off and their heads bowed in a circle of companionship, taking it really seriously—because death is possible just around the corner.'

That public displays of faith were acceptable in the armed forces was one thing. 'What was harder,' Chris acknowledges, 'was trying to reconcile the paradox between the legitimate use of violence and the love of your neighbour. That is hard.' He resolved it by determining right at the very beginning why he had joined the army. 'I was very clear that I was not in the military to kill people. My disposition was the reverse: I was prepared to put my life on the line for both the values of the State and the Christian ethic and more deeply the love of God and the love of neighbour: I thought that was worth dying for.' It was the height of the Cold War, when the Soviet threat was real. 'Nuclear annihilation, invasion across Europe—it was very serious, and all our military dispositions were governed towards deterring such an event. That fitted with my ethos—that I was there to stand the line and demonstrate that by good training, good equipment, good techniques, that it would be possible to convey a message to the Soviets that this was not on, and if necessary we would stand the line and take the shock.' There were people, he says, who join the military 'because it is socially advantageous', and a few 'who would actually quite enjoy killing', but he was clear what was his 'disposition'.

Chris served in a number of overseas operations, including some time in North Africa, the Far East, five tours in Northern Ireland and two in Yemen, where he learned an Arabic saying that summarises his own philosophy in life. 'In Yemen I met a wonderful group of tribesmen who helped us find our way around, and a senior tribal leader killed a goat, we had a meal together, and he said: "Trust in God and tether your camel." That is very good theology. God will work in His way, but it needs the collaboration of a human person to work in their way.'

As a Catholic serving in the British Army in Northern Ireland, one might have expected him to have had particular challenges, either within himself or in dealing with the Catholic community, but Chris says this did not occur. 'I didn't have a problem. I was trying to keep the peace and hold the line between the two factions. Although they claim Catholicism, it is really an historic definition to separate themselves from the incoming Protestants—going back to Oliver Cromwell. They were really Republicans and Unionists—that is a better way to describe the two tribes. So I did not see a contest between my faith and the people on the street,' he says. In fact, most of those who identified themselves as Catholic were not particularly practising, he explains. 'I did an interesting exercise. There is a very large conurbation in the centre of Belfast called the Ardoyne, which is a Catholic ghetto, surrounded by Protestant estates. At the very top of a hill overlooking the estate of the Ardoyne is a large church, the Holy Cross Church, and I thought I would do an audit of the number of Catholics who turned up for Mass. Out of the 12,000 Catholics who live in this ghetto, I counted 120. So if Mass-going is one of the criteria on which you would make a calculation about their Catholicism, they failed on that count.'

But it was the Falklands War for which Chris is best known, and it was a specific story of faith in action that caught my attention. After the Argentine invasion of the Falklands in 1982, Chris was part of the Task Force that was assembled and deployed immediately. While they assembled 'a great amphibious force', peace negotiations and shuttle diplomacy continued. 'In Whitehall there were those who were very pro-military intervention, and others totally against it. There was a political backdrop. Military operations are an extension of politics—they are not an end in themselves. It was the Prussian military thinker Carl von Clausewitz who said that war fighting is politics by other means,' says Chris. 'So as a soldier, one is constantly trying to think, when we act using state-sponsored violence, how it is contributing to the political endeavour. There came a moment in this amphibious build-up when the politicians wanted action, it became clear that the peace negotiations were going nowhere, and they wanted to get on with the campaign.'

This began the key episode of his military career, and perhaps his most significant spiritual encounter with God—something he prayed for the night before his deployment. 'The night before we went down to Portsmouth to get on the ship, I ran up onto the downland above my house on Salisbury Plain, and prayed among these ancient beech trees. My prayer was that the whole campaign would be a spiritual experience, that I would gain something spiritually from it all, and I really did.'

The campaign got under way in challenging, confusing circumstances. Chris's battalion, the 2nd Battalion of the Parachute Regiment, was given orders by the local commander to 'go down and raid a nearby settlement', Goose Green. 'We had a very forceful commanding officer who realised that when you communicate a mission, it has got to be understandable. The people who have to do it must understand what it means. However, the stated mission "to capture" Goose Green did not match the available resources. There always has to be a balance between the mission and the resources available. If you want to make a cup of tea, you need water and a tea bag. If you're only given a spoon, you can't do it. This particular battle started as a political initiative, with a lack of resources and a compromised mission.'

The battle lasted for 60 hours, in the course of which his commanding officer, Lieutenant-Colonel H. Jones, was killed. 'I was his second-in-command, so I took over command and carried on the battle. We outflanked the enemy defence around this settlement, closed in on them, and then it became clear to me that the enemy's will was going.' At this point, Catholic social teaching—which Chris defines as 'a body of thought and reflection and consideration for justice and peace for our social world, drawn from the circumstances of the modern world and the rich resources of Catholic thinking over 2000 years'—kicked in. 'If you go back to Catholic social teaching and the dignity of life, and you hold that seriously, you cannot use violence if the other side is not prepared to fight. The game's over.' So Chris decided to do something extraordinary. 'I decided to withdraw any more assault on the enemy, and to open up a line of negotiation. But it wasn't as simple as that because the clarity of what I have just said was not available to me on the battlefield: I hadn't slept for 40 hours, it was very cold, one in six of us was killed or injured, the whole cohesion of the battle had broken down, control had broken down because everybody was dispersed, radio batteries failed because they had been used up, and we were threatened with a counter-attack. So things were pretty bleak.' It was at that moment that Chris remembered what was in his pocket. A laminated copy of Charles de Foucauld's 'Prayer of Abandonment':

> Father,
> I abandon myself into your hands; do with me
>   what you will.
> Whatever you may do, I thank you:
> I am ready for all, I accept all.
> Let only your will be done in me, and in all
>   your creatures.
> I wish no more than this, O Lord.
> Into your hands I commend my soul;
> I offer it to you

with all the love of my heart,
for I love you, Lord,
and so need to give myself,
to surrender myself into your hands,
without reserve,
and with boundless confidence,
for you are my Father.

'I had made this ridiculous bargain with God, that if
I took this prayer with me, God would look after me,'
explains Chris. 'We do these things as if we attempt to
manipulate God. It's pitiful, really. But I thought that
I would say this prayer at this moment. I knew it by
heart. I spoke to my company commanders and they
asked "What are we going to do now, boss?" I said
"Just give me a moment".' He went down into a burning gulley, full of 'dead bodies and the detritus of the
battle around me', knelt down in the gorse and prayed.

'In a moment, I knew exactly what we needed to do,'
recalls Chris. 'And that terror and anxiety and sense
of loss and uncertainty was transformed. I just knew
precisely what I needed to do. I felt elated and inspired.
And so then I arranged for a ceasefire. I released a
couple of prisoners of war, and met the enemy. Their
first words to me were: "Thank God you've come."
They didn't want to be there either.'

That moment—a life and death moment, a decision
as to whether to keep fighting or to invite the enemy
to surrender—was not just a military decision. It was
a spiritual one. 'It was a seminal moment for me. I had
been pretty lukewarm in my faith until then. I had said
my prayers, went to Mass—but there is a world of
difference between that and abandoning yourself for
God and living each moment in that space which for
a moment I did. Christ wants us to abandon ourselves
to him—which I find hugely attractive. Ever since then

I have tried to deepen my understanding of what that really means.'

Central to the manner in which the battle ended was the way in which Chris treated the enemy. Having issued an ultimatum inviting their surrender, Chris walked across enemy lines to let them do so with dignity. 'We negotiated their surrender with honour. Without making them feel victimised or humiliated. They asked for a brief time of prayer, which we granted. They sang their songs, said their prayers, laid down their weapons and became our prisoners of war. And we cared for them—they had been very badly fed and clothed.' Chris sent away a BBC camera crew that had arrived on the scene, so conscious was he of the need to treat the Argentine surrender respectfully. 'We packed the BBC crew into a helicopter and sent them over a hill, and told a couple of Paras to pin them down and not allow them back. We didn't want a global spectre of these people being humiliated.'

Chris was highly decorated for his role in the Battle of Goose Green, receiving the Distinguished Service Order (DSO). But the war had caused him to question his future in the army. He was given a seven-month sabbatical at the National Defence College, which included a visit to the British Leyland car plant at Longridge as part of his course. 'The employees were a very unhappy group of people, and they were sabotaging the production line,' he recalls. 'I had to write a short paper on it, and I came to the conclusion that there was a principle that had been violated that work ought to be an agency for human development, and yet they had reversed that principle. In other words, human beings are intrinsically valuable, not instrumentally valuable. It was quite clear that the whole structure of this business was to take people and use them instrumentally to add value to the world of work, and I thought this was profoundly wrong.' Those observations, coupled with his experiences on the battlefield, inspired Chris to embark on a new path outside the army, providing consultancy and thought leadership for business on questions of ethics—built on Catholic social teaching.

Two other experiences deepened Chris's interest in Catholic social teaching. When he returned from the Falklands, he received a hero's welcome—but he felt a great burden of accountability. 'I had learned that the hardest problem I faced was trying to make right and good decisions, in a context that was wrong and bad. That paradox was the greatest challenge—and the burden is the accountability for those decisions, and the need to face the judgment of the people to whom you are accountable. That includes not only the State, but my regiment and the people I led, and my family and myself, especially the parents of those soldier-sons, who were killed while under my command.'

Five years after the Falklands War, Chris found himself on the other end of the forgiveness question, when an Argentine platoon sergeant, Horacio Benitez, came to Britain in search of reconciliation. He met Chris.

> He said to me: 'On behalf of myself, my platoon, battalion, army and country, I seek your forgiveness.' I found that very difficult to answer in a way that convinced him that he really was forgiven. I asked him what it would be like in Argentina if the Falklands War had not happened. He explained that the junta would still be in power, there would be no democracy, widows would still be wailing outside the Casa Rosada, people would still be disappearing, it would be a nightmare. I said: 'Horacio, we were

both on the same side. We had to go through
this suffering together in order that some greater
good could emerge, not only for the Falkland
islanders but for Argentina.' This links again back
to the idea of sacrifice, suffering, which is part
of the Catholic and Christian tradition: that if
you love, you will suffer. That made sense to
me, but it was a revelation. I understood it not
only strategically and politically, but spiritually,
and that tracks back to my original inspiration—
that our role as soldiers is to stand on the line on
behalf of the common good. And that takes us
back to Catholic Social Teaching.

In an interview with *The Guardian*, Benitez described
their encounter. 'It was very, very important for me to
meet Chris. I was very worried. I didn't know what he
would think meeting me, "the enemy". But he just held
out his hand, then embraced me. It was so emotional
I couldn't speak. I think this was the moment the war
really ended for me. It was the strangest feeling. He
seemed like an old, very deep friend.'[19]

Chris's work taking Catholic social teaching into secular businesses, governments and public institutions,
is what he believes is his vocation.

I just knew that this was what I was meant to do,
although I am not an academic, have no degree
in ethics, but I felt if this is what I am made to
do, why wouldn't it work? We have a loving God
who creates each person purposefully—not in
any time or place, but in this time and this place.
I would call that a calling, a vocation, and when
we pursue our vocation we contribute to our
flourishing—and our flourishing contributes to
our fulfilment. It seems pretty simple to me. If
you are pursuing your vocation, you are doing

the will of God—and the Holy Spirit is there to help you. So what's the problem? What's the anxiety? There isn't any. Not unless you don't really believe it—and that experience on the Goose Green Battlefield made it crystal clear that that's the way to live your life: to be held by the Holy Spirit. I am not smart enough or holy enough to do that all the time, but it is the thing that really moves me.

Of all the saints, martyrs, clergy and theologians throughout the ages, Chris says he is inspired by the Mother of God, by St Benedict, and by St Teresa of Avila—but the one he cites as his greatest inspiration above all is St Maria Faustina. 'Read her diary. She was the one who inspired the Catholic Church's attention to divine mercy. Divine Mercy Sunday emerged out of her diary and her mystic experiences with Christ. An ignorant Polish nun goes into a convent, writes this astonishing work, suffers terribly from tuberculosis, is in great pain, but says that she would suffer more if it would contribute to the world's understanding of the presence of divine mercy before judgement. Divine mercy—it is the one thing that will save the world. The invitation that nobody is beyond God's mercy, regardless of how awful they have been.' In a typical final moment of humility, he adds: 'But I hope I don't come across as some sort of "Holy Joe". Hypocrisy is terrible. I just try to tell the truth.'

James Mawdsley

The final person to mention in this chapter is the one who prayed longest and tried hardest for me to embrace the Catholic faith, my very good friend James Mawdsley.

James helped to introduce me to two causes that
have become central to my life: Burma and Catholicism. The first I embraced quickly, the second took
rather longer. We also shared a third common interest,
politics, and both stood as Conservative Party parliamentary candidates in the 2005 general election. In
2003 James and I co-authored a paper on foreign policy and human rights, called 'New Ground: Engaging
People with the Conservative Party through a Bold,
Principled and Imaginative Foreign Policy'. That led
to the establishment of the Conservative Party Human
Rights Commission, a body founded to advise the
party—including the leader and the foreign affairs
team while in opposition, and now in government
the prime minister and Foreign Secretary—on international human rights concerns.

I first met James when he came to Hong Kong in
2001, to address a conference I had organised for Christian Solidarity Worldwide. James had been arrested
in Burma for pro-democracy protests, not once but
three times. The first time he was deported, but that
thwarted his main objective—to see the inside of a
Burmese prison, and to look the regime in the eye. He
knew the only way he could achieve either was as a
prisoner, and so he returned in 1998, and was arrested
for handing out pro-democracy stickers, beaten for 15
hours, and sentenced to five years in jail, which was
suspended after 99 days. As if that were not enough,
he returned again a year later—and was jailed for 17
years. He served 416 days in solitary confinement,
before his release in October 2000.

James's story is told in full in his book *The Heart Must
Break*, and in my own previous book *Burma: A Nation
at the Crossroads*, among others. He recounts how his
Catholic faith not only sustained him in prison, but

deepened and became more alive. He read Thomas
à Kempis's *The Imitation of Christ* as well as almost all
of Pope St John Paul II's social encyclicals plus other
Church documents, which had been sent to him in jail.
Upon his return to Britain he told reporters how God
helped him endure torture and beatings. 'St Paul gave
me strength,' he said. 'God was protecting me every
moment, down to the most absurd details and in the
most unpredictable ways.'[20]

After James and I had got to know each other, he
showed almost the same single-minded and unrelent-
ing dedication to bringing me into the Catholic Church
as he had to the pursuit of democracy in Burma —
except that for much of the time I was as unresponsive
to his zeal as the Burmese regime. James wrote lengthy
letters to me making the case for Catholicism; we had
numerous conversations over dinner and drinks in
which I listened respectfully to his thoughts; and, cru-
cially, he gave me a copy of the *Catechism of the Catholic
Church*. For almost ten years, these exchanges went on,
I engaged with them out of interest and respect for
James, but I was not—at that time—remotely considering becoming a Catholic. I was happy where I was,
in the Church of England.

But those conversations, James's prayers and the
copy of the Catechism he had given me, eventually
bore fruit. It was to the Catechism that I turned when
my active, conscious journey of exploration began after
the conversation with Archbishop Bo in Rangoon in
2011, and for a whole year I read it almost every day.
And so I am indebted to as well as inspired by James.
His journey has taken him from activism and politics
into the priesthood, where God will undoubtedly use
his great characteristics of courage, principle, integrity
and the single-minded pursuit of truth to touch many.

Notes

1   Benedict Rogers, 'The conscience of Lord David Alton', *Crisis*, 1 November 2004.

2   Lord Alton and Baroness Cox, 'Building bridges, not walls: the case for constructive, critical engagement with North Korea', October 2010—http://www.jubileecampaign.org/BuildBridgesNotWalls.pdf.

3   *Nine Days that Changed the World* documentary film—http://ninedaysthatchangedtheworld.com/.

4   Benedict Rogers, 'The conscience of Lord David Alton'.

5   *Ibid.*

6   Alyssa McDonald, 'Ann Widdecombe—the extended interview', *The New Statesman*, 19 July 2010.

7   *Ibid.*

8   Ann Widdecombe, 'If only the Catholic church did PR', *The Guardian*, 7 September 2010.

9   Chris Whitehouse, 'Jim Dobbin—obituary', *The Tablet*, 13 September 2014.

10 Libby Copeland, 'Faith-based initiative: presidential hopeful Sam Brownback strives to be humble enough for a higher power', *The Washington Post*, 7 June 2006.

11 *Ibid.*

12 *The DC Spotlight Newspaper*, 'Top 10 most interesting: Congressman Chris Smith—how human rights became his value system', 1 October 2011.

13 Alton J. Pelowski, '"All in" for pro-life", The Knights of Columbus, Columbia online edition, 1 January 2015—http://www.kofc.org/en/columbia/detail/all-infor-pro-life.html.

14 *Ibid.*

15 Daniel Allott, 'Mr Smith's 30 years in Washington', *The Catholic World Report*, 1 May 2011.

16 *Ibid.*

17 Demetri Sevastopulo and Julie Zhu, 'Hong Kong democracy activists vent their anger against Beijing', *Financial Times*, 1 September 2014.

18 Martin Lee, 'Who will stand with Hong Kong?', *The New York Times*, 3 October 2014.

19   'Forgiveness out of war', *For a Change*, 4 April 2007—http://
     www.forachange.net/features/3266.html.
20   'James Mawdsley back home with a mission', *The Tablet*, 28
     October 2000.

The Writers, Thinkers and Priests

I can do things you cannot, you can do things I cannot;
together we can do great things.

Mother Teresa

MY JOURNEY INTO THE CATHOLIC CHURCH was initially inspired by the Catholics whom I have had the privilege of knowing personally, and who live out their faith with remarkable courage and integrity. But once my curiosity about Catholicism had been sparked by them, and after that conversation with Cardinal Bo in Rangoon in 2011, I embarked on an active journey of exploration, where my sources of inspiration, my companions along the way, were not people I knew personally but rather writers whose words and ideas engaged my heart, mind and spirit. For about two years, I read everything I could get hold of. Lord Alton gave me many suggestions, as did Cardinal Bo and my parish priest Fr Peter Edwards, and I read and read and read.

Scott Hahn

The first writer whose work captured my imagination was the American author Scott Hahn. Right at the beginning of my exploration, when I was first tentatively questioning Catholicism without any pre-determined view on where I might end up, a friend recommended *Rome Sweet Rome*, written by Scott Hahn and his wife Kimberly. Like me, Scott and Kimberly Hahn had been evangelical Christians. He was a Presbyterian minister and a Bible scholar, having been the top student in his Protestant seminary. Like me, as an evangelical he loved the Bible, the Word of God, placing it at the centre of his faith. Unlike me, however, he had been vigorously anti-Catholic, believing all the myths and false rumours that are sometimes put about in some Protestant circles—that Catholics don't read the Bible, that Catholics worship Mary, that the pope is the Antichrist. And then, completely unexpectedly, he began to investigate Catholicism for himself and after much soul-searching and theological study, he gradually came to the conclusion that what these falsehoods said about Catholicism were not true—and that the Catholic Church was in fact the true and fullest expression of Christian faith.

The Hahns' story is best read through their own writings, and I would recommend all their books. After *Rome Sweet Rome*, I turned to Scott Hahn's theological books, and one theme leaped out at me above all else: that everything the Catholic Church believes and teaches is rooted in Scripture. Far from not reading the Bible, as some Protestants claim about Catholics, the reality is the very opposite. There is nothing that the Church believes that cannot be traced to Scripture. While I was never anti-Catholic like Dr Hahn, as an evangelical I did believe in the centrality of Scripture and I did have questions about Mary, transubstantiation and the papacy. Dr Hahn helped address those questions.

Hail, Holy Queen: The Mother of God in the Word of God
helped me understand how Catholics view Our Lady.
Firstly, the suggestion that Catholics 'worship' Mary
was clearly rejected. Dr Hahn writes: 'As the Mother
of God, Mary is the mother par excellence ... A true
mother, Mary considers none of her glories her own.
After all, she points out, she is only doing God's bid-
ding: "Behold, I am the handmaid of the Lord; let it be
to me according to your word" (Luke 1: 38). Even when
she recognises her superior gifts, she recognises that
they are gifts: "All generations will call me blessed"
(Luke 1: 48). For her part, Mary's own soul "magnifies"
not herself but "the Lord" (Luke 1: 46).'[1] To understand
the Mother of God, he continues, 'we must begin with
God'.[2]

My parish priest had already told me that in Catholic
teaching, Mary always points the way to Jesus Christ,
so there can be no question of Catholics placing her
higher than Christ. And Dr Hahn's book helped me
see that. 'Do we detract from Christ's finished work
by affirming its perfect realisation in Mary?' he asks.
'On the contrary, we celebrate His work, precisely
by focusing our attention on the human person who
manifests it most perfectly.' Mary, he continues, 'is not
God, but she is the Mother of God. She is only a creature, but she is God's greatest creation. She is not the
king, but she is His chosen queen mother. Just as artists long to paint one masterpiece among their many
works, so Jesus made His mother to be His greatest
masterpiece. To affirm the truth about Mary does not
detract from Jesus—although refusing to affirm it *does*
detract from Him.'[3]

When Jesus looked at his mother and at his disciple John and spoke those words from the cross
shortly before he died—'Woman, behold your son,'

and to John 'Here is your mother'⁴—he gave the
Church and all who call themselves Christians a
relationship with Mary. 'And from that hour,' St
John tells us in his Gospel, 'the disciple took her
into his own home.' I had read those words many
times before but it was only now, actively exploring the Catholic faith through the works of Dr Hahn
and others, that I saw their true meaning. 'Mary is,'
writes Dr Hahn, 'in a real, abiding, spiritual sense—
our mother. If we are to know the brotherhood of
Jesus Christ, we must come to know the mother
whom we share with Jesus Christ. Without her, our
understanding of the gospel will be, at best, partial.'

Dr Hahn sets out in exciting detail the connection
between Mary and Eve, the traces that link the Old
Testament with the New Testament, the Immaculate
Conception and the Assumption. He also details how
the early Church, the Church Fathers, believed all of
these. It was only later that Protestants abandoned
Mary, and featured her just once a year in the nativity
scene, almost as a walk-on part. Yet she is the mother
of Christ, the mother of God, and—as I saw through
Dr Hahn's work—our mother too.

The Lamb's Supper: The Mass as Heaven on Earth
was the next of Dr Hahn's books that I tackled. Once
again, I could not put it down. Reading it was a key
part of the adventure on which I had embarked. He
describes the first Mass he witnessed, as a Protestant,
as an observer. 'For years, as an evangelical Calvin-
ist, I'd been trained to believe that the Mass was the
ultimate sacrilege a human could commit,' Dr Hahn
writes. 'The Mass, I had been taught, was a ritual that
purported to "resacrifice Jesus Christ". So I would
remain an observer. I would stay seated, with my Bible
open beside me . . . As the Mass moved on, however,

something hit me. My Bible wasn't just beside me. It was before me—*in the words of the Mass!*'[5]

When I started attending Mass as part of my exploration of the Catholic Church, the same observation struck me. In most Protestant services, you generally only have one reading from the Bible, perhaps two. And it isn't always necessarily one of the Gospels. Yet in every Mass, in every Catholic church in the world, there are at least three, often four readings: an Old Testament reading, a Psalm, a New Testament reading from one of the epistles or from the Acts of the Apostles, and the Gospel reading. I was also impressed that Catholics stand for the Gospel. And by the symbolism of the sign of the cross we make when the Gospel reading is announced: on our forehead, on our lips and on our chest. For a while I did not understand why we make the sign of the cross in that way when the Gospel reading begins, but its explanation is obvious and, when made with sincerity, beautiful: that the Gospel be in our minds, on our lips and in our hearts. 'When we cross ourselves,' Dr Hahn says, 'we renew the covenant that began with our baptism.'[6] Just as we do when we dip our finger into the holy water upon entering and leaving a Catholic Church, making the sign of the cross and in so doing renewing our baptismal vows.

Dr Hahn continues to the heart of the Mass:

> I remained on the sidelines until I heard the priest pronounce the words of consecration: 'This is My body . . . This is the cup of My blood.' Then I felt all my doubt drain away. As I saw the priest raise that white host, I felt a prayer surge from my heart in a whisper: 'My Lord and my God. That's really you!' . . . The experience was intensified just a moment later, when I heard the congregation recite: 'Lamb of God . . . Lamb of God . . . Lamb of

God,' and the priest respond, '*This* is the Lamb of God . . .' as he raised the host . . . From long years of studying the Bible, I immediately knew where I was. I was in the Book of Revelation, where Jesus is called the Lamb no less than twenty-eight times in twenty-two chapters. I was at the marriage feast that John describes at the end of that very last book of the Bible. I was before the throne of heaven, where Jesus is hailed forever as the Lamb . . . I would return to Mass the next day, and the next day, and the next. Each time I went back, I would 'discover' more the Scriptures fulfilled before my eyes . . . I saw the smoke of incense; I heard the invocation of the angels and saints; I myself sang the alleluias, for I was drawn ever more into this worship.[7]

I cannot claim to have had the same instantaneous understanding of the meaning of transubstantiation — leading to what Catholics call the 'Real Presence' — in the Eucharist. For me, it was a more gradual process. I attended Mass regularly and fell in love firstly with the deep reverence, the sense of mystery, the majesty of God exhibited in the Mass. In a sense I was content not to understand it all, because for me if God is fully understandable to human minds, he is no longer God. That sense of mystery that is often lacking in evangelical circles captured my imagination and my heart. And from that point, I gradually moved to a point where I could accept the central belief about what is happening in the Eucharist. When I read Luke 22: 19–20, I realised that Jesus at the Last Supper and the institution of the Lord's Supper does not say of the bread and the wine the words 'these are symbols'. Instead he says: 'This is My body . . . this is the cup of My blood.' And I reached a point, some while into my journey, where I believed this. I described in the second chapter how, praying in front of the Tabernacle in the chapel of Campion Hall on my retreat, I had a clear sense that Jesus really was present in the host.

Dr Hahn's book helped me to see that the teaching of the Real Presence was one which united the early Church, the Church Fathers. 'The witness to the Church's Eucharistic doctrines is unbroken, from the time of the Gospels till today,' he writes.[8] And from an evangelical perspective, this is not as hard to grasp as one might think. Christians of all strands are taught in Scripture that when two or more are gathered in the name of Christ, He is present with them.[9] So if He is present when we are praying, why would He not be present in the Eucharist?

Lord, Have Mercy: The Healing Power of Confession helped me understand what is known as the Sacrament of Reconciliation, Penance or 'Confession.' In the final chapter of this book I will reflect more on this sacrament, but I recommend Dr Hahn's book. He helped me understand the role of the priest in confession, and that one is confessing sins to God, through and not to the priest. 'Christ is still the Priest behind the priest. He is the Priest within the priest and he is the Priest acting through the priest,' he writes. 'So we don't go to the priest instead of going to Christ. We don't go to the confessional instead of going to the Lord of Mercy. We go to the Lord of Mercy, and He tells us to go to the confessional. Christ has instituted these creaturely means for the health of our soul. Sin is like an infection for which we need to go to the doctor to obtain the right prescription, for the right dosage; and then we follow the advice because we trust the authority.'[10]

The final book by Scott Hahn which I read on this journey was *Reasons to Believe: How to Understand,*

Explain and Defend the Catholic Faith. In this chapter it is not my intention to quote extensively from the authors who influenced me, but instead share brief extracts in the context of explaining why they influenced me—and to recommend that their works be read in full. Scott Hahn influenced me because he is able to explain Catholic beliefs from a biblical perspective. He writes in an engaging, indeed evangelical, style—explaining complex mysteries and perhaps controversial dogma in a way that is easily comprehensible. Coming from an evangelical Protestant background, he writes in a way that any Christian who reads the Bible and believes in it can understand. His works laid the foundation stones of my path of exploration, and drew me further along on my journey.

George Weigel

George Weigel is best known as Pope St John Paul II's biographer. His tome, 886 pages in length, called *Witness to Hope*, tells the story of one of the greatest men of the twentieth century, exploring his life, philosophy, theology and his message to the world. Translated into at least 12 languages including Chinese, this internationally acclaimed biography is widely regarded as the most authoritative account of John Paul II—not least because the author knew the pope personally and had direct access that other biographers could only dream of. I read *Witness to Hope* shortly before beginning my active journey of exploration, but with hindsight I am certain it was one of the stimuli for that journey.

Writing a biography of Pope John Paul II made Dr Weigel, in his own words, 'into a "Vatican expert"'— which, he told me, he had never intended to be. But being close to the pope had an impact on his faith and future. 'Spending a lot of time with a saint is obviously a faith-deepening experience, but that's true of a lot of saintly people I know, not just the one who was canonized,' he says.

However, George Weigel is much, much more than a papal biographer. Author of at least 20 other books and a public intellectual in his own right, he is one of the most influential thinkers in today's Church.

Born in Baltimore, Maryland, Dr Weigel's academic home today is at the Ethics and Public Policy Centre in Washington, DC. I had the privilege of meeting him in person in February 2014, and he encouraged me to write this book. But it was his books that aided my journey into the Church considerably.

'My family's Catholic roots go back to our native Germany, which is long ago and far away,' said Dr Weigel in response to a question about his own faith. 'I was raised in the faith, embraced it, and have always tried to deepen my understanding and practice of it. I've never had a "crisis of faith", nor have I had a "born again" experience. It's all been very supernaturally natural.'

The Truth of Catholicism: Ten Controversies Explored was enormously helpful in addressing some of the questions I had. The Church is often accused of being intolerant, and while history shows that Catholics have indeed been so—'to the point of coercion and bloodshed,' as Dr Weigel notes—the essence of Catholicism is the exact opposite:

> Pope John Paul II has become a leading exponent of international human rights, interreligious dialogue, and reconciliation because of his Christian faith, not despite it. As he put it in his first encyclical, *Redemptor hominis* (The Redeemer

of Man), the Catholic Church must exhibit a 'universal openness', so that 'all may find in her "the unsearchable riches of Christ" of which St Paul wrote' (Ephesians 3: 8). Tolerance, the Pope was suggesting, does not mean avoiding differences on the ground by affirming that there is 'your truth' and 'my truth' but nothing that both of us could ever recognise as *the truth*. Genuine tolerance means exploring and engaging differences, especially differences about ultimate things, within a bond of profound respect—a respect for all those whose very humanity compels them to search for answers to the deepest questions of life. That is the respect demanded by Catholic faith.[11]

On questions of morality, Dr Weigel puts the Catholic case beautifully. Contrary to popular opinion, Catholicism is not about following a set of commands, rules and duties—though they may be part of the infrastructure. No, he writes: 'Viewed from inside, morality is about happiness and the virtues that make for happiness. Love is the centre of the moral life for Catholics—love that disposes of itself as a gift, making us the kind of givers who can live for eternity with radically self-giving love.' In Catholic terms, he argues, 'the challenge is to make ourselves a gift to others. Everything else— including rules and laws, prescriptions and proscriptions—revolves around that. Giving ourselves equips us to be the kind of people who can live with God, a Trinity of self-giving Persons, forever.'[12]

Another theme Dr Weigel explores is ecumenism, or Christian unity—a theme that I hope emerges as a thread throughout this book and my story. Describing the opportunities and challenges, he highlights the moment in 1999 when the Catholic Church and the Lutheran World Federation jointly affirmed that, despite some differences in theological understanding, 'they held in common the truths involved in the doctrine that we are justified through faith in Christ— the issue that launched the Lutheran Reformation in 1517'. He also notes that the English Reformation, the separation of the Church of England from Rome, was 'an essentially political separation' and that at the time 'there were no grave doctrinal issues between Anglicans and Roman Catholics'.[13]

Catholics believe that 'there is only one Church because there is only one Christ, and the Church is his Body,' Dr Weigel states. At the same time, 'Christians don't create Christian unity. Christ creates the unity of the Church.' Catholics hold two beliefs in tandem. On the one hand, as he writes, 'the one Church of Christ "subsists" in the Catholic Church: that is, the Catholic Church understands itself to be the fullest, most rightly ordered expression in history of the Church of Christ, which transcends history'. Yet we also believe that

> the one Church of Christ is not completely identical with the Catholic Church: it does not 'stop' at the boundaries of the Catholic Church. The Catholic Church believes and teaches that there are 'many elements of sanctification and of truth' in Christian communities that lie outside Catholicism's visible borders ... Catholics have hundreds of millions of brothers and sisters in Christ who live their Christian lives outside the formal structure of the Catholic Church ... Whether other Christians think of Catholics as brothers and sisters in Christ, Catholics have no choice but to think of other Christians in that way. The Catholic Church has a unique position in world Christianity: it is the only Christian

communion whose self-understanding demands
that it be in ecumenical conversations with
everybody else, without exception.[14]

These beautiful words were immensely helpful to me.
As I have already described, from the very beginning
of my Christian journey I have had an ecumenical
outlook. I have never been particularly interested in
the institutional element of the Church; I am far more
interested in the question of communion and community, and of being the Body of Christ. So Dr Weigel's
clear and unambiguous description of the Catholic
Church's commitment to ecumenism and recognition
of Christians who follow Christ outside the structures
of the Catholic Church meant a lot to me. At the same
time, the belief that the Catholic Church is the fullest,
deepest expression of Christianity was a belief that I
was increasingly drawn to. A Church that traces its
roots directly to St Peter was a Church that I found
appealing in an age of modernity where we are rapidly
losing appreciation of history.

Dr Weigel goes on to explore the Church's teachings
on salvation and mission, and their relationship to freedom. And what I read from him on these themes spoke
absolutely to my own convictions. 'In the Church's mission to the nations, there must be complete respect for
human freedom,' he writes. 'The Church's missionary
method must be the method of freedom: as John Paul
wrote, underscoring the words for emphasis, "The
Church proposes; she imposes nothing ... She respects
individuals and cultures, and she honours the sanctuary of conscience."' Whilst holding firm to the truth
that the Church believes in, Catholics must engage the
world in 'conversation, not conflict'. Underpinning all
this is the Church's commitment to religious freedom.

'In the Catholic view of things,' says Dr Weigel, 'religious freedom is the first of human rights, not because it has something to do with the Church making the most of its opportunities but because it is the right that arises from what is most distinctively human about human beings—their thirst for the truth of life. The Catholic defence of religious freedom is a defence of the religious freedom of everyone.'[15]

The relationship between faith and politics, the Church and democracy is another theme in the book. While Dr Weigel emphasises that 'the proclamation of God's passionate love for the world is what the Church is for', at the same time the Gospel is not 'a private matter'. It has 'public implications', particularly because 'defending the inalienable dignity and infinite value built into human beings by their Creator is a public matter'. The Gospel helps form and shape cultures. 'A culture inspired by a Christian view of the human person will affirm certain kinds of politics as compatible with the dignity of men and women, and it will reject others for their incompatibility with that dignity,' argues Dr Weigel. 'The Church is not in the business of designing or running governments; the Church is in the business of forming the kind of people who can design and run governments in which freedom leads to genuine human flourishing. From evangelism to culture formation to political change: that is the public strategy of the Catholic Church in the twenty-first century.'[16] In the Catholic view, democracy is not just the systems and institutions—it is, as Dr Weigel puts it, 'a way of public life, a way of being a political community ... characterised by equality before the law, participation in decision making, civility, a passion for justice, and a commitment to both individual liberty and the common good'.[17] But such a democracy, like a house, must be 'built on a firm foundation ... a democratic culture.' Virtues and morality shape those foundations. 'That is why, in the Catholic view, "value-neutral democracy" is a contradiction in terms. And that is why the Catholic Church insists that religiously informed moral truths have a place in public life. The issue here is not the Church's desire to be a partisan political player. The issue is securing the foundations of the house of freedom.'[18]

For all these reasons, writes Dr Weigel, issues such as abortion are issues that affect the type of society we have. 'A society that permits lethal violence as a means of resolving a personal dilemma is not a society fully governed by the rule of law; it is a society governed in crucial respects by the rule of raw, unchecked power. If the legal principle that the strong have the right to declare the weak outside the boundaries of the community of common protection is firmly established, all of those whom the strong might someday declare unfit, unproductive, troublesome or inconvenient are in peril,' he contends. 'Abortion is a justice issue, not an issue of sexual morality.'[19]

Yet in all these matters, and perhaps contrary to popular perception, 'the Church proposes; she imposes nothing.' The Church, according to Dr Weigel, 'seeks to be the teacher of the nations, not the ruler of nations. On these questions she will propose, and propose, and then propose some more. The Catholic commitment to human dignity, and the Catholic commitment to democracy, demand it.'[20] These ideas were enormously appealing to me, not least because they were what I already believed. I was beginning to think that I had been a Catholic long before I ever made the decision to become one.

Several other books by George Weigel also inspired me. I read *Letters to a Young Catholic*, in which he describes Catholicism as 'a very tangible business—it's about seeing and hearing, touching, tasting, and smelling as much as it's about texts and arguments and ideas'.[21] It's about 'grittiness' and human frailty, weakness and failure.[22] It's about God's search for us—'and our "search" involves our learning, over the course of a lifetime, to take the same path through history that God does'.[23]

Letters to a Young Catholic, together with other books by other authors, helped me understand the correct Catholic view of Mary. True devotion to Mary 'necessarily' points us to Christ—'and through Christ (who is both son of Mary and Son of God) into the mystery of God himself, God the Holy Trinity'. Far from being an 'obstacle' to an encounter with Christ, as some Protestants and evangelicals might believe, 'Mary was and is a privileged vehicle for meeting Christ the Lord'.[24] She is also—as 'the first of disciples and thus the mother of the Church'—a role-model for Christian discipleship. 'How? Because it is in Mary's *fiat*—"Be it done unto me according to *your* word" (Luke 1: 38)—that we discover the pattern or form of all Christian discipleship. Mary's *fiat* makes possible the incarnation of the Son of God.'[25]

Catholics are people of hope, writes Dr Weigel; people of infinity, 'in which reason is enriched by imagination and imagination is disciplined by reason';[26] people who know when to laugh, when to gaze in wonder, when to pray, when to speak out for truth and against wrong, and always to love.

Two other works by Dr Weigel which I read on my journey were *Practicing Catholic: Essays Historical, Literary, Sporting, and Elegiac*, a wonderful collection of reflections on issues political, theological, moral, cultural, philosophical and spiritual, together

with *Evangelical Catholicism: Deep Reform in the Twenty-First-Century Church*. The message of *Evangelical
Catholicism*, Dr Weigel told me, is that 'we are entering a new phase of the Church's life, which is actually a very old "phase": it's the Church of apostolic
witness and fervent evangelization, a recovery in the
twenty-first century of the experience of the apostolic
Church. The difference today is that all Catholics in
the First World are called to be missionary disciples
in cultures that have been religiously bored or tone-
deaf, which was not the situation in the first-century
Mediterranean world.'

Through all his writings, I found Dr Weigel one of
the most engaging, thoughtful, challenging and inspiring of companions on my journey of exploration of
the Catholic faith. He exhibits a rare gift of combining fierce intellect with beautiful prose, tackling deep,
sometimes complex, often controversial topics with a
narrative that draws the reader on. I recommend his
books very highly indeed. Asked what his message
to people exploring Catholicism would be, he replies
simply: 'Meet the Church by "coming inside", as Evelyn Waugh said, not by judging it from the outside,
according to the world's terms.'

Malcolm Muggeridge

As a journalist and someone deeply interested in politics, I found Malcolm Muggeridge a convert to whom
I could relate well. His life as a foreign correspondent, a Fabian socialist, an author and commentator, a
television presenter, with a colourful personal life is
itself fascinating. His journey into the Church is even
more interesting.

Born in 1903, he was finally received into the Church on 27 November 1982 — at the age of 79. For decades he had stood on the fringes of the Church, gazing sympathetically but reluctant to make the commitment. During the Second World War, for example, he used to meet regularly with the writer Lettice Cooper. According to his biographer Richard Ingrams, she recalled, considering 'Malcolm with such obvious yearning towards the Roman Catholic Church that I was surprised that it took him so long to get there'.[27] And even earlier, in the 1930s, the Fabian socialist Beatrice Webb — a friend and associate of Muggeridge — wrote in her diary: 'If you see much of the Devil and idiot in human society, you had better believe in a god to set it right. And confession and absolution would suit poor Malcolm's complexes; he needs spiritual discipline and he would find peace in religious rites. "Malcolm would do well in the Roman Catholic Church," I suggested.'[28] Yet it took another half century to get there.

For much of his life, Muggeridge showed a fascination with Christianity in general — and Catholicism in particular — without identifying himself as a follower. Once asked by Auberon Herbert whether he would become a Catholic, he replied negatively. 'I see the force and importance of the Roman Catholic Church, but I could not, in honesty, accept its dogma. In reciting the creed I should have to add "not" to most items,' he said.[29] In a letter to the archbishop of Canterbury in 1956, he wrote: 'I am, alas, not myself a believing Christian. I wish I were. But one thing I can say with the utmost sincerity, and that is that I grow evermore convinced that the Christian gospel was the most wonderful thing that ever happened to the world; that it represents the nearest to ultimate truth that has ever been revealed to mankind; that our civilisation was born of it, is irretrievably bound up with it and would almost certainly perish without it.'[30]

According to Richard Ingrams, in a profile by Hugo Charteris in *London Life* in 1965 he was still not prepared to say that he was a Christian. 'At this stage in his life he was still unable to subscribe to any of the dogmas in the Creed,' writes Ingrams. '"All I can say is that, in my travels, Christianity is about the best thing I have come across," said Muggeridge. The specific appeal of Christianity lay in its call to the spiritual. "I see life," he told Charteris, "as an eternal battle between two irreconcilable opposites, the world of the flesh and the world of the spirit."'[31]

It is fair to say, without being judgmental or cruel, that Muggeridge took to both worlds — of flesh and spirit — with enthusiasm and energy. A heavy drinker, who had numerous adulterous affairs and yet throughout his life was devoted to his wife Kitty, Beatrice Webb wrote of him in her diary on 19 January 1931: 'He is the most intellectually stimulating and pleasant mannered of all my "in-laws". An ugly but attractive and expressive face, a clever and sympathetic talker. Ultra-modern in his view of sex ... yet I think Malcolm is a mystic.'[32] Describing one particular period of his life, he admitted: 'That was my worst period: drinking, smoking, insomnia, barbiturates and the fleshpots — high society.'[33]

Raised in an agnostic, socialist family and educated at Cambridge, he initially engaged in left-wing politics — hence his association with Beatrice and Sidney Webb. British socialists in the 1920s and 1930s had an extraordinarily distorted admiration for communist Russia, which blinded them to Stalin's horrific inhumanity. The Russian Revolution had been an inspiration for the left in Britain, including Muggeridge. Sent off as a young foreign correspondent to Russia, Muggeridge became the first Western journalist to report on the famine in Russia in 1933, an experience which altered his political views. He then spent a period in India. In the Second World War, he served with MI6 in Sierra Leone, Mozambique and South Africa, as well as a stint at the famous Bletchley Park in Buckinghamshire, where the Enigma Code was cracked, enabling British intelligence to monitor German activities—in Ingrams's view, 'in its way the most important British victory of the war'.[34] After the war he joined *The Daily Telegraph*, served as Washington correspondent, and travelled in Asia, including to Burma. He went on to be editor of the satirical journal *Punch*, and then to work in television, on BBC's *Panorama*.

One woman made more impact than any other on Muggeridge's growing fascination with religion, and perhaps can be credited with inspiring him to finally enter the Church: Mother Teresa. In March 1968, Muggeridge was asked by the BBC's head of religious broadcasting if he would interview an Albanian nun involved in missionary work in Calcutta. He had never heard of Mother Teresa, but he agreed to do the interview, which was broadcast on the BBC's *Meeting Point* programme in May that year. A review in the Irish *Independent* noted that Muggeridge had talked to Mother Teresa 'with a degree of sympathy that almost reached personal involvement. And in a sense it was because you somehow felt that this was another minor incident drawing Muggeridge along his circuitous journey to Catholicism.'[35]

That interview—which resulted in a remarkable response from viewers, sending in donations for the work of Mother Teresa's Missionaries of Charity—inspired Muggeridge to do a full-length documentary. Mother Teresa initially resisted, but was finally

persuaded and wrote: 'If this TV programme is going
to help people to love God better, then we will have it,
but with one condition—that the Brothers and Sisters
be included as they do the work.' She told Muggeridge:
'Let us now do something beautiful for God.'[36]

Something Beautiful for God became a television
documentary and a book, and it was the book which
was one of the first things I read on my own journey.
By the time he had made the film, Muggeridge's religious position, according to Ingrams, was 'that of a
Christian who had no commitment to any particular
Church'. If he had a leaning, it was towards Catholicism, but he struggled with teachings on confession, the intercession of saints, and with the rosary.[37]
Nevertheless, the time he spent with Mother Teresa
radically changed his perceptions. 'She appealed to
him because she was simple and unsophisticated and
reduced the Christian Gospel to its bare essentials of
love in action ... Malcolm himself, for once humble
and enquiring, personified the quest of the modern
man for faith and hope.'[38]

Muggeridge went on to make other films—on the
life of St Paul, and on saints such as St Augustine, as
well as a film about Jean Vanier, Catholic founder of
a community for disabled people called 'L'Arche'. He
began to write and speak about Christianity. Besides
his relationship with Mother Teresa, 'nothing in the
course of Malcolm's life could have been more bizarre'
than his encounter with Svetlana Stalin, daughter of
Joseph Stalin, who had become a Christian. She first
made contact with Muggeridge after reading his book
Jesus Rediscovered.[39]

Of his many books, the three which I read on my
journey were *Conversion: The Spiritual Journey of a
Twentieth-Century Pilgrim*, *Jesus: The Man who Lives*

and *The End of Christendom*, in addition to *Something Beautiful for God*. I found his honesty and search for truth compelling. 'In the stress of life, collectively in the chaos of politics, individually in the clamorous demands of the ego and the flesh, it is always open to us to wait on God,' he writes. 'All we have to do is, as it were, to make a little clearing in the wild jungle of our human will, and then keep our rendezvous with our Creator. He is sure to come; His presence falls like a comforting shadow, and then we are at peace.' A little later, he adds: 'God signifies an alternative impulse – to sacrifice rather than grab, to love rather than lust, to give rather than take, to pursue truth rather than promote lies, to humble oneself rather than inflate the ego. In all creation the hand of God is seen; in every human heart, in a blade of grass as in great trees and mountains and rivers; in the first stirring of life in a foetus and in the last musings and mutterings of a tired mind.'[40]

Who in his 'right mind' would believe the story of the birth, death and resurrection of Jesus Christ, Muggeridge asks. The answer? 'The greatest artists, mystics, sculptors, saints, builders – for instance, builders of the great medieval cathedrals – over the Christian centuries, not to mention the Christians of all sorts and conditions whose lives, generation after generation, have been irradiated, given a meaning and a direction, through this great drama of the birth, ministry, death and resurrection of Jesus of Nazareth.'[41]

In *Jesus: The Man who Lives*, Muggeridge writes: 'There are such moments in life; when a truth crystallises, from being implicit becoming explicit, and all creation seems to participate – the sun shining more warmly, the air breathed in more exhilaratingly, the grass greener, the trees taller and the flowers brighter. The addition of clouds opening, a dove descending, a voice speaking, is not, after all, in the circumstances so very out of the way.'[42]

Muggeridge describes his reception into the Church with words that could be used to describe my own sentiment: 'A sense of homecoming, of picking up the threads of a lost life, of responding to a bell that had long been ringing, of taking a place at a table that had long been vacant.'[43]

Ingrams describes Muggeridge as 'a man who told the truth,' and that shines through in his writings. 'The power of truth is very great,' Muggeridge writes, 'as even those who, preferring fantasy, hate it and seek to pollute and destroy it, are in the last resort forced to acknowledge. Their sense of its power is manifested by their very proneness to shout it down and stamp it out.'[44] And what is the greatest truth of all? The truth that Muggeridge throughout much of his life toyed with, respected, was drawn to, questioned, and then ultimately embraced: 'The Risen Christ is the image of Fallen Man redeemed; of his ultimate, and only enduring, liberation; of the elusive freedom he has sought so ardently, so valiantly and so vainly at hustings and on battlefields, in disputes and in debates, and in the secret strivings of rebellious minds, now at last attained.'[45]

If you haven't already read Malcolm Muggeridge's books, please do so. I fell in love with Muggeridge—and through him, renewed my love for Jesus Christ and, like him, finally embraced the truth of the Catholic Church as the fullest expression of the Body of Christ.

G. K. Chesterton

It is almost impossible to be English and Catholic and not read G. K. Chesterton. Together with C. S. Lewis, he is perhaps the greatest popular Christian apologist of the twentieth century, certainly among those who approached apologetics in a literary way. Indeed, it was Chesterton who had been a significant influence on Lewis.

An accomplished writer of fiction, Chesterton became a Catholic in 1922, having embraced Christianity at least 20 years earlier and worshipped in the Church of England. One of his greatest works, *Orthodoxy*, was published in 1908 when he was an Anglican. According to a biographer, Karl Schmude, whose short booklet on Chesterton is published by the Catholic Truth Society, the 'explanation for the delay' in becoming Catholic 'seems to have been more personal than intellectual'. Chesterton had 'scarcely any mental obstacles' on his path to Rome. 'Even the matter of spiritual author- ity, and the Church as the earthly repository of that authority—an issue over which many potential con- verts have agonised—did not present difficulties. To Chesterton it was perfectly reasonable that the Church which Christ had founded should speak with the same authority as Christ Himself did on earth.' Yet conver- sion is ultimately 'a matter of grace rather than reason, a conclusion of the will and not merely a conclusion of the mind; and Chesterton, whose mind was so unim- aginably swift, was fairly slow to act'.[46]

Together with *Orthodoxy*, I read some of Chesterton's other major works—particularly *The Everlasting Man*, *The Thing: Why I am a Catholic*, *The Catholic Church and Conversion*, and a collection of essays under the title *In Defence of Sanity*, as well as his superb biography of St Francis of Assisi. One of my first impressions of Chesterton was the way he carries profundity lightly. A wordsmith able to convey deep truths clearly, he was also a *bon-viveur* who spent many an evening in the Old Cheshire Cheese pub in Fleet Street with his brother Cecil and friend Hilaire Belloc, and who once said that 'Wherever the Catholic sun doth shine, there's always laughter and good red wine. At least I've always found it so. Benedicamus Domino!' Dr Weigel notes in *Letters to a Young Catholic* that Chesterton and Belloc were 'convinced that the truths God wants us to find in this world were to be found, not only in churches and lecture halls, but in places like the Olde Cheshire Cheese—places that provided the good food and good drink that enabled good fellowship and good conversation.'[47] They were men who knew, in the words of Belloc's biographer Joseph Pearce, that 'love and laughter were linked in a mystical unity' because 'beyond the mere love of laughter was to be found the laughter of love'.[48]

Associated with this was a deep sense of awe and wonder at the miracle of life. 'From the beginning,' Chesterton told a reporter, 'I think I was staggered by the stupendous marvel of existence—by the miracle of sunlight coming through a window, by the miracle of people walking on legs through the streets, by the miracle of people talking to each other.'[49]

Mankind, however, has violated this miracle of God's creation. 'God had written, not so much a poem, but rather a play,' says Chesterton in *Orthodoxy*; 'a play he had planned as perfect, but which had necessarily been left to human actors and stage-managers, who had since made a great mess of it.'[50]

During my retreat at Campion Hall in January 2013, in preparation for my reception into the Church, I read *The Catholic Church and Conversion*. Chesterton describes the 'three stages or states of mind' through which the convert passes, and I identified very closely with these. 'The first is when he imagines himself to be entirely detached, or even to be entirely indifferent, but in the old sense of the term, as when the Prayer Book talks of judges who will truly and indifferently administer justice,' he writes. 'The first phase is that of the young philosopher who feels that he ought to be fair to the Church of Rome. He wishes to do it justice; but chiefly because he sees that it suffers injustice.'[51] That is not precisely what I felt, but it comes close to my mentality when I first began my journey of exploration of Catholicism—I genuinely had no pre-determined decision in mind, at least not consciously, but wanted to give Catholicism a fair hearing. I could not say I was 'indifferent', or entirely detached. Rather I was actively exploring but with an open mind. I was conscious that some evangelicals had perceptions of Catholicism that might perhaps have been doing the Church an injustice.

The second phase is when the convert 'begins to be conscious not only of the falsehood but the truth, and is enormously excited to find that there is far more of it than he had ever expected'.[52] That certainly was true—the more I read and the more I talked with Catholic friends, the more I realised that not only was Catholicism far more deeply rooted in Scripture than I had previously appreciated, but much of it was what I already believed. 'This process, which may be called discovering the Catholic Church, is perhaps the most pleasant and straightforward part of the business; easier than joining the Catholic Church and much easier than trying to live the Catholic life. It is like discovering a new continent full of strange flowers and fantastic animals, which is at once wild and hospitable,' suggests Chesterton.[53] 'It is, broadly speaking, the stage in which the man is unconsciously trying to be converted.'[54]

The third stage is 'perhaps the truest and most terrible' —a time in which 'the man is trying not to be converted'. He has, says Chesterton, 'come too near to the truth, and has forgotten that truth is a magnet, with the powers of attraction and repulsion. He is filled with a sort of fear, which makes him feel like a fool who has been patronising "popery" when he ought to have been awakening to the reality of Rome.' I never experienced this third stage in such stark terms, but of course I went through a period of soul-searching and asking: is this really the path for me? 'The moment men cease to pull against it they feel a tug towards it,' continues Chesterton. 'The moment they cease to shout it down they begin to listen to it with pleasure. The moment they try to be fair to it they begin to be fond of it. But when that affection has passed a certain point it begins to take on the tragic and menacing grandeur of a great love affair. The man has exactly the same sense of having committed or compromised himself; of having been in a sense entrapped, even if he is glad to be entrapped.'[55]

The parallel with a love affair is certainly what I felt. I fell in love with the Catholic Church. But it was rather like falling in love with someone I had known about for a long time, admired, perhaps even become friends with. And as with falling in love, there are several stages—similar but slightly different to Chesterton's three stages. When you first fall in love with another person, you love absolutely everything about that person, and you won't hear any criticism whatsoever. After a while, once you have come to know the person better, you realise firstly that there is a lot that you still do not know, much that you do not understand and perhaps—if we are really honest—some things that you do not particularly like: some of their views, habits, hobbies and preferences. There may be moments when they do or say something that irritates you. You have disagreements. But you love them anyway. And then, perhaps, a third stage—where you learn new things, and you begin to understand why they think or act in a certain way, and whether or not you agree with it, you accept that that is part of their nature.

In some ways this is true with the Church too. After the initial phase of falling in love, I discovered that there are aspects of the Church—whether in teaching, in practice, in structure and management, and among people—that made me think: 'Why do they do it that way? Why do they teach that? If I were founding a Church, I wouldn't do it that way.' But then I reached a point where I had two thoughts. First, thank God, I am not founding a Church—because the one I have joined, regardless of what I think about particular issues, practices or structures, has stood the test of time. And second, while there may be aspects that I question or even disagree with or find difficult to defend, the fundamental core beliefs I love and embrace and give my life to: as we do when we really love a person.

One of the discoveries upon entering the Church is how much broader—indeed universal—it is than it might appear to the outsider. 'Becoming a Catholic broadens the mind,' writes Chesterton. 'It especially broadens the mind about the reasons for becoming a Catholic. Standing in the centre where all roads meet, a man can look down each of the roads in turn and realise that they come from all points of the heavens.'[56] For me, when asked the question 'Why did you become a Catholic?' I cannot give a sound-bite answer. There were a whole multitude of paths that brought me into the Church—the inspiration of others, a yearning for the deep mysteries of the Church, an appreciation of the transcendent reverence and majesty, a love for Catholic social teaching and the Church's commitment to human dignity and justice. These roads, these points of the heavens, culminated in one decision-point.

'At the last moment of all, the convert often feels as if he were looking through a leper's window,' writes Chesterton. 'He is looking through a little crack or crooked hole that seems to grow smaller as he stares at it; but it is an opening that looks towards the Altar. Only, when he has entered the Church, he finds that the Church is much larger inside than it is outside.'[57] That I have found to be very true. While the Mass is in essence the same everywhere in the world, the variety of forms of Mass, local cultural elements and diverse charisms amount indeed to a many-roomed mansion. 'The Church is the natural home of the Human Spirit,' concludes Chesterton.[58]

Why has Christianity survived, Chesterton asks in *The Everlasting Man*. 'Because it fits the lock, because it is like life. It is one among many stories, only it happens to be a true story. It is one among many philosophies, only it happens to be the truth ... We are Christians and Catholics not because we worship a key, but because we have passed a door and felt the wind that is the trumpet of liberty blow over the land of the living,' he writes.[59] 'If it were an error, it seems as if the error could hardly have lasted a day. If it were a mere ecstasy, it would seem that such an ecstasy could not endure for an hour. It has endured for nearly two thousand years.'[60]

David Mills, in an article for *Catholic Exchange* titled 'G. K. Chesterton: rhetoric, genius and holiness,' writes: 'In Chesterton I discovered a man who told me truths I needed to know. These truths were of two sorts: truths I did not see at all or truths I only intuited. In reading him I kept saying "Aha" or "So that's it" when he showed me something I had not seen, and "Yes" and "Exactly" when he showed me clearly something I'd only seen dimly.'[61] I agree. He was unique. At his funeral in 1936 his close friend Hilaire Belloc was overheard muttering: 'Chesterton will never occur again.'[62]

Hans Urs von Balthasar

With the exception of Scott Hahn, the authors featured here so far are not theologians, but journalists and public intellectuals. Coming from a journalistic background myself, it is not surprising that Dr Weigel, Muggeridge and Chesterton engaged my mind as they did. But serious theology was also on my agenda as I continued my journey towards Rome, and Hans Urs von Balthasar was influential in this.

The Swiss theologian is widely considered one of the greatest theologians of the twentieth century. He is the author of over 60 works. Three of his books were important in my journey: *Engagement with God, Love Alone is Credible* and a book co-authored with Cardinal Joseph Ratzinger as he then was—Pope Benedict XVI to be—called *Mary: The Church at the Source*.

For an eminent theologian, von Balthasar writes clearly, beautifully and comprehensibly. His writing is simple without being simplistic. One of the most moving passages in *Engagement with God* is a section on God as the 'Source in whom all truth reposes'. Yet he continues:

On the other hand, however, this source cannot simply be treated as if it were an established fact to be relied on, nor regarded as an abstract truth to be pondered or a work of art to be admired, nor dismissed with only a word of thanks. For the source is not a thing, nor an abstract truth nor a work of art, but God himself, eternally involved in Christ crucified for my sake and for the sake of the whole world. I myself cannot, in the face of this, stand by as a mere spectator. I am involved, though involved only insofar as I involve myself. To put this less concisely, in the process of God's involving himself for my sake, I am already affected by his involvement. But it is not just the result of God's efforts that benefits me; for through becoming involved, I have inevitably entered into partnership with that eternal love which is manifested as such in all the tremendous work that love does in the world. Hence what we call the gift to the world of the free, unmerited grace of God is in fact his involvement on behalf of the world, in which, however, the world itself is already and eternally involved.

In a strange way, this removes the dualism between prayer and works, between contemplation and action. One normally imagines that for a Christian (as for every person who has some religion), action is the fruit of contemplation though contemplation can and must continue throughout the action and fertilise it. This much is not untrue; for in Christianity, as in every religion, God as the Absolute enjoys the primacy that is due to him, and we must therefore, first of all, turn to him in order that we may know him and be able to proclaim him to others. All our actions in the world should echo and correspond to this initial experience of God; for the grace of God is prior to all our involvement, undertaken for God in the world, and for the needs of the world for his sake. But this golden rule, to which there is no exception, is substantially modified in Christianity by the fact that the source of grace at which I as an individual must first of all drink is nothing less than God's total involvement, everything he does in fact for the salvation of the world. Were I not involved in this saving action of his, I would never learn that God is love, the love of three Persons in One. For I can never strip away the whole dramatic action of the Incarnation, Cross, and Resurrection in the attempt to contemplate 'behind all this' God as he fundamentally 'is', everlastingly at rest, and content in himself. What we are looking at when we contemplate the love of God is 'Christ, giving himself in love' and this 'urges us on, because we are convinced that one has died for all: therefore all have died' (2 Corinthians 5: 14). In contemplating this, we suddenly realise that we have been made to take our part in the action as a whole and that we are therefore participants in this action. God's active work 'urges us on' to active works. For since he has laid down his life for us, we too ought to lay down our lives for the brethren.[63]

As someone very engaged in 'active works' and yet appreciative of contemplation and the importance of prayer, I found this passage encouraging. I was also inspired by this passage on love:

For Christianity has shed the light of love over humanity and in this light the unique worth of every individual person is made manifest. Without this light the general principles of human rights could not have been formulated, principles that are normative indeed for us, even though in practice they are frequently trodden underfoot. But the darkness falls on Christianity deepest

of all when ostensibly Christian nations pay no
heed to these principles, whereas others that do
not call themselves Christian seek to conform
themselves on the whole to such principles. In
vain we shall search the world before Christ for
this kind of outlook of man on his fellow man; we
shall find it neither in Plato, who speaks nobly of
Eros, nor in the treatises of Aristotle and Cicero
on friendship nor even in the writings of the
Stoics. In none of these will we find the kind of
respect for the person of one's neighbour that
can only be established as a principle for the first
time by the Christian revelation. For God, in his
boundless involvement, has indeed always the
individual in mind (though all in community are
just as much his preoccupation); and as he moves
toward the individual, so he lights up his unique
dignity as a person.[64]

In *Love Alone is Credible*, von Balthasar writes with stark
honesty: 'When man encounters the love of God in
Christ, not only does he experience what genuine love
is, but he is also confronted with the undeniable fact
that he, a selfish sinner, does not himself possess true
love. He experiences two things at once: the finitude
of the creature's love and its sinful frigidity.'[65]

How true. How many times have I undertaken an
act of service or love not in an attitude of love but
instead grumbling, grudging, wishing I were doing
something else; or worse, how often have I decided not
to help someone in need because it was not convenient,
because I had other priorities; or, having carried out an
act of service or love, looked for praise and gratitude,
turning the act into a self-serving act of gratification
for the ego instead of a humble act of love? How often?
Too often.

'It is only when we look the Crucified One in the eye that we recognise the abyss of selfishness—even of that which we are accustomed to call love,' concludes von Balthasar. 'When the question is most seriously put to us, we say No where Christ, out of love, said Yes, and in our nonlove, we say Yes without a second thought to Jesus's bearing our sins ... At a deeper level, man is aware of his heart's paralysis, fallenness, and frigidity, his incapacity to meet the demand of any law of love, no matter how generally postulated.'[66]

Several times already in this book I have mentioned Mary, and how as an evangelical Protestant I had rarely even thought about her. Once a year, in the Nativity scene, evangelicals and other Protestants are reminded that Mary gave birth to Jesus Christ—but then for the rest of the year she does not feature. So when I began exploring the Catholic faith, I began to discover not only the truth of what Catholics believe about Mary, and how we do not worship her, as some Protestants claim, but instead 'venerate' or 'honour' her, but I also began to discover Mary herself—and why we venerate her. And one of the most important guides for me in this was a book von Balthasar co-authored with Cardinal Ratzinger, before he become Pope Benedict XVI, called *Mary: The Church at the Source*. It is a captivating book, which helped draw together in my mind, heart and soul everything that I was discovering about the Mother of God.

'Veneration of a human being must in no way be confused with the adoration shown to God alone,' write von Balthasar and Cardinal Ratzinger. Veneration, they explain, is what the Jews in the Old Testament show to their forefathers, the patriarchs, Moses, and the prophets—'without thereby offending in the least against the worship of God'.[67] The

veneration of Mary, they contend, 'is the surest and
shortest way to get close to Christ in a concrete way.
In meditating on her life in all its phases we learn
what it means to live for and with Christ—in the
everyday, in an unsentimental matter-of-factness
that nonetheless enjoys perfect inner intimacy. Contemplating Mary's existence, we also submit to the
darkness that is imposed on our faith, yet we learn
how we must always be ready when Jesus suddenly
asks something of us.'[68]

At the heart of a relationship with Mary is the
Magnificat, her 'song of praise' set out in Luke 1:
46–56. It begins: 'My soul magnifies the Lord, and
my spirit rejoices in God my Saviour.' Reflecting on
this, von Balthasar and Cardinal Ratzinger write:
'To magnify the Lord means, not to want to magnify ourselves, our own name, our own ego; not to
spread ourselves and take up more space, but to
give him room so that he may be more present in
the world. It means to become more truly what we
are: not a self-enclosed monad that displays nothing
but itself, but God's image. It means to get free of the
dust and soot that obscures and begrimes the trans-
parency of the image and to become truly human by
pointing exclusively to him.'[69]

But while Mary's purpose in our faith and
spiritual lives is always to point the way to God,
at the same time without Mary, Jesus Christ would
not have set foot on the earth as a man. 'For without Mary,' write von Balthasar and Ratzinger, 'God's
entrance into history would not achieve its intended
purpose. That is, the very thing that matters most in
the Creed would be left unrealised—God's being a
God with us, and not only a God in and for himself.
Thus, the woman who called herself lowly, that is

nameless (Luke 1: 48), stands at the core of the pro-
fession of faith in the living God, and it is impossible
to imagine it without her. She is an indispensable,
central component of our faith in the living, acting
God. The Word becomes flesh—the eternal Meaning grounding the universe enters into her. He does
not merely regard her from the outside; he becomes
himself an actor in her. It needed the Virgin for this
to be possible, the Virgin who made available her
whole person, that is, her embodied existence, her
very self, as the place of God's dwelling in the world.
The Incarnation required consenting acceptance.
Only in this way do Logos and flesh really become
one ... A body is prepared for the Son through Mary,
in that she gives herself over wholly to the Father's
will and thus places her body at his disposal as the
tabernacle of the Holy Spirit.'[70] It is so obvious when
it is put like that. To reinforce the point: 'Her Yes
becomes the meeting place in which God obtains
a dwelling in the world. God, who does not dwell
in buildings of stone, dwells in this Yes given with
body and soul; he whom the world cannot encom-
pass can come to dwell wholly in a human being ...
It is upon her that the Holy Spirit descends, thereby
making her the new Temple. Joseph, the just man,
is appointed to be the steward of the mysteries of
God, the paterfamilias and guardian of the sanctuary, which is Mary the bride and the Logos in her.'[71]

Von Balthasar explores the scriptural basis for the
Hail Mary, the Angelus and the Rosary—three dis-
tinctly Catholic forms of prayer. None of them, he
argues, 'go a single step beyond the pattern laid down
in the Bible'.[72]

Von Balthasar and Ratzinger end the book with
reflections on Mary and Peter: Mary, the Mother of

God and the Mother of the Church, and Peter, the rock on whom the Church was founded. In my evangelical, Protestant days these two key figures in the Church's very origin rarely featured—Peter usually only as the disciple who denied the Lord three times and then wept, Mary as the woman holding the baby in the Nativity scene. As a Catholic, discovering the Marian and Petrine roots of the Church was like unlocking a hidden treasure, and von Balthasar was one who helped me find the key.

Thomas Merton

Some years before I began my conscious journey of exploration of Catholicism, I discovered Thomas Merton. I read the American Trappist monk's famous book, *No Man is an Island*, and found it profoundly beautiful. The prologue begins: 'No matter how ruined man and his world may seem to be, and no matter how terrible man's despair may become, as long as he continues to be a man his very humanity continues to tell him that life has a meaning.'[73]

And that meaning links us to others for, as Merton goes on to write, 'my successes are not my own. The way to them was prepared by others. The fruit of my labours is not my own: for I am preparing the way for the achievements of another.'

My own story reflects that—certainly in that, as this book illustrates, many others helped prepare and guide my path, and I hope therefore that this book will contribute, in however small a way, to influencing others in their journeys. 'Therefore,' says Merton, 'the meaning of my life is not to be looked for merely in the sum total of my own achievements. It is seen only in the complete integration of my achievements and failures with the achievements and failures of my own generation, and society, and time. It is seen, above all, in my integration in the mystery of Christ.[74]

Merton's words jumped off the pages at me. The importance of silence and rest was particularly striking, and inspired me in my practice of taking annual retreats, regular breaks, and keeping some evenings free from engagements. 'If we have no silence, God is not heard in our music,' Merton says. 'If we have no rest, God does not bless our work. If we twist our lives out of shape in order to fill every corner of them with action and experience, God will silently withdraw from our hearts and leave us empty.'[75]

I embraced Christ in 1994 at university, but not because I went looking for Him, and not without many questions, doubts and a process of questioning. Similarly, just under two decades later, I entered the Catholic Church not because I sought her but because she sought me, and again, not without two years of questioning.

'If I find Him with great ease, perhaps He is not my God,' writes Merton. 'If I cannot hope to find Him at all, is He my God? If I find Him wherever I wish, have I found Him? If He can find me whenever He wishes, and tells me Who He is and who I am, and if I then know that He Whom I could not find has found me: then I know He is the Lord, my God: He has touched me with the finger that made me out of nothing.'[76] At the same time, he continues, 'we cannot find Him unless we know we need Him. We forget this need when we take a self-sufficient pleasure in our own good works. The poor and helpless are the first to find Him, Who came to seek and to save that which was lost.'[77]

A little later, I read his famous spiritual auto-biography, *The Seven-Storey Mountain*, in which he tells of his conversion to Catholicism and his sub-sequent entry into the Cistercian abbey of Our Lady of Gethsemane, in Kentucky. As Matteo Pistono says, 'single-handedly, he restored credibility to the very possibility of contemplative virtue which had long been denigrated by liberal intellectuals and tradi-tional Christians alike. His was a voice of sanity, filled with sacred wonder, and replete with inquiry and contradiction.'[78] His was a voice that drew me, gently, towards the Church.

Pope Benedict XVI

There were plenty of others. Long before my active journey of exploration I read St Augustine's *Confessions*, Thomas à Kempis's *The Imitation of Christ*, St Thérèse of Lisieux's *The Story of a Soul* and several works by Henri Nouwen. All of them sowed their seeds.

During the more active journey I read Jean-Pierre de Caussade's *Abandonment to Divine Providence*, Dor-othy Day's *The Long Loneliness*, Jacques Maritain's *Christianity and Democracy* and *The Rights of Man and Natural Law*, Henri de Lubac's *Catholicism: Christ and the Common Destiny of Man* and John Henry New-man's *Loss and Gain: The Story of a Convert* and *Apolo-gia pro Vita Sua*.

In the months after my reception into the Church, I read Blaise Pascal's *Pensées* and discovered the beauti-ful and inspiring work of Fr Timothy Radcliffe, whose books *What is the Point of Being a Christian?*, *Why Go to Church?: The Drama of the Eucharist*, *Take the Plunge: Living Baptism and Confirmation*, *I Call You Friends* and

Sing a New Song: The Christian Vocation are among the best books I have read.

Later on, I read Abbot Christopher Jamison's *Finding Happiness* and *Finding Sanctuary*, and Fr Raniero Cantalamessa's *In Love with Christ: The Secret of Saint Francis of Assisi*, and *Sober Intoxication of the Spirit*.

I discovered the poetry of Gerard Manley Hopkins. All of these books have helped me in my journey to, into and within the Catholic Church. But there is one author, theologian and priest who perhaps more than any other caught my imagination, and he happened to be the pope at the time I made my decision to become a Catholic.

The world was unkind and unfair to Pope Benedict XVI. Portrayed as a tough, hard-line conservative—nicknamed 'God's Rottweiler'—his writings indicate a very different person: one who possesses not only a fierce intellect and a devout commitment to orthodoxy, but also a deeply sensitive, spiritual, thoughtful mind whose absolute devotion to Jesus Christ shines through more than anything else. When he visited the United Kingdom in September 2010, I was captivated. I watched most of his engagements on television, particularly the Mass in Birmingham for the Beatification of John Henry Newman, the Mass in Westminster Cathedral, his address to both Houses of Parliament in Westminster Hall, and the Prayer Vigil in Hyde Park. I followed the media coverage closely and it was clear that during his visit he won people over, including some of the media who had wrongly predicted a visit marred by protests and hostility. The so-called Rottweiler had been revealed as the German Shepherd.

Observing his visit to the United Kingdom was, with hindsight, another stepping stone on my journey

into the Church, although it was at least six months
before my first conversation with Cardinal Bo in Rangoon which unlocked the gates to what I call my 'conscious journey of exploration.' But I had already been
drawn to Benedict XVI some years previously. I read
his trilogy on Jesus of Nazareth—a truly remarkable
set of books which display his rare gift of commu-
nicating deep theological beliefs in easy, engaging
language, giving a simple—though by no means sim-
plified or simplistic—message. This work, entitled,
Jesus of Nazareth, looks at Christ's birth and infancy,
his life and teachings, and his arrest, trial, execution and resurrection in a tone that is ecumenical,
indeed evangelical, and one which any Christian of
any tradition would appreciate.

'God is the issue,' writes Benedict XVI. 'Is he real,
reality itself, or isn't he? Is he good, or do we have to
invent the good ourselves? The God question is the
fundamental question, and it sets us down right at the
crossroads of human existence.'[79]

He continues: 'If we had to choose today, would
Jesus of Nazareth, the son of Mary, the Son of the
Father have a chance? Do we really know Jesus at all?
Do we understand him? Do we not perhaps have to
make an effort, today as always, to get to know him
all over again?'[80]

Enmity with God, says Benedict XVI, 'is the source
of all that poisons man; overcoming this enmity is the
basic condition for peace in the world. Only the man
who is reconciled with God can also be reconciled
and in harmony with himself, and only the man who
is reconciled with God and with himself can establish
peace around him and throughout the world.'[81]

Love comes from God, and is 'the true morality'
of Christianity.[82] 'In the end,' he reiterates, 'man just

needs one thing, in which everything else is included;
but he must first delve beyond his superficial wishes
and longings in order to learn to recognise what it is
that he truly needs and truly wants. He needs God.
And so we now realise what ultimately lies behind
all the Johannine images: Jesus gives us 'life' because
he gives us God. He can give God because he himself
is one with God, because he is the Son. He himself is
the gift—he *is* "life".'[83]

After my conversation with Cardinal Bo in Rangoon
in March 2011, the first book I read on my more active
journey towards the Church was a book he gave me,
*Light of the World: The Pope, the Church, and the Signs of
the Times*, a set of interviews of Pope Benedict XVI in
conversation with Peter Seewald. The more I read of this
pope, the more drawn towards him and the Church I
felt. I read his books *Called to Communion: Understanding
the Church Today*, *Heart of the Christian Life: Thoughts on
Holy Mass*, *On the Way to Jesus Christ*, *Credo for Today:
What Christians Believe* and two of his beautiful com-
pilations of reflections on the saints: *Holiness is Always
in Season* and *Great Teachers*. And of course, these are
just a fraction of the books he has authored.

Heart of the Christian Life helped me understand the
Eucharist. For many Protestants, Communion is not a
regular feature of worship. It may happen fortnightly,
monthly, even quarterly in some traditions. Yet for
Catholics it is the very epicentre of our faith, and the
heart of the Mass. Why?

'The Body and Blood of Christ are given to us so
that we ourselves will be transformed in our turn. We
are to become the Body of Christ, his own Flesh and
Blood,' Benedict XVI writes. 'We all eat the one bread,
and this means that we ourselves become one. In this
way, adoration, as we said earlier, becomes union.

God no longer simply stands before us as the One who is totally Other. He is within us, and we are in him. His dynamic enters into us and then seeks to spread outward to others until it fills the world, so that his love can truly become the dominant measure of the world.'[84]

But the Eucharist is not only for Sunday, nor even only for Mass. Eucharistic Adoration is an important part of Catholic spirituality—a time of prayer in front of the consecrated Host. For an evangelical Protestant, sitting in front of what appears to be a wafer and 'adoring' it appears a strange activity. But when one realises that it is in fact the 'Real Presence' of Christ, it becomes more comprehensible. 'When, in adoration, we look at the consecrated Host, the sign of creation speaks to us,' writes Benedict XVI. 'And so, we encounter the greatness of his gift; but we also encounter the Passion, the Cross of Jesus and his Resurrection. Through this gaze of adoration, he draws us toward himself, within his mystery, through which he wants to transform us as he transformed the Host.'[85]

Some Protestants object to icons, statues and other images in Catholic spirituality, but once again, Benedict XVI has a very clear explanation: 'The icon must not become an idol that is free-standing and reduces God to something positively material and tangible. It must rather bear within itself the dynamic of transcendence, of pointing beyond itself; it must be an invitation that sets us on the way, on the search for the face of the Lord—an invitation that leads us beyond all material things and keeps us continually on the journey of following after, which in this life is never completed.'[86]

In *On the Way to Jesus Christ*, Benedict XVI describes the importance of faith in action—loving your neighbour, serving the poor, reaching out to the oppressed. 'Listening to God becomes living with God, and it leads from faith to charity, to the discovery of one's neighbour,' he writes.[87]

In 2010—again, before my active journey of exploration began—I read Benedict XVI's three encyclicals: *Deus caritas est* ('God is Love'), *Spe salvi* ('Saved in Hope') and *Caritas in veritate* ('Charity in Truth'). As with his books, he demonstrated a rare talent for going deep but not getting lost in the woods. His encyclicals were for me yet another tug along the path.

'Being Christian is not the result of an ethical choice or a lofty idea,' begins *Deus caritas est*, 'but the encounter with an event, a person, which gives life a new horizon and a decisive direction.'[88]

The encyclical goes on to explore different forms and meanings of love, the 'unbreakable bond between love of God and love of neighbour', and the responsibility of the Church to love in action. 'For the Church, charity is not a kind of welfare activity which could equally well be left to others, but is a part of her nature, an indispensable expression of her being' he writes. The Church has a responsibility to speak up for justice, including religious freedom. 'The Church cannot and must not take upon herself the political battle to bring about the most just society possible,' he argues. 'She cannot and must not replace the State. Yet at the same time she cannot and must not remain on the sidelines in the fight for justice.'

Spe salvi focuses on the hope that we have when we have faith. 'To come to know God—the true God— means to receive hope,' he says.[89] 'Man needs God, otherwise he remains without hope.' And key to discovering that hope is prayer. 'When no one listens to me any more, God still listens to me. When I can no longer talk to anyone or call upon anyone, I can always talk to God. When there is no longer anyone to help me deal with a need or expectation that goes beyond the human capacity for hope, he can help me.'

Caritas in veritate looks at the Church's social doctrine, and concludes that 'love is God's greatest gift to humanity, it is his promise and our hope'.[90] But love, or charity, must always be based on truth. 'Truth is the light that gives meaning and value to charity. That light is both the light of reason and the light of faith ... Without truth, charity degenerates into sentimentality. Love becomes an empty shell, to be filled in an arbitrary way. In a culture without truth, this is the fatal risk facing love.'

And love is two-way. 'Charity is love received and given,' according to this encyclical. 'As objects of God's love, men and women become subjects of charity, they are called to make themselves instruments of grace, so as to pour forth God's charity and to weave networks of charity.' But again, truth: 'Without truth, without trust and love for what is true, there is no social conscience and responsibility, and social action ends up serving private interests and the logic of power, resulting in social fragmentation, especially in a globalised society at difficult times like the present.'

Justice is important, but 'charity goes beyond justice' because 'to love is to give, to offer what is "mine" to the other; but it never lacks justice ... Justice is inseparable from charity and intrinsic to it.'

Caritas in veritate is packed with an agenda that addresses many of the world's challenges today: the economy, poverty, violations of religious freedom, the family, social breakdown, technological advances and the environment. Benedict XVI concludes:

As we contemplate the vast amount of work
to be done, we are sustained by our faith that
God is present alongside those who come
together in his name to work for justice. Only
if we are aware of our calling, as individuals
and as a community, to be part of God's family
as his sons and daughters, will we be able to
generate a new vision and muster new energy
in the service of a truly integral humanism.
The greatest service to development, then, is
a Christian humanism that enkindles charity
and takes its lead from truth, accepting both as
a lasting gift from God ... Development needs
Christians with their arms raised towards God
in prayer, Christians moved by the knowledge
that truth-filled love, caritas in veritate, from
which authentic development proceeds, is not
produced by us, but given to us.

Throughout 2012–13, the Year of Faith, I read almost all
of Benedict XVI's General Audience addresses, and his
Apostolic Letter *Porta fidei*, which begins: 'The "door of
faith" (Acts 14: 27) is always open for us, ushering us
into the life of communion with God and offering entry
into his Church. It is possible to cross that threshold
when the word of God is proclaimed and the heart
allows itself to be shaped by transforming grace. To
enter through that door is to set out on a journey that
lasts a lifetime.'[91] I had begun that journey about seven
months before Benedict XVI initiated the Year of Faith,
and I entered through the doors of the Church just
towards the end of the Year of Faith. The journey is of
course far from over—it will last a lifetime—but Benedict XVI was an instrumental guide for a significant
part of my journey so far.

For that reason I was, along with almost everyone else in the world, stunned when Benedict XVI

announced on 11 February 2013 that he was resigning. When a colleague first told me the news, I assumed it was a joke. Then, as the truth became clear, I went through a mixture of emotions.

Firstly, sadness—I had already made the decision to become a Catholic and was preparing to be received into the Church just over a month later. I had been looking forward to entering the Church led by Benedict XVI, one of the greatest theologians of our time—and on a more trivial note, sharing a name with the Holy Father was rather appealing. But then as the news sank in, my already profound respect for this particular Holy Father grew even deeper.

What a step of humility, honesty, and courage. To recognise that due to ageing and failing health, he was no longer able to serve the Church in the way he would wish the Successor of St Peter to serve, and therefore to step aside and give the Church the opportunity to choose a new pope, is the mark of a man who is called by God.

In his final address to 200,000 faithful in St Peter's Square on his last full day as pope, he said that: 'The Lord has really guided me. He has been close to me: daily could I feel His presence.' He concluded: 'Dear friends! God guides His Church, maintains her always, and especially in difficult times. Let us never lose this vision of faith, which is the only true vision of the way of the Church and the world. In our heart, in the heart of each of you, let there be always the joyous certainty that the Lord is near, that He does not abandon us, that He is near to us and that He surrounds us with His love.'[92]

For a pope reviled by some as a 'Rottweiler', it is amazing how his theme consistently was 'love, hope and charity'. George Weigel says: 'Benedict XVI will be remembered in time as the greatest papal preacher since Gregory the Great.'

Catholic Teachings

Among the vast amount of reading that I engaged with over the two-year journey of exploration were other encyclicals from previous popes: notably Leo XIII's 1889 encyclical *Quamquam pluries*, on devotion to St Joseph, and *Rerum novarum* in 1891, 'On Capital and Labour'; John XXIII's *Pacem in terris*, on peace 'in truth, justice, charity and liberty' in 1963; and many, though not all, of John Paul II's encyclicals—*Redemptor hominis* in 1979, *Laborem exercens* in 1981, *Centesimus annus* in 1991, *Veritatis splendor* in 1993, *Evangelium vitae* in 1995 and *Fides et ratio* in 1998.[93] I also read many Apostolic Letters and Apostolic Exhortations, and of course some of the documents of the Second Vatican Council, particularly the Church's 'Pastoral Constitution' known as *Gaudium et spes* and the declaration on religious freedom—*Dignitatis humanae*. The Latin titles may not sound very enticing, but I fell in love with this amazing, beautifully written body of writing over the decades and indeed centuries, that sets out in depth what the Church teaches on a whole range of theological, doctrinal, moral, ethical and social themes. In the space of this book, I simply cannot capture the essence of these writings, but if you have never read them, whether you are a Catholic or someone exploring the Catholic faith or someone seeking insight, direction or, indeed, truth, I would urge you to do so.

Scott Hahn, George Weigel, Malcolm Muggeridge, G. K. Chesterton, Hans Urs von Balthasar, Thomas Merton, Pope Benedict XVI and a whole range of other

Catholic writers and Church documents mentioned here were all very important guides on my journey. Through their words, they answered some of the questions I was asking, brought into focus some of the thoughts I already had, and inspired new perspectives on the God whom I had been worshipping already for almost two decades. But if I have to single out two single volumes that contained the fuel that drove me on into the Church, there is little doubt that it would be two works which hardly have the catchiest of titles but have the most exciting of contents: the *Catechism of the Catholic Church*, and the *Compendium of the Social Doctrine of the Church*.

I read the Catechism, in full, over the course of a year. Typically I would begin each day with a time of prayer and reflection. I would read the Scripture readings for the day and the commentaries, either from *Every Day with Jesus*[94] which I used to subscribe to, or latterly from the Catholic *Bible Alive* devotional;[95] I would say the prayers and hymns from the wonderful Catholic devotional *Magnificat*;[96] and then I would read a page or two or a section of the Catechism.

I was struck by the beauty of the prose in the Catechism; and by how much of it was what I already believed. I fell in love with the Church through the Catechism, as much as through other influences.

The Compendium of the Social Doctrine of the Church similarly grabbed me. The title is unenticing, but I have never seen any other Christian tradition set out as comprehensively and persuasively such a view of the world, its challenges and the best ways forward. It is a combination of spiritual nourishment and political platform: it is a manifesto for the values which should underpin approaches to every key topic in society—the economy, the environment, human rights, the family, foreign policy, war and peace, life. As a human rights activist I read it as a mandate for the work I was already engaged in.

When I started this book, I thought I would include a whole reflection on the Catechism and the *Compendium of the Social Doctrine*, with plenty of extracts quoted. But on reflection, I would rather simply challenge the reader to overcome any sense of intimidation from either the laborious nature of the titles or the sheer volume of the publications, and go ahead and read both these volumes, in full, as I did. If you are a Catholic and you have never read them in full, I have a hunch that they will enrich your Catholic faith. If you are not yet a Catholic, but are curious, I have a hunch that you might find them as absorbing as I did. Either way, at least give it a go. A page or a paragraph or a section a day, for a year or so, and see what happens. Why not, in the words of Jean-Pierre de Caussade, abandon yourself to divine providence?

Notes

1   Scott Hahn, *Hail, Holy Queen: The Mother of God in the Word of God* (London, Darton, Longman and Todd, 2001), p. 6.
2   *Ibid.*, p. 7.
3   *Ibid.*, p. 33.
4   John 19: 27.
5   Scott Hahn, *The Lamb's Supper: The Mass as Heaven on Earth* (London, Darton, Longman and Todd, 2003), p. 8.
6   *Ibid.*, p. 4.
7   *Ibid.*, pp. 8–9.
8   *Ibid.*, p. 30.
9   Matthew 18: 20.
10 Scott Hahn, *Lord, Have Mercy: The Healing Power of Confession* (London, Darton, Longman and Todd, 2003), p. 4.

[11] George Weigel, *The Truth of Catholicism: Ten Controversies Explored* (Leominster, Gracewing, 2001), p. 5.

[12] *Ibid.*, p. 5.

[13] *Ibid.*, pp. 32–3.

[14] *Ibid.*, pp. 34–6.

[15] *Ibid.*, pp. 47–8.

[16] *Ibid.*, p. 55.

[17] *Ibid.*, p. 56.

[18] *Ibid.*, pp. 60–1.

[19] *Ibid.*, pp. 64–5.

[20] *Ibid.*, p. 67.

[21] George Weigel, *Letters to a Young Catholic* (Leominster, Gracewing, 2004), p.xii.

[22] *Ibid.*, p. 1.

[23] *Ibid.*, p. 1.

[24] *Ibid.*, p. 5.

[25] *Ibid.*, p. 7.

[26] *Ibid.*, p. 1.

[27] Richard Ingrams, *Malcolm Muggeridge: The Biography* (London, Harper Collins, 1995), p. 21.

[28] *Ibid.*, p. 9.

[29] *Ibid.*, p. 59.

[30] *Ibid.*, pp. 79–80.

[31] *Ibid.*, p. 93.

[32] *Ibid.*, p. 7.

[33] *Ibid.*, p. 93.

[34] *Ibid.*, p. 24.

[35] *Ibid.*, p. 10.

[36] *Ibid.*, p. 11.

[37] *Ibid.*, pp. 13–14.

[38] *Ibid.*, p. 14.

[39] *Ibid.*, pp. 31–2.

[40] Malcolm Muggeridge, *Conversion: The Spiritual Journey of a Twentieth-Century Pilgrim* (Eugene, Wipf and Stock, 1988), pp. 6–7.

[41] *Ibid.*, pp. 5–6.

[42] Malcolm Muggeridge, *Jesus: The Man who Lives* (London, Collins, 1975), p. 9.

[43] Muggeridge, *Conversion*, p. 3.

44 Muggeridge, *Jesus: The Man who Lives*, p. 67.
45 *Ibid.*, p. 86.
46 Karl Schmude, *G. K. Chesterton* (London, Catholic Truth Society, 2008), p. 4.
47 Weigel, *Letters to a Young Catholic*, p. 4.
48 *Ibid.*, p. 5.
49 Schmude, p. 10
50 G. K. Chesterton, *Orthodoxy* (Chicago, Moody, 2009), p. 18.
51 G. K. Chesterton, *The Catholic Church and Conversion* (San Francisco, Ignatius Press, 1990), p. 2.
52 *Ibid.*, p. 5.
53 *Ibid.*, p. 7.
54 *Ibid.*, p. 7.
55 *Ibid.*, pp. 8–9.
56 *Ibid.*, p. 80.
57 *Ibid.*, p. 2.
58 *Ibid.*, p. 9.
59 G. K. Chesterton, *The Everlasting Man* (Peabody, Hendrickson Publishers, 2007), p. 37.
60 *Ibid.*, p. 57.
61 David Mills, 'G. K. Chesterton: rhetoric, genius and holiness', 23 April 2015—http://catholicexchange.com/g-k-chesterton-rhetoric-genius-holiness.
62 Schmude, p. 5.
63 Hans Urs von Balthasar, *Engagement with God* (San Francisco, Ignatius, 1975), pp. 6–8.
64 *Ibid.*, pp. 4–5.
65 Von Balthasar, *Love Alone is Credible* (San Francisco, Ignatius, 2004), p. 1.
66 *Ibid.*, pp. 6–7.
67 Von Balthasar and Joseph Cardinal Ratzinger, *Mary: The Church at the Source* (San Francisco, Ignatius, 1997), p. 16.
68 *Ibid.*, p. 17.
69 *Ibid*, p. 5.
70 *Ibid.*, p. 4.
71 *Ibid.*, pp. 7–8.
72 *Ibid.*, p. 18.
73 Thomas Merton, *No Man is an Island* (Boston, Shambhala, 2005), p. xi.

74 *Ibid.*, p. xxii.
75 *Ibid.*, p. 34.
76 *Ibid.*, p. 45.
77 *Ibid.*, p. 48.
78 Matteo Pistono, 'Thomas Merton in the Himalayas: interview with Harold Talbott', October 15 2014—http://www.matteopistono.com/blog.htm?post=972759.
79 Pope Benedict XVI, *Jesus of Nazareth* (London, Bloomsbury, 2007), p. 9.
80 *Ibid.*, p. 1.
81 *Ibid.*, p. 5.
82 *Ibid.*, p. 9.
83 *Ibid.*, pp. 53–4.
84 Benedict XVI, *Heart of the Christian Life: Thoughts on Holy Mass* (San Francisco, Ignatius, 2010), p. 3.
85 *Ibid.*, p. 5.
86 Benedict XVI, *On the Way to Jesus Christ* (San Francisco, Ignatius, 2004), p. 8.
87 *Ibid.*, p. 9.
88 Pope Benedict XVI, *Deus caritas est*, 2005.
89 Pope Benedict XVI , *Spe salvi*, 2007.
90 Pope Benedict XVI *Caritas in veritate*, 2009.
91 Apostolic Letter 'Motu proprio data', *Porta fidei*, 2011.
92 'Full text of Benedict XVI's last address', *The Catholic Herald*, 27 February 2013.
93 Encyclicals and other writings of John Paul II.
94 A devotional published by CWR. See http://www.cwr.org.uk/store/t-edwj.aspx for more information
95 Published by Alive Publishing.
96 Published by Magnificat.

✧ 6 ✧

Return to Retreat

The rose is a mystery—where is it found?
Is it anything true? Does it grow upon ground?
It was made of earth's mould but it went from men's
eyes
And its place is a secret and shut in the skies.

In the gardens of God, in the daylight divine
Find me a place by thee, mother of mine.

But where was it formerly? Which is the spot
That was blest in it once, though now it is not? —
It is Galilee's growth: it grew at God's will
And broke into bloom upon Nazareth hill.

In the gardens of God, in the daylight divine
I shall look on thy loveliness, mother of mine.

from Gerard Manley Hopkins, 'Rosa mystica'

Lift up your sick self just as you are, and through your
longing strive to touch good, gracious God just as he
is. Touching him is eternal health, which is the point
of the story of the woman in the Gospel who said, 'If
I touch but the hem of his garment I shall be whole.'

The Epistle of the Privy Counsel
in The Cloud of Unknowing and Other Works

That they may be one.

John 17: 21

E LEVEN DAYS before I was received into the Church in Burma, a new pope was elected. It is difficult to imagine a more exciting time to join the Catholic Church. Almost overnight, Pope Francis changed the Church's image, through symbolic but significant gestures: washing the feet of female prisoners, having lunch with the homeless, holding a severely disfigured man in an embrace. Theologically, he has not said anything that is different from the message of Benedict XVI or John Paul II, but he has chosen to emphasise, in word and deed, the Church's message of grace, mercy and love.

On 24 March 2014 I was on a flight to Rome. I had been invited to attend a conference on religious freedom. As I looked out of the window, I suddenly recalled the date. It was the first anniversary of my reception into the Church. Exactly one year after travelling to Rome spiritually and theologically, I was arriving in Rome physically as well. A few days later, I was privileged to attend a General Audience with Pope Francis, in St Peter's Square. We were allocated special seats, very close to the Holy Father, and while I did not meet him in person, I could observe him closely. Most moving was when he went to greet a group of disabled people in wheelchairs, at the foot of the steps to St Peter's. One by one he talked to them, embraced them, blessed them, not simply shaking hands for a second and moving on but spending several minutes with each one. This pope, I thought, acts like Jesus.

I had been to Rome several times previously, but only once since becoming a Catholic. That was in June 2013. The highlight of that visit was to be given a private tour of the Scavi, underneath the Basilica, and to be shown the resting place of St Peter's bones, which were discovered directly beneath the high altar. The seminarian who gave me the tour, a friend of mine, and I, were alone, undisturbed by the tour groups for a quarter of an hour or so, and so he led us in a time of prayer at the tomb of St Peter.

After the experience of the retreat at Campion Hall prior to my reception into the Church, I decided to make this an annual fixture, and so on 2 January 2014 I returned to Oxford and to Fr Nicholas King. As with the previous retreat, I kept an account, writing it more or less as I went along, each evening reflecting on the day, rather like a diary. When the Lord speaks in clear and beautiful ways as He does when one takes the time to stop and be still and listen to Him, I did not wish to forget what He said.

I arrived for the retreat with no agenda. I did have three subjects I hoped I might hear from the Lord on—namely, my continuing growth as a Catholic, my vocation, and this book. But despite having these three topics loosely in mind, I also hoped to begin the retreat with an open heart, mind, soul and spirit, eager for the Lord to set the agenda, for Him to speak as He wished, and completely open to the possibility that He might have things to say to me on completely different and unexpected topics. Indeed, who am I to come to the Lord and say: 'Lord, I'd like to hear from you on this or that, but preferably leave out the other'? That would be absurd. I came, I hope, to retreat simply saying: 'Speak, Lord, your servant is listening.'

After arriving at Campion Hall, opposite Christ Church and next to Pembroke College, on 2 January, I had lunch and then met with Fr Nicholas, as I was to do once a day each day, for about half an hour each time. He asked me about my spiritual and prayer life over the course of the past year since we had last met,

and then suggested three 'exercises' or 'ways of praying' (based on the principles of the Spiritual Exercises
of St Ignatius of Loyola, the founder of the 'Society of
Jesus' or the Jesuits). These were: reflecting on the 'season' of Christmastide in the Church, and preparation
for Epiphany, praying over the readings for the day;
'praying with pen in hand,' reflecting on the events
of the past 12 months; or contemplating my favourite
verse in the Bible. Fr Nicholas encouraged me to do
five periods of prayer and contemplation, each one
no less than 20 minutes and no more than one hour,
over the course of the subsequent 24 hours or so. We
arranged to meet again at 5.30pm the following day
and each day after that. And so off I went.

The weather was unusually sunny and beautiful
on my first afternoon, and so for my initial session I
decided to combine prayer with walking (Fr Nicholas
encouraged me to take lots of walks). I walked around
Christ Church Meadow, spent time in the Botanical
Gardens, and strolled along the river. As I watched
the river flowing, I had an overwhelming sense of how
tired I was, how I could at last 'let go' for a few days,
how restful the gently flowing river was. The river
spoke of peace, rest, refreshment. I watched the current
as it flowed in one direction, and felt God saying: 'Go
with the flow—flow with me.' In a river, the water
all flows in one direction—no parts of the water are
attempting to flow in the opposite way. It should be the
same with our journey with God—He is the current,
and we need to flow with Him.

The water became a repeated theme. Christ Church
Meadow was flooded, in parts, but instead of seeing the flooding as a negative, God used the water
to remind me that He is the 'living water' (John 4:
10–14). 'I am the water of life,' He told me. Then the

words from Matthew 11: 28–30 came to me—'Come
to me, all you that are weary and are carrying heavy
burdens, and I will give you rest. Take my yoke upon
you, and learn from me; for I am gentle and humble
in heart, and you will find rest for your souls. For
my yoke is easy, and my burden is light.' The words
'Drop thy still dews of quietness, till all our strivings
cease' came to mind. They come from the famous
hymn 'Dear Lord and Father of mankind', quoted in
the second chapter.

I was amazed at how ordinary aspects of life, which
in our normal busy days we would rush past without
giving a second thought, took on a whole new meaning. Ordinarily, I wouldn't think much of a river or a
water-logged meadow. Similarly, as I looked at the
grass on the lawn in the Botanical Gardens, I reflected
on how amazing it is that every single blade of grass
is created by God, just as every hair on my head, and
yours, is known to Him. Indeed, a couple of times I
became slightly distracted by the other people who
were around, and felt momentarily irritable with them
(entirely unreasonable of me, for they had every right
to be there). My irritation turned to wonder, however,
when I felt an overwhelming reminder that each and
every one of them—each and every one of us—is
made in the image of God: *Imago Dei*. It is a remarkable thought.

As I walked down the tree-lined avenue towards
Christ Church, I saw in the distance a light in the arch-
way of the college. Again, ordinarily I wouldn't give it
a second thought, but as I walked down the avenue,
trees either side of me, I had a real sense of God saying that in my life I should 'keep walking towards the
light', that He is 'the light in the darkness', and that
His light is always with me.

The readings for the day were very interesting. 1 John 2: 22–8 says 'Keep alive in yourselves what you were taught in the beginning'. This reminder is repeated in 2 Timothy 3: 14, which came up later in the day in a separate reflection, when I was reading St Jerome's writings: 'Continue in what you have learned and firmly believed, knowing from whom you learned it.' But at the same time, another of the day's readings was Psalm 97, which begins 'Sing a new song to the Lord, for He has worked wonders'. I had a sense of the Lord saying to me as I walked along the river in Christ Church Meadow: 'I am with you, and I will show you new things.' To summarise, He was saying keep hold of the essentials, but be open to change, to new songs. Perhaps that is, in a different context, what God is saying to the Church through Pope Francis also?

I came back to my room, and read for a while. I read Gerard Manley Hopkins's poems 'To Oxford' (appropriately), 'The habit of perfection' and 'Nondum'. I also read some of his sermons and prose, including a reflection on the Spiritual Exercises written in 1880.

In my second session, I began to reflect on 2013. I sensed that God was saying to me that my life is a 'many-roomed mansion.' That phrase is used about heaven and about the Church, but God was saying that in my own life there are many rooms: family; friends; Burma; Indonesia; North Korea; freedom of thought, conscience, religion or belief for all; politics; my new Catholic faith. He reminded me of what He had shown me in a 'mansion' on my last retreat (see Chapter 2). Then He took me through the key events of the year and with some of them said 'I did that' and at other times said 'We did that together, Ben.' The highlights included some of the amazing experiences in Burma, which would have been inconceivable a short time ago: in March 2011 and May 2012 I was deported from Burma, but in 2013 I gave training workshops not only in Rangoon but in Myitkyina (Kachin State) and Hakha (Chin State) focused on human rights and religious freedom advocacy and documentation, a lecture at the British Council on religious freedom, speeches at public events hosted by the National League for Democracy (Aung San Suu Kyi's party) alongside Lord Alton and Cardinal Bo, and began to work with Buddhist monks to promote religious freedom and counter intolerance. The completion of a major report on Indonesia, called *Indonesia: Pluralism in Peril — The Rise of Religious Intolerance across the Archipelago*, which is 60,000 words and took much of the year to research and write, was another highlight. Visiting my atheist friend Alexander Aan for the second time, and being greeted by him with a warm hug, was yet another. Alex was jailed in 2012 for two-and-a-half years for declaring himself an atheist. The UN Human Rights Council's unanimous decision in March to establish a Commission of Inquiry to investigate North Korea's dire human rights crisis is another, particularly as it came as a result of more than six years of sustained advocacy by CSW, in collaboration with others.

Of course my reception into the Catholic Church was the biggest highlight of the year. I reflected on the Catholic beliefs which I have now embraced, which are new to me: specifically, the veneration (which simply means 'honouring') of Mary, the Mother of Christ; Eucharistic adoration; Confession; and praying the Rosary. On my previous retreat, which was before I became a Catholic, the Lord spoke very vividly to me about Mary, Our Lady, and about the Eucharist, and I describe this in Chapter Two. In preparation for becoming a Catholic I embraced these beliefs and, after a long process of study, thought, questioning, and prayer, I believe I grasped them intellectually, theologically and spiritually. They became alive for me during my last retreat. But it is fair to say that as a new Catholic, it takes time to develop a relationship with Mary and participate in regular Eucharistic adoration. During this session of this retreat, however, the Lord spoke very clearly. In reference to Mary, He said to me: 'She is my mother.' Of the Eucharist: 'This is my body.' On Confession, or the Sacrament of Reconciliation: 'I love you.' Then Mary took my hand, and said: 'Come, Ben, let us go and see my Son, the Lord.' We sat at the foot of the cross. I had further encounters with Our Lady which I will describe shortly, but each time she always pointed me to the Lord. Fr Nicholas affirmed this: 'She always does,' he said.

I went to bed early that night, as I was very tired. I had several very vivid dreams, including a beautiful dream of my mother and my next-door neighbour, both of whom are very keen gardeners, sitting in a garden amidst an assortment of beautiful, colourful flowers. I was sitting there too, with them. I don't know what, if anything, it signified, except the beauty of creation, motherhood, neighbourliness, love, hope. I had a second, less beautiful dream in which two people I love and admire enormously told me that they did not believe Jesus had ever existed. They were surprisingly emphatic and aggressive in this. Initially, in the dream, I did not want to respond, as I did not want to get into an argument, but I was surprised at their insistence and felt I had to reply. I can understand people who doubt Jesus's divinity, the Resurrection, the Virgin birth but, I said, the historical evidence of the existence of a man called Jesus, and the historical evidence of his crucifixion, is solid. Furthermore, I never hear Western secularists questioning the historical existence of Buddha or Mohammed, or even any of the quite difficult-to-grasp Hindu religious figures!

I awoke unexpectedly and inexplicably at 5am on the second day, which was rather irritating, because I'd hoped for a much-needed long night's sleep. I had resolved I would keep my e-mail contact to a bare minimum (ideally just a brief check of my mobile phone once a day, in case of emergencies), but waking at 5am I switched on my phone to find an urgent message which required some attention—temporarily (but not disastrously) unsettling and disturbing the intended pattern of peace and focus on God.

I went back to sleep for a little while, and then got up, and after breakfast saw that the sun was shining. I had always wanted to try to find C. S. Lewis's home, The Kilns, near Headington Quarry, and so I decided to set off there. I wanted to make it a prayerful walk, and took with me my copy of *Magnificat* and a book of poems of Christian mystics, called *For Lovers of God Everywhere*. On the way, I stopped at St Mary's, the University Church, where great preachers such as C. S. Lewis and John Wesley had once spoken and where Blessed John Henry Newman had been Vicar when he was an Anglican, before he became Catholic. I said a few prayers, but did not linger long—in a strange way, I did not want to. I still love many things about the Anglican tradition, and love my Anglican brothers and sisters, but it is no longer my spiritual home. I felt a visitor, and decided to move on.

I had only a very vague sense of how to get to Headington Quarry, and made no attempt to find a map, but I followed my nose. I ended up going in the right direction, but after about 40 minutes the sun disappeared, the dark clouds gathered, and it began to pour. I had no umbrella. Initially I shrugged my shoulders, smiled and persevered. Then the rain turned to hail. Still I kept going. Then I reached Headington, and found the right turn-off to Headington Quarry. The rain, which had shown signs of easing, then bucketed down, and I lost my determination. I could not find Lewis's house, or his grave, and gave up, taking a bus back to the city centre. I started to feel irritated—that I had gone out in the rain without an umbrella and got drenched; gone in search of Lewis's home with no map and no idea how to find it, and failed; in effect 'wasted' the morning—and not even had much of a time of prayer, as the route took me along a busy main road which was neither peaceful nor attractive nor particularly conducive to contemplation and prayer. But once again, the Lord interrupted my inner grumblings. 'Why are you expending energy on negative thoughts?' He said. 'Think of the good exercise and fresh air you have had on this walk. Think of the warmth you are going back to, where you can sit inside and pray, contemplate, meditate and read. Think of the millions who do not have such shelter, or such opportunities.' At this, my spirits lifted again.

Back in my room, I reflected on what the morning had taught me. Sometimes, I felt the Lord say, we don't always find what we're looking for, at the time we want—perhaps because we're looking in the wrong place, or looking without direction or purpose, or looking in the wrong way, or we allow the storms of life to blow us off track. When we follow our own agenda or plan, and not God's, it comes to nothing. Perhaps the morning's aimless, vague venture in search of Lewis's home, with no specific reason and no map or directions, which was then blown off course by hail and rain and a lack of perseverance, is a parable illustrating this thought.

The day, Friday, 3 January, was the Feast of the Most Holy Name of Jesus—and the Jesuits' feast day. I reflected on the readings for the day, and on a passage by Richard Rolle in which he says this: 'If you think the name "Jesus" continually, it purges your sin and kindles your heart; it clarifies your soul; it removes anger and does away with slowness. It wounds in love and fulfils in charity. It chases the devil and puts out dread. It opens heaven, and makes you a contemplative. It puts all vices and phantoms out from the lover.' And St Bonaventure, who writes:

> This name is powerful, because it brings down our enemies, restores our strength, and renews our mind. It is grace-filled, because in it is contained the foundation of faith, the ground of hope, and the fulfilment of holiness. It is joyous, because it is gladness to the heart, music to the ear, honey to the tongue, and splendour to the mind. It is delightful, because it nourishes when it is recalled, soothes when it is uttered, anoints when it is invoked, refreshes when it is written, and instructs when it is read. It is a truly glorious name, because it gives sight to the blind, makes the lame walk, brings hearing to the deaf, speech to the dumb, and life to the dead. O blest name endowed with such powers! Devout soul, whether you are writing, reading, or teaching or whatever you are doing—may nothing have taste for you, nothing please you, apart from Jesus.

I was then taken in my meditations to the manger, where I stood and looked at the infant Christ child. And I reflected on my two nephews and what parallels there may be. A baby conveys an adorable, angelic,

beautiful demeanour. I reflected on how we grow, the
challenges we face as we begin to develop, the inno-
cence of childhood, the beauty and the struggles of life,
the differences between the Christ-child and humanity,
the perfection of Christ and the imperfection of the
human race. Then Our Lady came and said: 'Behold,
my Son.' And Jesus said: 'Behold my mother.' I had
a clear sense that one cannot understand one without
the other. Finally, in this image, I was holding the baby.
Then I had a sense of Jesus holding me. We hold him
in our hearts, and He holds us in the palm of His hand.

From there, a new image. A hand upon my head,
and a voice: 'I am here.' Then He picked me up and
stood me on a table. I was there like a miniature doll,
or a Lilliputian, with the enormity of God, like some
huge friendly giant, in front of me. 'Look at me, Ben,'
He said. Then an image of Christ on the cross. 'Look
always at me.'

I spent the rest of the time praying the Rosary, which
is still new to me, still difficult, but clearly beautiful
and powerful. Then the sun came out again, and after
lunch I went out for another walk. I walked along the
river towards Littlemore, where John Henry Newman
had lived, and which I had visited on my last retreat. I
took the book of poems, *For Lovers of God Everywhere*,
and read St John of the Cross's words: 'If a man wishes
to be sure of the road he travels on, he must close his
eyes and walk in the dark.'

As I returned to Campion Hall, I reflected on the
contrasts of Oxford: the dreaming spires and glorious
architecture of the university buildings and city centre,
versus the less attractive, and in parts poor, residen-
tial areas just a few minutes away. They illustrate the
contrasts of life, between moments of spiritual 'highs'
and the more regular hard grind of daily life; and the

contrasts between the beauty of God and the imperfections of humankind.

In my final session of the day, I sat in the main chapel in Campion Hall and reflected on my favourite passage, Isaiah 58: 6–12. Where do I feel closest to God, other than on retreat? It is without doubt when I am in a prison visiting a jailed atheist, or in a camp for displaced Ahmadiyya people, or in a burned-down church, or with dissidents in a dirty, sparse apartment in Rangoon, or with Kachin refugees and displaced people, or in the remote Chin Hills, or with Rohingya friends who are marginalised and even dehumanised and stateless. Then Mary came again, and took me by the hand. 'There's my Son, riding on a donkey,' she said. 'There's my Son, multiplying the loaves and fishes. There's my Son, washing the disciples' feet. Imitate Him.' Then she came again. 'There's my Son, speaking to the Samaritan woman at the well. There's my Son, healing the sick. There's my Son, dining with the tax collector. Imitate Him.'

Sitting in the chapel, I began to ponder the extraordinary nature of the Gospel message. If you were writing a story about God's salvation of the world, I thought, would you really — really — write one that has God coming to the world born as a baby in a manger (because there is no room in the inn) to a virgin, causing scandal for her and her husband who is not the father of the child and who wasn't even yet married to the mother when she became pregnant; becomes a carpenter; is crucified; and his followers are persecuted then and throughout the ages? And, moreover, would so many people, throughout the ages, be willing to die for such a story — if it were not true? And then I thought of the Eucharist, and that, if He can be born of a Virgin then, as He says, the Bread can certainly be His Body. And then the words of Luke 4: 16–21 came to me, where our Lord quotes Isaiah 61 and says: 'Today this scripture has been fulfilled in your hearing.'

In between these wonderful times of contemplation, reflection and prayer, I read—poetry, prayers, a wonderful book by a Franciscan priest, Richard Rohr, called *Falling Upward*; and St Augustine's *City of God* and Simone Weil's *Waiting on God*.

On the third day, I started with the Wedding at Cana (John 2: 1–11). I was struck by the way Jesus speaks to his mother, in an apparently irritable, disrespectful, dismissive tone. My first thought was that if I ever spoke to my mother like that, or if my nephews ever spoke to my sister in that way, neither my mother nor my sister would tolerate it. Poor Mary was just being helpful, and motherly, by pointing out that there was no more wine. Yet I was also struck by how Mary responds to Jesus's rebuke. She doesn't reprimand him—indeed, quite the opposite. She tells the servants: 'Do whatever he tells you.' Somehow she knows that he has it all under control, even though he tells her 'my hour has not yet come'. She has that quiet confidence, that patience—a patience that says even if you don't understand, even if you don't see clearly, you can know that Jesus is the truth, and Jesus is in control. I was reminded of the words in 1 Corinthians 13: 12—'For now we see in a mirror, dimly, but then we will see face to face. Now I know only in part; then I will know fully, even as I have been fully known.' Interestingly, that verse is preceded and succeeded by verses focused on 'love.' Mary then turned to me, after speaking to the servants, and said: 'Ben, do whatever he tells you.'

After my first session of prayerful contemplation, I read some of Gerard Manley Hopkins's poetry. I was struck by the last verse of his poem 'Easter', which reads:

Seek God's house in happy throng;
Crowded let his table be;
Mingle praises, prayer and song,
Singing to the Trinity.
Henceforth let your souls alway
Make each morn an Easter Day.

I thought back to the wedding at Cana, the celebration of a wedding, and the celebration of Easter, and felt God saying clearly: celebrate, every day!

I also read Hopkins's poem 'Jesu dulcis memoria', and noted the second verse in particular:

No music can touch the ear,
No news is heard of such sweet cheer
Thought half so dear there is not one
As Jesus God the Father's Son.

His poem 'Oratio Patris Condren: O Jesu vivens in Maria' also spoke to me:

Jesu that dost in Mary dwell,
Be in thy servants' hearts as well,
In the spirit of thy holiness,
In the fullness of thy force and stress,
In the very ways that thy life goes,
And virtues that thy pattern shows,
In the sharing of thy mysteries;
And every power in us that is
Against thy power put under feet
In the Holy Ghost the Paraclete
To the glory of the Father. Amen.

I also loved his poems 'O Deus, ego amo te'; 'Rosa mystica' (which I particularly recommend); and the fifth and seventh verses of 'S. Thomae Aquinatis Rhythmus ad SS. Sacramentum':

O thou our reminder of Christ crucified,
Living Bread the life of us for whom he died,
Lend this life to me then: feed and feast my
  mind,
There be thou the sweetness man was meant to
  find.

Jesu whom I look at veiled here below
I beseech thee send me what I thirst for so,
Some day to gaze on thee face to face in light
And be blest forever with thy glory's sight.

In my next period of prayer, I reflected on the passage in Luke 2: 19–51, and the words: 'Mary treasured all these words and pondered them in her heart'—words which occur twice, in verse 19 and verse 51. I felt the Lord saying: 'Treasure all these things—and all that I have shown you, on this retreat, on your previous retreat, and throughout your life—and ponder them in your heart, Ben.'

I also reflected on the prediction of the suffering of Christ, and Mary, by Simeon in verses 34–5—that Christ would 'be a sign that will be opposed' and, to Mary, that 'a sword will pierce your own soul too.' This passage contrasts with the joy of the wedding at Cana, and taken together, they give us the complete message of the Gospel and the Christian faith: joy mingled with suffering, celebration juxtaposed with pain.

Then I sat looking at Jesus as he was in the temple 'sitting among teachers, listening to them and asking them questions' (verse 46). I felt that is what I have been doing for much of the past two years or so, as I have journeyed in my faith into the Catholic Church, and what I have been doing on this retreat. I have sat at the feet of teachers—sometimes literally, in person, with priests and friends whom I trust and who have guided me, and sometimes spiritually, through the books and writings I have read. Each time, I have been listening to them and asking questions. I felt Mary telling me to continue doing this. 'Imitate Him,' she said again. St Bonaventure (1221–74) speaks of 'the journey of the mind to God'.

In between sessions, I read quite a bit of Alister McGrath's excellent new biography of C. S. Lewis. One quotation from Lewis seemed very relevant to this retreat. Much of this retreat was alive with what one might call 'imagination', God-centred and God-directed I believe, but at odds with what the world would view as 'rational'. Lewis has just the right words for this, writing of how he viewed such matters when he was an atheist:

> On the one side a many-islanded sea of poetry and myth; on the other a glib and shallow 'rationalism'. Nearly all that I loved I believed to imaginary; nearly all that I believed to be real I thought grim and meaningless.

The truth, as Lewis goes on to contend and as I believe with all my heart, is precisely the reverse. What I have seen and experienced so far on this retreat is real; it is the world's ways which are imaginary, in the sense that they will come to nothing. As J. R. R. Tolkien said, God has willed that 'the hearts of men should seek beyond the world and should find no rest therein'.

Alister McGrath, recounting Lewis's conversion, describes how Lewis came to the realisation that following Christ does not mean having to declare all other faiths and beliefs 'totally false', but rather it means recognising that other faiths may be 'echoes or anticipations of the full truth', but that the full truth 'was made known only in and through the Christian faith'. Christianity 'brings to fulfilment and completion imperfect and partial insights about reality scattered abroad in human culture'.

Then in my final session, I was back at the wedding in Cana, this time tasting the wine myself. 'Taste and see that the Lord is good' were the words that came to me. Then He took me to the Last Supper, and I had a sense of real, deep sadness that not all Christians are in communion with each other, and a longing for us all to be one, to be able to sit together at the Lord's table and share His body and His blood together. I pray this may happen one day. I pray perhaps God may use Pope Francis to bring us closer to that point. From the Last Supper, the scene changed, in that same Upper Room, to Christ's post-resurrection appearance to His apostles, where he held out his hands and said: 'See the nail marks in my hands and feet' (John 20: 26–9). At that point, the words of a famous hymn, 'When I survey the wondrous cross', came to me: 'Love so amazing, so divine, demands my love, my life, my all.'

For much of 2013, I had been reading the great medieval devotional classic *The Cloud of Unknowing*. I had finished it a few weeks previously, but in the Penguin Classics edition I have, there are several other writings by the same author (who is unknown). One evening on retreat, I read *The Epistle of Privy Counsel*, which contains several passages directly relevant to this retreat. In particular, the instruction in the opening paragraph, as follows:

> Do not pray with words unless you feel you have to, and even then, if you do, do not bother about their being many or few ... See that nothing occupies your thoughts except an utter determination to reach out to God: no special thought about what he is, or how he works, but

only that he is as he is. Let him be himself, please,
and nothing else. You are not to go probing into
him with your smart and subtle ideas. That belief
must be your foundation.

A little later, the author writes:

Lift up your sick self just as you are, and through
your longing strive to touch good, gracious God
just as He is. Touching Him is eternal health,
which is the point of the story of the woman in
the Gospel who said, 'If I touch but the hem of
his garment I shall be whole.

That is a perfect way to sum up the purpose of this
retreat—to come to God as I am, and touch Him as He
is, or even just the hem of his garment.

I woke up at 2am on the fourth day, having had an
extraordinary dream—or several. I had found myself
initially meeting Pope Francis, but not in a formal audience—instead, in a very informal comfortable friendly
chat at a coffee table before lunch. We discussed freedom of religion or belief. He expressed his concern
about the persecution of Christians, but also his sadness about divisions between Catholics and Christians
of other denominations. He expressed concern about
any persecution of one by another, Catholic and Protestant, but particularly commented on anti-Catholic
attitudes held by some Protestants. I shared with him
my vision to be a voice for freedom of conscience, and
freedom of religion or belief, for all people, whatever
their beliefs, and he affirmed and encouraged me in
that. This scene was followed by lunch with Pope
Francis, in which a group of other people joined us. I
sensed that perhaps God was affirming, through this
dream, both my calling to advocate for freedom of conscience, religion and belief for all, but also a calling to

encourage Christian unity, to help foster closer friendship and fellowship between Catholics, Protestants and Evangelicals—Christians of all stripes and colours.

Secondly a scene involving my local parish priest and members of the parish in a celebration for the priest's birthday.

The last scene in my dream—or perhaps another dream—found me in some kind of Catholic social gathering—a dinner, an event of some sort. In the scene, I was talking to a woman who asked me how I ended up doing the work I do now. I told my story, starting with the occasion when I first heard Baroness Cox speak in my university chapel in 1994—20 years ago. I have been working closely with her, and in the field of human rights and religious freedom, ever since. Then Baroness Cox herself appeared, and the scene moved to some sort of group visit with her (in real life I've had the privilege of travelling with her many times). She told the assembled group that it was 'time to go', and we left the venue with her.

I made a note of these dreams, as they were vivid and detailed, and I sensed spoke to me about my vocation, my rootedness in the Catholic Church which I have just joined and to ecumenical unity and 'community'. After noting them down, I managed to get back to sleep for another six hours or so.

After breakfast and before Sunday Mass, I devoted my first session of prayer and contemplation to the Passion of Christ, reading the events leading up to his crucifixion, in Matthew 26. I focused particularly on two key scenes: the garden of Gethsemane, and Peter (verses 31–5; and again 69–75). I went for a walk through the University Parks, and found myself in Gethsemane.

There, I was struck by the disciples sleeping, and Christ's question to them: 'So you could not stay awake with me one hour?' I saw myself as one of the sleeping disciples, and asked myself how many times have I been like them? Failing to spend time awake with the Lord, or coming to him so sleepy or rushed that I am inattentive and it is poor quality time? Too many times.

Then I reflected on the scenes with Peter, his promise to the Lord not to deny Him, the Lord's prediction that before the cock crows Peter would indeed deny Him three times, Peter in the courtyard doing just that, and then Peter as he 'went out and wept bitterly.' I realised I am Peter. How many times have I deserted or denied Christ? Maybe not literally, verbally denying the Lord, but through action or inaction—by laughing at inappropriate or blasphemous jokes told by others, by telling such jokes myself, by engaging in unedifying conversation, by staying silent when the Lord's name is abused, by thinking unkind thoughts about others, or saying unkind words? I could identify with Peter weeping bitterly. And yet I was reminded that the Lord went on to use Peter to build His Church (Matthew 16: 18–19). I was reminded that every Pope is a 'successor of Peter.' I was reminded how many examples there are in the Bible of people who did some awful deeds and yet went on to do great deeds: Moses, David and Paul, for example.

I came back to Gethsemane and the arrival of Judas, the crowd, the chief priests, armed with 'swords and clubs'. And I thought how many times in our world today do crowds of thugs, and police, come armed with weapons, sometimes accompanied by religious clerics (think of some Muslim clerics in Pakistan, Indonesia, Syria, Egypt, Nigeria, or Buddhist monks in Burma and Sri Lanka), to attack or arrest an unarmed, non-violent, peaceful Christian, or follower of another religious minority such as the Ahmadiyya or Baha'i, or a political dissident.

I was also struck by how a garden can often be a place of life, beauty and hope, and yet, as we see in Gethsemane and also in Eden, how it can become a place of sorrow and suffering. And that, once again, is the amazing juxtaposition at the heart of the Christian story: joy mingled with sorrow, love and suffering, life and death.

As I walked back, I noticed a number of beautiful, historic church buildings that are Church of England churches, and I felt a twinge of sadness. Many of them would once have been Catholic churches, before Henry VIII's break with Rome, and it would be so wonderful if the Church of England could be reunited with the Catholic Church. I didn't feel any regret whatsoever about becoming a Catholic, nor did I feel any sense of 'missing' the Church of England, and nor did I feel a particular wish for the buildings per se to be part of one 'Church' (the Church is about the people, the body of Christ, far more than the buildings, however beautiful and historic they may be), but I just felt a simple desire to see them reunited and as one. As I continued to walk, Handel's Messiah played in my head. 'Hallelujah! Hallelujah!' ... 'And He shall reign forever and ever ... Hallelujah, Hallelujah, Hallelujah!'

I went to Sunday Mass in the Catholic Chaplaincy next door to Campion Hall, for the Feast of Epiphany. Interestingly, the first prayer during the intercessions was a prayer for Christian unity, a prayer that Christians of all denominations would be one—echoing one of the repeated themes of my retreat.

I was delighted that one of my favourite hymns or carols was sung at the end of Mass. It is a hymn that contains so much meaning, relevant to the themes I work on and that have arisen in this retreat. I refer to it in Chapter 2, and quote it in full here:

> It came upon the midnight clear,
> That glorious song of old,
> From angels bending near the earth,
> To touch their harps of gold:
> 'Peace on the earth, goodwill to men
> From heaven's all gracious King!'
> The world in solemn stillness lay
> To hear the angels sing.
>
> Still through the cloven skies they come,
> With peaceful wings unfurled;
> And still their heavenly music floats
> O'er all the weary world;
> Above its sad and lowly plains
> They bend on hovering wing.
> And ever o'er its Babel sounds
> The blessed angels sing.
>
> Yet with the woes of sin and strife
> The world has suffered long;
> Beneath the angel-strain have rolled
> Two thousand years of wrong:
> And man at war with man hears not
> The love-song which they bring:
> O hush the noise, ye men of strife,
> And hear the angels sing.
>
> For lo! the days are hastening on
> By prophet bards foretold,
> When, with the ever-circling years
> Comes round the age of gold.
>
> When peace shall over all the earth
> Its ancient splendours fling,
> And the whole world give back the song
> Which now the angels sing.

The third verse particularly speaks to me, and during this retreat all I have tried to do is once again to 'hush the noise' for five days, so I can hear the love-song that the angels sing.

After lunch, I went for another long walk through the University Parks, stopping off to look from the outside at Lady Margaret Hall (my mother's alma mater) briefly. In an amazing irony—or perhaps God's sense of humour—as I walked down Norham Gardens, who should cycle past but one Professor Richard Dawkins! I said a prayer for him.

Through the afternoon, I read and contemplated the crucifixion of Christ, and the events immediately before it, told in Matthew 27. As I walked through the University Parks, unlike the previous day, the flood-water did not speak to me of life-giving water. Instead, the scene felt like Narnia after Aslan has gone, without the snow. Winter. Perhaps a glimpse of what the world may have looked like after Christ died on the cross, the curtain of the temple was torn in two, the earth shook, the rocks split and the tombs opened (Matthew 27: 50–2). Forlorn, grey, overcast, the trees bare with no leaves and the river brown, muddy and high. An atmosphere of death.

Then I was standing among the crowd, at the foot of the cross, watching Christ crucified. I felt outrage, righteous anger, anguish, grief. I was weeping. Then from the cross, despite his agony, the Lord caught my eye and gave me a smile. I could not smile back; I kept weeping. He caught my eye again, still smiling, and beckoned me to come to him. I went, and he stretched down from the cross and put his hand gently on my head.

From there, I was at the tomb. It was surrounded by guards, and I watched as they ensured that it was completely secured. I felt angry, but helpless—completely helpless. In the work I do, we frequently have to respond to cases of individuals jailed, or facing execution, for their beliefs. Of course there are often times when we cannot do anything, but often there is something we can do: sometimes to actually secure their release, or to delay or lift the death sentence, or at the very least to let the world know. But at the tomb in which Our Lord was buried, what could I do? Then he spoke to me: 'Even in your work: yes, there are things you can do. But if you don't fuse what you can do with what I can do, put your gifts and abilities and opportunities together with my power, then it is of limited or no use.' How true.

The next moment, nails were being hammered into my hands, and I felt the impact. How could He have endured that?

Then I was with the Lord as he washed the disciples' feet, and I was among them, having my feet washed. But the water turned bloody.

Then a map of the world, with crucifixes covering it. Then 'North Korea'.

A real affirmation of my vocation, a renewal of my love for the Lord, and a preparation for confession. C. S. Lewis once said: 'I believe in Christianity as I believe that the Sun has risen, not only because I see it but because by it I see everything else.'

In the evening, after supper, I finished reading a beautiful short biography of Dominic Barberi (1792–1849), published by the Catholic Truth Society (CTS) as part of a series on 'Saints of the Isles'. Dominic Barberi was born in Pallanzana, near Viterbo, about 50 miles from Rome, in 1792, 'one year after the passing of the "Relief Act" in England, by which Catholics were once more allowed to practise their religion openly, after three centuries of persecution'. He is perhaps most famous as the priest who received John Henry Newman into the Catholic Church, at Newman's home in Littlemore (which I visited on my last retreat). Newman had grown up as an evangelical within the Church of England, and his journey is of course an inspiration to me, having travelled down a similar path. But Dominic Barberi was so much more than just the priest who made Newman a Catholic. For decades God had given him a specific heart for England, and he joined the Passionists, an order founded by St Paul of the Cross in Italy in 1720, to 'preach the love and suffering of the Crucified Christ'.

The biography concludes with these words, which relate to some of the themes that have come up during this retreat:

> The life of Dominic Barberi is well chronicled by both himself and his contemporaries. In essence it is a love story; a passionate love story for England. It began in Italy and after a long period of maturing it developed in Belgium and blossomed in England. It is not a romantic story as it is marked by suffering, deprivation, frustration and disappointment. Some may believe that it is a failure, just as Calvary appeared to be a failure. Dominic only worked in England for eight years, made relatively few converts, established three communities of his Order, gave a small number of missions and retreats, and crucially failed to see the conversion of England. So why should he be declared a saint? What is there in his life that is worthy of imitation?
>
> Like Jesus of Nazareth, much of Dominic's life was hidden; only God knows, but it is probable he achieved far more for England in the trials

and sufferings of his hidden life before he ever came to these islands. Like Jesus he died almost alone and in apparent failure. Like Jesus he constantly proclaimed the love of the Crucified God. Like Jesus he always acted in total charity, and even in his darkest hours never lost his trust and confidence in God. Like Jesus he had great love for Mary, and was always eager to have her interceding for him — and there is ample evidence that she listened to him.

... Holiness shone through, and he was so attractive to others; be it the great intellectuals of his day, or the smallest of children; be it members of his own community or people from other Christian denominations. His driving ambition for the unity of all Christians gave purpose and meaning to his pastoral work.

... Ultimately Dominic was a man of deep prayer. Yes, he had been blessed with many graces by God, but unlike most people who give up when the going gets tough, he not only persevered, but thanked God for his many crosses. He is a model of trust and perseverance, a man filled with a sense of patience as he waited to learn the will of God, and through it all, a sense of gratitude that God would have anything to do with him.

Dominic had spent most of his life praying, through the intercession of Mary, for England ... With Father Ignatius Spencer he embarked on a huge mission to bring England back to 'Unity in the Truth' ... Their model was the Christ of the Passion, and they believed that it was not so much their preaching, but their example and above all their prayer that would bring about an answer to the prayer of Jesus: 'That they may all be one.'

After breakfast on the final day of my retreat, I spent some time in prayer in my room, including praying the Rosary. It is very striking how the 'Hail Mary' is straight from the Bible. That may sound strange to my Catholic friends who know this very well, but as a new Catholic, and for my Protestant friends, it is worth noting. It comes from Luke 1, the passage immediately preceding the Magnificat, where Mary visits Elizabeth, her cousin and the mother of John the Baptist: 'When Elizabeth heard Mary's greeting, the babe leapt in her womb. And Elizabeth was filled with the Holy Spirit and exclaimed with a loud cry, 'Blessed are you among women and blessed is the fruit of your womb ... Blessed is she who believed what was spoken by the Lord' (verses 42–5). And so hence we pray: 'Hail Mary, full of grace, the Lord is with thee. Blessed art thou among women, and blessed is the fruit of thy womb, Jesus. Holy Mary, Mother of God, pray for us sinners, now and at the hour of our death. Amen.' A beautiful, biblical prayer.

After this time of prayer, I walked once again around Christ Church Meadow. I had hesitated about going out, because the skies were yet again grey and overcast and threatened rain. But it was not actually raining, and so I decided to go. As I walked onto Christ Church Meadow, I saw a full sun had broken through the clouds, and a strong beam of sunlight fell almost across my path. I felt the Lord was saying: 'This is the day of the Resurrection.' Having spent yesterday with the Lord in His Passion, it was my intention, Fr Nicholas's recommendation and indeed the right stage in the Spiritual Exercises of St Ignatius, to be focusing on the Resurrection, and this was a beautiful beginning to the day. For the rest of the walk, my head was filled with a contemporary version of the Gloria that we had sung in Mass the day before: 'Glory to God, Glory to God, Glory to God in the highest; and on earth, peace on earth, peace to people of goodwill. We praise you, we bless you, we adore you, we glorify you, we give you thanks for your great glory, Lord God, heavenly King, O God, almighty Father!'

Then I came back to my room, and spent some time in the Campion Chapel contemplating the account of the Resurrection in John 20 and 21. I found myself in the garden at the empty tomb, and the gardener (Jesus) beckoned me to him, hugged me, and then said: 'I am the gardener of your life.' Interesting how the image and theme of gardens keeps recurring.

I then had a sense of a link between the Resurrection and Burma—Burma is not yet fully 'resurrected', but there is more hope in Burma now than there has been for several decades, and perhaps it may be moving towards its resurrection. That certainly is my prayer.

A beam of light then came, and I was kneeling at the Lord's feet. He blessed me. 'Now go out into the world,' He said.

Then I was walking with Him, through the garden, hand-in-hand.

I asked the Lord: 'Where will you take me now, Lord?' This was met with a picture of myself at a desk, with a pen and a computer keyboard, followed by a scene of walking through a poor, possibly bombed or conflict-ridden area with children in tow. Further affirmation of my vocation to justice, human rights, peace, religious freedom, and to writing. Then the Lord said: 'I'll tell you more later. Follow me.'

Our Lady appeared again, saying: 'Imitate Him, do as He says, try to do what He does.'

Some of my favourite words from Thomas à Kempis's *The Imitation of Christ* then came: 'Those who love stay awake when duty calls, wake up from sleep when someone needs help, keep burning, no matter what, like a lighted torch. Those who love take on anything, complete goals, bring plans to fruition. Those who do not love faint and lie down on the job.'[1]

Mary put her hand on my head and said: 'Go now, my son.' I held her hand for a few moments.

Later, I was back in the garden at the empty tomb, with Peter and John. I love the way John runs ahead of Peter, but does not go into the tomb. When Peter comes up from behind, he goes straight in. Then I was with the seven disciples, when Jesus appears while they are fishing (John 21: 1–14). Again, I love Peter's enthusiasm, where he puts on his clothes and jumps into the water to wade ashore when he realises it is the Lord on the beach, even though the boat is not far from the shore. I echo something of Peter's enthusiasm. In my head came the carol 'Tomorrow shall be my dancing day', and then 'I am the Lord of the dance', a popular hymn.

When Jesus tells Peter 'feed my sheep', I had an inkling that perhaps the Lord was directing those same words to me in relation to my writings, and particularly this new book—that He wishes to use the book to 'feed' people with 'food for thought'. Then: 'Be still and know that I am God; I am the Lord that leadeth thee; In thee O Lord do I put my trust.'

Just as the Lord asks Peter three times 'Do you love me?' He asked me three times: 'Do you love me, Ben?' The first time I replied 'Yes, Lord', he responded: 'Write.' The second time, he said: 'Speak.' The third time: 'Go to my people.' Another affirmation of my calling to go to the oppressed and then be a voice for them, in spoken and written word. I was then in a field of sheep, with the Lord. He was very clearly the shepherd, but I was assisting him. One sheep ran off towards the neighbouring field, where danger lurked, and I went and brought it back. Then a panoramic, aerial view of beautiful landscape—fields, hills, forests—ending up in mountains. In between times of prayer and contemplation, I read some more poetry. I read Gerard Manley Hopkins's long poem 'The wreck of the *Deutschland*', and was struck by the first verse:

> Thou mastering me
> God! Giver of breath and bread;
> World's strand, sway of the sea;
> Lord of the living and dead;
> Thou hast bound bones and veins in me,
>   fastened me flesh,
> And after it almost unmade, what with dread,
> Thy doing: and dost thou touch me afresh?
> Over again I feel thy finger and find thee.

I then read an extract from W. H. Auden's 'For the time being—A Christmas oratorio':

> He is the Way:
> Follow Him through the Land of Unlikeness;
> You will see rare beasts, and have unique
>   adventures.

> He is the Truth:
> Seek Him in the Kingdom of Anxiety;
> You will come to a great city that has expected
>   your return for years.

> He is the Life.
> Love Him in the world of the Flesh;

And at your marriage all its occasions shall
   dance for joy.

And then George Herbert's 'Love (III)':

Love bade me welcome: yet my soul drew back,
Guilty of dust and sin.
But quick-eyed Love, observing me grow slack
From my first entrance in,
Drew nearer to me, sweetly questioning
If I lacked anything.

'A guest,' I answered, 'worthy to be here':
Love said, 'You shall be he.'
'I, the unkind, ungrateful? Ah, my dear,
I cannot look on Thee.'
Love took my hand, and smiling did reply,
'Who made the eyes but I?'

'Truth Lord, but I have marred them: let my
   shame
Go where it doth deserve.'
'And know you not,' says Love, 'who bore the
   blame?'
'My dear, then I will serve.'
'You must sit down,' says Love, 'and taste my
   meat.'
So I did sit and eat.

After lunch, I went for another long walk. As I walked
through Christ Church Meadow, along the path past
the walls of Christ Church and Merton, the hymn in
my mind was: 'He is Lord, He is Lord, He is risen
from the dead, and He is Lord. Every knee shall bow,
every tongue confess, that Jesus Christ is Lord.' It kept
repeating and repeating, with ever-growing enthusiasm,
until I was bursting to sing it out-loud. Being English,
I didn't, but instead I was joined in this chorus in my
head by Mary, and then by St Benedict (whose name I

share), St Charles Borromeo (my patron saint, taken at my baptism and confirmation in Rangoon), St Ignatius of Loyola, St Francis of Assisi, St Dominic, all the saints, all the angels, in a heavenly chorus: 'He is Lord, He is Lord, He is risen from the dead and He is Lord.'

I reached Magdalen College by this point, and decided to go in. I saw the outside of the rooms where C. S. Lewis had lived and worked, I visited the beautiful chapel and said a prayer, I walked the cloisters, and I went to the deer park, where Psalm 42 — 'As the deer pants for the water' — came to mind. There's a song based on Psalm 42, which has the lyrics: 'You're my friend and you are my brother, even though you are a King; I love you more than any other, so much more than anything; You alone are my strength and shield, To you alone may my spirit yield.' Those words came to mind and became a prayer as I watched the deer elegantly and gracefully moving around on the grass. I then visited St Edmund Hall (my father's alma mater) briefly, before returning to Campion Hall.

Returning to the Campion Chapel, I was back with the disciples on the beach with Jesus (John 21). Jesus invited me to join them, cooking fish. It turned into a bit of a party. We played football and went swimming. I had a sense of the Lord speaking to me in this, but am unsure whether He was saying that I should take more time for recreation, to spend time with friends, to have fun, to cook more (which I enjoy doing), or whether He was speaking about 'community' and vocation. It is unclear, and I simply offer it back to Him and ask Him to continue to speak.

As the day drew to a close and I prepared to end my retreat with a final session with Fr Nicholas and the Sacrament of Reconciliation (Confession), followed by evening Mass, I asked the Lord if He would speak to me about my calling. 'Stay where you are for now,' He said. 'Stay doing what you're doing. And I will show you the way. It will unfold.' Finally, the Lord said to me as I completed my final period of prayer in the main chapel: 'Go in peace.' What a wonderful way to end a retreat.

After my final session with Fr Nicholas, Confession, and Mass, I formally ended the retreat and ended my silence. I was invited to join the brethren at their table for dinner, had drinks and conversation with them after the meal, and went to bed feeling deeply content and at peace.

The words 'Thank You' seem so inadequate an expression of gratitude for what I received over these five days, but I am full of thankfulness to God for a beautiful beginning to 2014. At the beginning of the retreat, Fr Nicholas told me that in my sessions with him at the end of each day, I should share what had gone on in the prayer times, both the positives and the times when I may have felt bored or frustrated. I can honestly say that the words 'bored' or 'frustrated' do not describe any moment of the retreat—at any point. There was the earlier brief irritation on the second day, but that was in relation to circumstances rather than the prayer life, and soon passed. There were moments of silence, for sure, when nothing happened, but I was in anticipation, rather than boredom. Never once was I bored or frustrated. The days were beautifully unrushed, peaceful, calm, still, quiet, refreshing and enriching. I came to God just as I am, and touched Him 'just as He is'. What more could I ask for?

And as for my future, I conclude with the words of Simone Weil, who writes in *Waiting for God*: 'It is not my business to think about myself. My business is to think about God. It is for God to think about me.' I await His direction and give Him all the glory.

In July 2015, I embarked on an eight-day Ignatian retreat at St Beuno's Jesuit retreat centre in north Wales—but that is another story, for another day.

Note

[1] Thomas à Kempis, *The Imitation of Christ*, ed. Donald E. Demaray (New York, Alba House, 1994), p. 3

Epilogue

S O THIS IS MY TALE. Except it is much, much more than that. It is God's tale, and the tale of the many people who were guides, signposts and influences along the journey.

Becoming a Catholic opens up a whole new world. It is a joy to be in communion now with the saints from all the ages, from St Augustine, St Thomas à Kempis and St Thomas Aquinas to St Benedict, St Dominic and St Francis of Assisi, from St Thomas More and St Edmund Campion to St Ignatius of Loyola and St Teresa of Avila, from St Teresa Benedicta of the Cross (Edith Stein) to St Maximilian Kolbe. For much of the time since I became a Catholic, I have been discovering the saints, reading their biographies, and requesting their intercession.

It is also a privilege to be in communion now with contemporary Catholics who may one day be recognised as saints: from those no longer with us in this world, such as Shahbaz Bhatti and Cecil Chaudhry, to those still living out their faith in action, such as Sister Lourdes and Cardinal Bo.

And it is a delight to be in communion with those who, through the ages, have made the same journey from Protestant Christianity, in my case evangelical Anglicanism, into the Catholic Church: men and women like John Henry Newman, Gerard Manley

Hopkins, G. K. Chesterton, Malcolm Muggeridge, Ann Widdecombe and Scott Hahn.

One of the riches of the Church that I have discovered is that it has universality, but certainly not uniformity. In the time since I was received into the Church, I have attended Mass in different churches in Britain, from my own home parish of St Joseph's in New Malden to the parish of St Edward's in Shaftesbury, Dorset, where I grew up, from Westminster Cathedral and St George's Cathedral in Southwark to the Mayfair headquarters of the Jesuits at Farm Street, from the Catholic chaplaincy in Oxford to the Oratory School near Reading. But I have also attended Mass around the world—in Paris, Brussels and Stockholm, in Rome, Positano, Venice and Assisi, in Dubrovnik, in Washington, DC, in San Diego and Laguna Niguel, California, in Naples, Florida, in Seoul, in Jakarta and Surabaya, Indonesia, and in Rangoon, Mandalay, Hakha, Myitkyina and Putao, Burma. I have even been to an Eritrean Mass in Stockholm. What I love is the fact that, wherever you are in the world, the readings and the basic liturgy are the same, so whatever the language, if you have a Missal or the Order of Mass and the readings for the day in your own language, you can follow the liturgy. And you know that around the world, millions of people are praying the same prayers and reflecting on the same readings. On the other hand, no Mass is identical. Even within the same country, there are a variety of forms of Mass, from the Solemn Mass with incense and Latin to a contemporary, charismatic Mass with guitars; and then around the world, local customs and cultures can be seen influencing the Mass. A universality that embraces diversity is part of what makes the Church beautiful.

I am discovering Catholic humour too. A Church in which Chesterton and Belloc found a home must have something going for it. In Rome after Cardinal Bo's installation, an evangelical Christian attending a celebratory lunch with the cardinal and a small group of his close friends was amused at the flow of wine and the waves of laughter. 'I had no idea Catholics could be so much fun,' she remarked. 'We have only just started,' retorted one of the other guests. In Catholicism everything has its place. In church, especially in the Mass, it is a time for reverence, for worship, and yes, for solemnity. But outside, there is a place for revelry. I once gave a Catholic priest two gifts: some religious books and a bottle of whisky. Pointing at the books, he noted that they were 'spiritual'. Pointing to the bottle, he observed that it was 'spirit'. That caused him to conclude: 'Spirit and spiritual—we need both in life!'

Yet of course no journey of this kind is a constant stream of easy discoveries and spiritual highs. As I have described in this book, I had to work through what I believed—and what the Church teaches—about Mary, papal infallibility, transubstantiation. By the time I entered the Church I had of course embraced these beliefs, but I still need to develop my understanding of them, and deepen my relationship with Our Lady and my adoration of the Eucharist. As David Mills writes in an article titled 'The convert's unnecessary worries', 'we become Catholics not actually knowing a great deal about the Faith and keep finding ourselves suddenly realising, "Oh, *that's* it. That's why the Church teaches this." Acceptance comes first, then practice, then understanding.'[1]

If you were to ask me what three aspects of Catholicism I have found most difficult, the answer is clear to me: the sacrament of confession, the exclusion of non-Catholic Christians from receiving communion, and the rosary. The first of course is essential and fundamental; the second is the Church's teaching; while the third is more optional.

My difficulty with confession was human, not theological. Of course I have no difficulty accepting that I am a sinner, and that I need to confess my sins and be reconciled with God. Every day, through what I do or think or say or what I fail to do, I am reminded of this fact. Even the idea of going to confess to someone else, a priest, who then, on behalf of God, gives you absolution, was not too difficult to embrace. No, the difficulty was at a human level. Speaking your sins, telling another person, is not easy. It is a blow to one's pride. It can be embarrassing. As one priest put it to me, it is a bit like going to the dentist and having a filling or worse, a root canal: it is never pleasant, it can be painful, but it is absolutely necessary.

And yet when we think of confession as the sacrament of reconciliation, a name by which it is sometimes known, that puts a whole new perspective on it. And when we think of 'penance' not as 'punishment' but as putting into action that reconciliation with God, it becomes something beautiful. I discovered that Confession becomes a conversation. The priests to whom I have made my Confession have always responded sympathetically, occasionally asking some helpful questions or making some constructive suggestions about how to avoid repeating the sin. And the penance has not been a penalty, it has been a prayer—for the person I may have offended, or for my own relationship with God.

When some of my evangelical Christian friends have occasionally come to Mass with me, or when I have visited their churches, the fact that we are no longer in communion with each other is painful. I have to explain to them that while they are very welcome to go forward for a blessing, with their arms crossed across their chest, they cannot receive Holy Communion. And likewise, when I visit Anglican or Baptist or evangelical churches, often to speak or simply to accompany friends, I cannot go up to receive holy communion myself. I wish I could. I wish they could. I long for unity. 'That they may be one', as we are told in John 17: 21. One day.

Why is this the Church's position? Well, as uncomfortable as it is, it does make sense. We have different perspectives on what actually is happening at holy communion. For Protestants, the bread and the wine are mere symbols, representing the body and blood of Christ. For Catholics, we believe that in a mysterious, miraculous way, they become the body and blood of Christ—His real presence. To receive holy communion without sharing the belief of what it actually is would, in a Catholic view, be sacrilegious.

I still have a feeling of fondness for the Church of England. While there is much that is helpful about the clarity of the Catholic Church's teachings, there is something comfortable about Anglicanism's liberalism. As Edward Norman wrote after he left the Church of England to become Catholic, while joining the Catholic Church 'induces not only a feeling of coming home but a sensation of cleansing,' at the same time 'humanly speaking, nevertheless, gratitude to Anglicanism is still experienced and a large degree of lasting affection'. The Church of England, says Norman, 'provides a masterclass in equivocation; it also, however, is the residence of very many good and faithful Christian people who deserve respect—for their perseverance in so many incoherent spiritual adventures. To leave their company is a wrench; to adhere to the Catholic faith is to join the encompassing presence of a universal body of believers in whose guardianship are the materials of authentic spiritual understanding. After lengthy preparation I have immense gratitude.'[2]

The rosary has been a challenge again not at a theological level, but at a practical one. Co-ordinating all the elements of the rosary—fingering the beads, reading and meditating on the passages of Scripture, and saying the prayers—all at once has been difficult. I have not generally found it, yet, to be a form of prayer that draws me closer to God, perhaps because I am so busy trying to co-ordinate everything. But whilst it is a form of prayer that clearly can be beautiful, and which the Church promotes, priests have told me that it is by no means essential. It is more important to pray in ways that work well for one's own spirituality, that draw one closer to God, than to worry about mastering particular forms of prayer.

One of the wonderful aspects of my journey, for which I am deeply grateful, was the support and encouragement of evangelical Christian friends. Not a single Christian friend expressed opposition to my exploration, or to my ultimate decision. Many were surprised, some raised some questions, but no one showed hostility. The Reverend Simon Downham, vicar of the church I had been worshipping at for ten years, St Paul's Church in Hammersmith, which is associated with Holy Trinity, Brompton, one of the most famous evangelical, charismatic Anglican churches in the country, could not have been more gracious. I met him for lunch soon after my retreat in January 2013, and shared my decision to become a Catholic. I had sent him a copy of my reflections on my retreat prior to meeting him, so he had some idea of my journey. At the conclusion of our conversation, he said to me: 'This is a wonderful decision. I can see that it has deepened your own spiritual life, and is therefore a blessing to you. It will be a blessing to the Catholic Church to have you among its ranks. And it is a blessing for us, because now we have another friend in the Catholic Church.'

Of course, some friends asked questions. One close friend asked me whether I had thought through two particularly serious points: the sexual abuse scandal, and the question of the Church's own wealth. I took those points seriously, and turned to Catholic friends for advice.

On the first, every Catholic I spoke to was absolutely unequivocal in expressing how truly horrific and appalling the sexual abuse scandal was. They were outraged. Yet they also assured me that contrary to some of the portrayals in the media, the Church had taken it extremely seriously. Pope Benedict XVI had made numerous statements, had met personally with some victims, and had taken action against those involved, both the perpetrators and those who had covered it up. In March 2009, for example, he wrote a letter to Catholics in Ireland, in which he said: 'You have suffered grievously, and I am truly sorry. I know that nothing can undo the wrong you have endured. It is understandable that you find it hard to forgive or be reconciled with the Church. In her name, I openly express the shame and remorse that we all feel.'[3]

Catholic friends told me that the Catholic Church is now, today, one of the safest places for a child to be, because of the action the Church, in collaboration with the authorities, has taken to address the crisis.

On the question of the Church's riches, and how they are used, I initially identified with the questioner. Working in some of the poorest parts of the world,

I regarded the opulence of the Vatican with some suspicion. Yet Catholic friends pointed out that the Church is in fact the world's second largest provider of humanitarian aid in the developing world after the United Nations. Its aid agencies, such as Caritas, its religious orders, many of its priests are engaged in amazing work with the poorest of the poor. Furthermore, in worshipping God we want to give Him all the glory, honour and praise—hence, over the centuries, the place of fine art and great music, beautiful architecture and ornate vestments. I know that even in the poorest parts of the world, Christians who have very little will give their best, turning out in their smartest clothes for Sunday worship, creating incredible flower arrangements, singing their hearts out. The Vatican's resources come from faithful Catholics, often widows offering their mite, who have given funds for the purpose of ornate and beautiful worship—'doing something beautiful for God', to quote Mother Teresa. For the Church to refuse this would be an insult.

One friend made these points in an email:

> I think a central answer is that one cannot separate Mother Teresa's life and work from her theology (the same is true of St Francis and all the great saints). I might suggest he (and you) read the marvellous biography of Mother Teresa, Brian Kolodiejchuk's *Come Be My Light*. It describes the years of darkness during which she felt utter alienation from Christ, whom she had met personally in the early years, and with whom she had fallen deeply in love. For years she could not find Him—in prayer, in reflection, or in work. Only her deep, profoundly developed Catholic faith protected her from despair, and permitted

her to understand the grace she was being given—
to experience personally the spiritual desolation
that assailed others, including the desperate poor
of Calcutta. In short, during all those years she
was not only serving the bodily needs of the
sick and dying. Far more importantly, she was
teaching them that the Light of Christ burns
even in the deepest darkness. This has been an
important lesson in my life.

[It is a mistake to think] that Mother Teresa can
or should be understood outside her devotion to
the Catholic Church. She was utterly committed
to its teachings—the Eucharist, the Petrine
supremacy and the Magisterium, apostolic
succession, obedience, the centrality of Mary,
purgatory—all of it. She also understood that the
Church here below has always included terrible
sinners, including popes, priests who have
abused children and bishops who have covered
it up. She understood that the earthly Church has
required, and will periodically require, reform
through the action of the Holy Spirit.

I have already noted to you my delight in the
tactile, sensuous nature of Catholic liturgy at its
most beautiful. In its expression of the divine
mystery of the Eucharist, the Church employs
finery of all kinds: soaring columns and majestic
paintings, exquisite vestments, fragrant incense,
the glorious music of Mozart sung by silver-toned
voices, the splendid language of the liturgy, and
(most magnificent of all) the touch of Christ
Himself—body, blood, soul, and divinity. While
I recognize that those (clergy and lay) who are
granted such richness are all subject to corruption,
that is no argument for its diminution, much less
its elimination. These are things that reflect the
incarnation itself. They lift our souls to God. I see
them as a great gift, not a liability.

Another friend, who helped me a lot in my journey, wrote this:

> Something that is worth pointing out Ben is that there will always be aspects that one needs to polish up. There will always be areas of the faith, public debate, or indeed one's life, that one has to pray, read and ponder about to better believe with the Church. It is beautiful to think that the Church is the new people of Israel—Christ's bride. In that sense, the Church opens the way for us to believe; we believe with the Church. When one grasps that, then faith and reason are harmonious. They don't do violence to each other. They, on the contrary, nourish each other so that we can carry believing to deepen into the truths of the faith.
>
> The reason why I say this is because you will find that we always need to keep on getting more and more formation about the faith. There does not come a point when one can say 'Aha, I got it all!' We have often mentioned how God has a lot of sense of humour. This affects the way we live. We keep on discovering the awe and beauty of the faith. This might range from re-discovering an amazing aspect in the faith; to having to think things through so that one can defend the Church/faith in a more dynamic, attractive and truthful way.
>
> Often it is important to remember that the Church as such is holy. It is, however, formed by sinners, whose sins often do not do a service to spreading the faith. This is important to remember as there might be aspects that come up—as most notably the child abuse scandal. The holiness of some of the Church's members is reassuring and edifying. However, my faith is not confined to the fact that, for instance, Padre

Pio was a great man. Our faith has to be rooted in Jesus Christ, in the fact that he left the Church as an instrument of Salvation. This might seem as slightly off topic but it is in fact central. Indeed, there are a large number of people that criticised the Church because of the abuse scandals, which are indeed absolutely appalling. However, it helps to throw back the question (once of course one has dealt with the scandals) and ask oneself or the other person 'if the scandals had not taken place, would you believe?' The answer has to go back to the aspect that we were mentioning before—it has to be rooted in Jesus Christ. There will always be wrong-doings carried out by Catholics for which the Church might be held accountable; the Crusades, the Inquisition, the Dark Ages, and, unfortunately, a whole lot of other aspects. Once one has established that we follow Jesus Christ and we believe in the Church, one can start dealing with aspects to be able to defend the Church. The more formation one gets the more one is able to defend the Church. With formation one's faith and love for the Church matures and grows. This helps when it comes to aspects of science. We are not afraid to discuss things, as we don't believe our faith violates the realms of reason. The same might apply to past human mistakes.

The case of abuse scandals is a sad one. Whilst it might not in itself be the main 'defence', I think many do not recognise the work the pope [Benedict XVI] has done to heal the wounds of people affected. No doubt a great number of people have been harmed. In some cases the wounds might take time to heal. The Church had mechanisms to deal with possible abuses. In some circumstances they were perhaps mishandled by the local ecclesiastical authorities, and it is something that has done harm. However, the case in the Church might have also been a reflection of what was in fact a deeper social problem—as we have unfortunately seen in other institutions.

Your friend is right when he says that not everyone that says Lord, Lord will enter the Kingdom of Heaven. There are in fact Catholics that better start pulling their socks up. We can never rest on our laurels as without the grace of God we are all capable of committing the worst crimes.

Regarding the riches case I think that one is a more straight forward one. There are two aspects. One—the humanitarian help that the Church gives to countries. It is the second largest humanitarian body in the world—second only to the whole of the UN—and it is present in many areas where people do not even want to be involved: HIV in Africa, looking after the poorest of the poor, chronically ill people, and a long list of other things. The finances for these projects many times come from funds raised in Rome. A second aspect is the Liturgy. If one really believes that the Mass is Heaven on Earth, then one does not cut corners when it comes to embellishing the Liturgy—it is a beautiful manifestation of love for God; to be able to offer nice vestments, and sacred vessels exclusively dedicated to worship and giving Him glory.

Some decades ago, a journey like mine would have contributed to greater division among Christians. John Henry Newman, for example, lost almost all his Anglican friends when he became Catholic. In contrast, however, while it is too soon to make this claim definitively, my journey may contribute to building some bridges. That certainly is my hope.

In October 2013, I travelled to Chin State, Burma, one of the poorest and most remote parts of the country. My hosts were all Chin Baptists. I worshipped with them, and spoke in one of their churches. But I quietly asked one of my Chin friends if I could also visit the Catholic church, and attend Mass. I had wondered if this would be an awkward cause of contention, but quite the opposite. The Chin Baptists told me that they did not know the Catholic bishop and priests, even though they were less than a mile away, but that they would like to. A Baptist pastor helped set up an appointment with the new bishop of Hakha for me, and accompanied me. The meeting went very well, both were eager to establish ecumenical relations, and the Baptist pastor told me at the end that I had helped facilitate that simply by my presence.

My hope for this book is that it too will help build unity—by addressing misperceptions of Catholicism, and by emphasising that what we have in common is far, far more significant than our differences. It has been exciting to come into the Church at a time when Pope Francis is emphasising this same message: meeting regularly with Pentecostal and evangelical pastors, speaking at charismatic gatherings, preaching a simple message of Jesus Christ.

Like many converts to Catholicism, my journey was guided by a multitude of people and factors. David Mills describes his journey, and it resonates with mine: 'My own experience of conversion was partly intellectual, but partly and probably mostly affective, in the sense that I came to feel the attraction and beauty of the whole, and that here was a body and a life into which I wanted to—had to—enter. The "converging probabilities" that drew me in, to use John Henry Newman's term, came from all sides, from observation and pro-life activism and participation in the liturgy and growing Marian devotion and visiting churches as much as from reading and reflection. This was my own experience, but I'm fairly sure it is also true for all but the most intellectual converts I've known, and perhaps true of them as well in ways others can't see.' And like Mills, while I grasped many things intellectually, I fell in love with the mystery which is Catholicism. 'As I read them,' he writes, 'I found that the Catholic answers were always deeper than the questions I was asking.'[4]

In the time since my reception into the Church, I have continued to read, and to ask questions. I have read almost everything Pope Francis has written or said, in homilies, media interviews and his Apostolic Exhortation, *Evangelii Gaudium*, and his encyclical, *Laudato Si'*. His words sum up how I see faith: 'An authentic faith—which is never comfortable or completely personal—always involves a deep desire to change the world, to transmit values, to leave this earth somehow better than we found it. We love this magnificent planet on which God has put us, and we love the human family which dwells here, with all its tragedies and struggles, its hopes and aspirations, its strengths and weaknesses ... All Christians, their pastors included, are called to show concern for the building of a better world. This is essential, for the Church's social thought is primarily positive: it offers proposals, it works for change and in this sense it constantly points to the hope born of the loving heart of Jesus Christ.'[5]

It was that message of the Church, expressed in different ways and through different people, which captured my heart. I had become a Christian in 1994 under the influence of a Methodist. I had worshipped for nineteen years as an Anglican. And now I have come home, to the mother Church of both Anglicans and Methodists, to Rome.

Three months after becoming a Catholic, I visited Assisi. It was absolutely beautiful to walk in the footsteps of St Francis, and particularly to walk in the countryside and forests surrounding the town. On one particular walk I found myself journeying deeper and deeper into the woods, losing the path and for a time having no idea where I was. Eventually I found my way out, crashing through undergrowth, into a stunning field of sunflowers. It felt like a parable for my journey of faith, and my arrival home in the mother Church.

Two and a half years after I was received into the Church, I experienced a privilege that millions of lifelong Catholics around the world can only dream of and that I had never dared imagine: I met the Holy Father. It was during a private audience with Pope Francis, as one of over hundred delegates at the International Catholic Legislators Network (ICLN) conference in Rome, immediately after the Angelus in which that day he chose to issue a two-fold appeal: for persecuted Christians and for all people forced to flee their homes in search of peace and security. 'Even today, dear brothers and sisters, in the Middle East and other parts of the world, Christians are persecuted,' said the Pope. 'There are more martyrs [in this day and age] than there were in the first centuries [of the Church].' He urged governments to protect religious freedom everywhere, and called on the international community 'to put an end to violence and oppression'. Given my work for religious freedom, particularly in Burma, Indonesia and North Korea, with Christian Solidarity Worldwide, this made the occasion particularly special.

We were told in advance that the one thing we can expect in a private audience with Pope Francis is a surprise. We were told to prepare for the possibility that we might each have a few moments with the Holy Father. I had therefore prepared carefully in my mind what I would say if given the opportunity—I wanted it to be meaningful but concise, and to touch on issues of religious freedom while containing a personal dimension.

The moment Pope Francis entered the room, it was as if a spirit of pure love and happiness swept in. Smiling, he exuded warmth—just as he does everywhere he goes. He took his seat, and the president of the ICLN, Christiaan Alting von Gesau, delivered a short speech to the Holy Father on behalf of us all, in fluent—and impressive—Spanish, highlighting our main message, the defence of the most vulnerable people in the world: the unborn child and family life, persecuted Christians, and refugees and migrants. Then the African contingent—parliamentarians from Kenya, Zimbabwe and Malawi—sang an 'Alleluia', African-style, for the pope. The Holy Father then addressed us, expressing his appreciation for the work of Catholics in politics. And then, a line began to form for each individual present to meet Pope Francis personally.

When I joined the line, I had a fluttering in my heart—it is not every day, after all, that one meets the pope. But when I reached him, and was suddenly looking into his eyes, I felt only peace and joy. A deep inner calm filled me and I said: 'Holy Father, thank you for speaking up for persecuted Christians and other minorities. I work for religious freedom and human rights in Asia. I work especially closely with Cardinal Bo of Burma. I became a Catholic two years ago, received into the Church in Burma by Cardinal

Bo.' At the mention of Burma's first-ever cardinal, the pope's face lit up in recognition and approval: "Bo!" he exclaimed with a big smile.

I was face to face with the pontiff for no more than a minute, but it was an experience of a lifetime. The personality the world has come to love over the past two years is every bit as unique as his media portrayal. An aura of humility, compassion, mercy and joy surrounds him—indeed, the spirit of Christ shines through him. I left with gratitude in my heart—knowing that I could say he is not just *the* pope, but for me he is *my* Holy Father.

Notes

1. David Mills, 'The convert's unnecessary worries', *Catholic Pulse*, 6 November 2014: http://www.catholicpulse.com/en/columnists/mills/110614.html.
2. Edward Norman, 'This is why I have decided to join the Catholic Church', *The Catholic Herald*, 16 November 2012.
3. Peter Stanford, 'Pope resigns: the pope who was not afraid to say sorry', *Daily Telegraph*, 11 February 2013: http://www.telegraph.co.uk/news/worldnews/the-pope/9862770/Pope-resigns-The-pope-who-was-not-afraid-to-say-sorry.html.
4. David Mills, 'The anatomy of conversion', *New Oxford Review*, April 2010: http://www.newoxfordreview.org/article.jsp?did=0410-mills.
5. Pope Francis, *Evangelii Gaudium*, p. 93.

Cardinal Charles Maung Bo

Cecil Chaudhry

Shahbaz Bhatti

Sister Maria Lourdes Martins da Cruz

Lieutenant Colonel Christopher Keeble, DSO

Rangoon Cathedral

Bibliography

Books

Alton, David, and Caroline Cox, *Building Bridges, Not Walls*—a report on a visit to the Democratic People's Republic of Korea (DPRK), October 2010

Augustine, *Confessions*, a new translation by Henry Chadwick, Oxford, Oxford University Press, 1991

Anderson, Clare and Joanna Bogle, *John Paul II: Man of Prayer—The Spiritual Life of a Saint*, Leominster, Gracewing, 2014

Benedict XVI, *Jesus of Nazareth*, London, Bloomsbury, 2007

Benedict XVI, *Jesus of Nazareth—Holy Week: From the Entrance into Jerusalem to the Resurrection*, London, Catholic Truth Society, 2011

Benedict XVI, *Jesus of Nazareth: The Infancy Narratives*, London, Bloomsbury, 2012

Benedict XVI, *Called to Communion: Understanding the Church Today*, San Francisco, Ignatius Press, 1991

Benedict XVI, *Heart of the Christian life: Thoughts on Holy Mass*, San Francisco, Ignatius Press, 2010

Benedict XVI, *On the Way to Jesus Christ*, San Francisco, Ignatius Press, 2004

Benedict XVI, *Light of the World: The Pope, the Church and the Signs of the Times—A Conversation with Peter Seewald*, San Francisco, Ignatius Press, 2010

Benedict XVI, *Credo for Today: What Christians Believe*, San Francisco, Ignatius Press, 2009

Benedict XVI, *Holiness is Always in Season*, San Francisco, Ignatius Press, 2009

Benedict XVI, *Great Teachers*, Huntingdon, Our Sunday Visitor Publishing, 2011

Benedict XVI, Encyclical Letter, *Deus caritas est*, Rome, 2005 — http://w2.vatican.va/content/benedict-xvi/en/encyclicals/documents/hf_ben-xvi_enc_20051225_deus-caritas-est.html

Benedict XVI, Encyclical Letter, *Spe salvi*, Rome, 2007 — http://w2.vatican.va/content/benedict-xvi/en/encyclicals/documents/hf_ben-xvi_enc_20051225_deus-caritas-est.html

Benedict XVI, Encyclical Letter, *Caritas in veritate*, Rome, 2009 — http://w2.vatican.va/content/benedict-xvi/en/encyclicals/documents/hf_ben-xvi_enc_20090629_caritas-in-veritate.html

Benedict XVI, Apostolic Letter Morta Propio Data, *Porta fidei*, Rome, 2011 — http://w2.vatican.va/content/benedict-xvi/en/encyclicals/documents/hf_ben-xvi_enc_20090629_caritas-in-veritate.html

Cantalamessa, Raniero, *Sober Intoxication of the Spirit: Filled with the Fullness of God*, Cincinnati, Servant Books, 2005

Cantalamessa, Raniero, *Sober Intoxication of the Spirit: Part Two—Born Again of Water and the Spirit*, Cincinnati, Servant Books, 2012

Caussade, Jean-Pierre de, *Abandonment to Divine Providence*, Notre Dame, Ave Maria Press, 2010

Chesterton, G.K., *Orthodoxy*, Chicago, Moody Publishers, 2009

Chesterton, G.K., *The Catholic Church and Conversion*, San Francisco, Ignatius Press, 1990

Chesterton, G.K., *The Everlasting Man*, Peabody, Hendrickson Publishers, 2007

Chesterton, G.K., *In Defense of Sanity*, San Francisco, Ignatius Press, 2011

The Cloud of Unknowing and Other Works, trans. Clifton Wolters, London, Penguin, 1978

Day, Dorothy, *The Long Loneliness*, New York, Harper Collins, 1952

Evans, Edward, *The History of the Catholic Church in Burma 1856–1966*, San Vito di Cadora (BL): Graf. Sanvitese, 2012

Francis, Apostolic Exhortation, *Evangelii gaudium*, Rome, 2013 — http://w2.vatican.va/content/francesco/en/apost_exhortations/documents/papa-francesco_esortazione-ap_20131124_evangelii-gaudium.html

Hahn, Scott and Kimberly, *Rome Sweet Rome: Our Journey to Catholicism*, San Francisco, Ignatius, 1993

Hahn, Scott, *Hail, Holy Queen: The Mother of God in the Word of God*, London, Darton, Longman and Todd, 2001

Hahn, Scott, *The Lamb's Supper: The Mass as Heaven on Earth*, London, Darton, Longman and Todd, 2003

Hahn, Scott, *Lord, Have Mercy: The Healing Power of Confession*, London, Darton, Longman and Todd, 2003

Hahn, Scott, *Reasons to Believe: How to Understand, Explain and Defend the Catholic Faith*, London, Darton, Longman and Todd, 2007

Hahn, Scott, *Ordinary Work, Extraordinary Grace: My Spiritual Journey in Opus Dei*, London, Darton, Longman and Todd, 2007

Hahn, Scott, *Angels and Saints: A Biblical Guide to Friendship with God's Holy Ones*, London, Darton, Longman and Todd, New York, Image, 2014

Ingrams, Richard, *Malcolm Muggeridge: The Biography*, London, Harper Collins, 1995

Jamison, Christopher, *Finding Sanctuary — Monastic Steps for Everyday Life*, London, Phoenix, 2007

Jamison, Christopher, *Finding Happiness — Monastic Steps for a Fulfilling Life*, London, Phoenix, 2009

John Paul II, encyclicals and other writings — http://www.papalencyclicals.net/JP02/

à Kempis, Thomas, *The Imitation of Christ*, ed. Donald E. Demaray, New York, Alba House, 1996

Kohen, Arnold, *From the Place of the Dead: The Epic Struggles of Bishop Belo of East Timor*, New York, St Martin's Press, 1999

Lubac, Henri de, *Catholicism: Christ and the Common Destiny of Man*, San Francisco, Ignatius Books, 1988

Maritain, Jacques, *Christianity and Democracy and the Rights of Man and The Natural Law*, San Francisco, Ignatius Books, 2011

Merton, Thomas, *No Man is an Island*, Boston, Shambhala, 2005

Merton, Thomas, *The Seven-Storey Mountain*, New York, Harvest, 1998

Muggeridge, Malcolm, *Conversion: The Spiritual Journey of a Twentieth-Century Pilgrim*, Eugene, Wipf and Stock, 1988

Muggeridge, Malcolm, *Jesus: The Man who Lives*, London, Collins, 1975

Muggeridge, Malcolm, *The End of Christendom*, London, Wm. B. Eerdmans Publishing Company, 1980

Muggeridge, Malcolm, *Something Beautiful for God: Mother Teresa of Calcutta*, London, Lion Publishing, 2009

Newman, John Henry, *Loss and Gain: The Story of a Convert*, Teddington, Echo Library, 2008

Newman, John Henry, *Apologia pro Vita Sua*, London, Penguin, 2004

Pascal, Blaise, *Pensées and Other Writings*, a new translation by Honor Levi, Oxford, Oxford University Press, 1995

Radcliffe, Timothy, *Why Go to Church? The Drama of the Eucharist*, London, Continuum, 2008

Radcliffe, Timothy, *What is the Point of Being a Christian?*, London, Continuum, 2005

Radcliffe, Timothy, *Take the Plunge: Living Baptism and Confirmation*, London, Continuum, 2012

Radcliffe, Timothy, *Sing a New Song: The Christian Vocation*, London, Templegate Publishing, 1999

Radcliffe, Timothy, *I Call You Friends*, London, Continuum, 2012

Ratzinger, Joseph, *The Ratzinger Report: An Exclusive Interview on the State of the Church*, San Francisco, Ignatius Press, 1985

Russell, Claire, *Glimpses of the Church Fathers*, London, Scepter, 1996

Schmude, Karl, *G. K. Chesterton*, London, Catholic Truth Society, 2008

Von Balthasar, Hans Urs, *Engagement with God*, San Francisco, Ignatius Press, 1975

Von Balthasar, Hans Urs, *Love Alone is Credible*, San Francisco, Ignatius Press, 2004

Von Balthasar, Hans Urs and Joseph Cardinal Ratzinger, *Mary: The Church at the Source*, San Francisco, Ignatius, 1997

Waal, Esther de, *Seeking God: The Way of St Benedict*, Norwich, Canterbury Press, 2014

Weigel, George, *The Truth of Catholicism: Ten Controversies Explored*, Leominster, Gracewing, 2001

Weigel, George, *Letters to a Young Catholic*, Leominster, Gracewing, 2004

Weigel, George, *The Courage to Be Catholic: Crisis, Reform and the Future of the Church*, New York, Basic Books, 2004

Weigel, George, *Practicing Catholic*, New York, Crossroad Publishing, 2012

Weigel, George, *Evangelical Catholicism: Deep Reform in the Twenty-First-Century Church*, New York, Basic Books, 2013

Williams, Paul, *The Unexpected Way: On Converting from Buddhism to Catholicism*, London, T&T Clark, 2002

Articles

Abhaya: Burma's Fearlessness (website), 'The activist and the uninvited guests', 7 April 2011

Allott, Daniel, 'Mr Smith's 30 years in Washington', *The Catholic World Report*, 1 May 2011

Anon., 'James Mawdsley back home with a mission', *The Tablet*, 28 October 2000

Asia News, 'Pope Francis encourages Cardinal Zen, "the one who fights with a sling"', 24 October, 2014

BBC News, 'Profile: Cardinal Zen'

BBC, 'Pakistan Minorities Minister Shahbaz Bhatti shot dead', 2 March 2011

Becker, Stuart Alan, 'Myanmar's first cardinal strives to be a "voice for the voiceless"', *The Myanmar Times*, 1 April 2015

Benedict XVI, 'Full text of Benedict XVI's last address', *Catholic Herald*, 27 February 2013

Bo, Charles Maung and Benedict Rogers, 'Religious violence threatens to tear Myanmar apart', *Mizzima*, 3 May 2013

Bo, Charles Maung and Benedict Rogers, 'Myanmar's religious diversity: dialogue trumps violence', *The Myanmar Times*, 23 August 2013

Bo, Charles Maung, 'Burma needs tolerance to reach its potential', *The Washington Post*, 13 June 2014

Bradsher, Keith, 'Gentle cleric's stature grows as he risks ire of China', *The New York Times*, 8 July 2006

Copeland, Libby, 'Faith-based initiative: presidential hopeful Sam Brownback strives to be humble enough for a higher power', *The Washington Post*, 7 June 2006

The Guardian, Obituary: Father Chico Fernandes, 14 October 2005

Khoo Thwe, Francis, 'Yangon cardinal calls for dialogue between military and ethnic militias to end conflict in Myanmar', Asia News, 2 March 2015

Lee, Martin, 'Who will stand with Hong Kong', *The New York Times*, 3 October 2014

Mahtani, Shibani, 'Myanmar's Cardinal Charles Maung Bo to work toward religious tolerance', *The Wall Street Journal*, 7 January 2014

McDonald, Alyssa, 'Ann Widdecombe—extended interview', *The New Statesman*, 19 July 2010

Mills, David, 'G. K. Chesterton: rhetoric, genius and holiness, *Catholic Exchange*, 23 April 2015

Mills, David, 'The convert's unnecessary worries', *Catholic Pulse*, 6 November 2014

Mills, David, 'The anatomy of conversion', *New Oxford Review*, April 2010

Norman, Edward, 'This is why I have decided to join the Catholic Church', *The Catholic Herald*, 16 November 2012

Pelowski, Alton J, 'All in for pro-life', *The Knights of Columbus Columbia online edition*, 1 January 2015

Pistono, Matteo, 'Thomas Merton in the Himalayas: interview with Harold Talbott', www.matteopistono.com, 15 October 2014

Pomfret, James and Yimou Lee, 'Hong Kong clashes, arrests kick-start plans to blockade city', *Reuters*, 27 September 2014

Rogers, Benedict, 'The conscience of Lord David Alton', *Crisis Magazine*, 1 November, 2004

Rogers, Benedict, 'Uninvited visitors', *The International Herald Tribune*, 3 April 2011

Rogers, Benedict, 'Is it a crime to write a book?' *Democratic Voice of Burma*, 7 April 2011

Roughneen, Simon, 'With Burma's first Catholic saint possible, archbishop hopes for papal visit', *The Irrawaddy*, 19 December 2013

Sevastopulo, Demetri and Julie Zhu, 'Hong Kong democracy activists vent their anger against Beijing', *Financial Times*, 1 September 2014

Smith, Michael, 'Forgiveness out of war', *For a Change*, 4 April 2007

Stanford, Peter, 'Pope resigns: the pope who was not afraid to say sorry', *Daily Telegraph*, 11 February 2013

Thompson, Wendy, 'Top 10 most interesting: Congressman Chris Smith—how human rights became his value system', *The DC Spotlight Newspaper*, 1 October 2011

Vatican Radio, 'Pope Francis to new cardinals: presiding flows from charity', 15 February 2015

Vatican Radio, 'Pope Francis: cardinals are servants of the Church', 15 February 2015

Whitehouse, Chris, 'Jim Dobbin—obituary', *The Tablet*, 13 September, 2014

Widdecombe, Ann, 'If only the Catholic Church did PR', *The Guardian*, 7 September 2010

More comments on *From Burma to Rome*

This is a remarkable story of a journey with God, one that has brought Benedict Rogers to risk his life in the service of the poor and the despised, and find his fulfilment and peace in a homecoming to the Catholic brand of Christianity.

Fr Nicholas King, SJ

This unique book describes not only the personal and intellectual elements of Catholicism but also the social and political forces currently shaping the life of the Church. The author's journey of faith is a guide to the Church in today's world.

Fr Christopher Jamison, OSB

Benedict Rogers's story is extraordinary. It is a pilgrimage towards justice and authentic spirituality. But in his journey he surrounds himself with other spiritual giants — past and present. Ben's compelling journey from Burma to Rome is entirely lacking in egotism and overflowing in courage.

The Rev. Joel Edwards,
writer, broadcaster and former director of
Micah Challenge International

'Becoming a Catholic opens up a whole new world', writes Benedict Rogers. From Burma to Rome provides evidence for that bold assertion by illuminating and vindicating Pope Francis's image of the Church as 'Field Hospital'. Part biblical exegesis, part spiritual reflection, and part *tour d'horizon* of the deepening worldwide crisis of religious freedom, the book showcases Rogers's heroes, and Rogers himself, as hospital workers striving to love God in the world — to say 'Yes!' to Him — by loving and serving His creation. Learned, pastoral, humorous, and deeply inspiring, Benedict Rogers has written a classic in the genre of Catholic conversion stories.

Dr Thomas Farr,
former Director of the United States Office
of International Religious Freedom
and Senior Fellow, The Berkley Center for Religion,
Peace, and World Affairs at Georgetown University

Lightning Source UK Ltd.
Milton Keynes UK
UKOW04f1339151115

262765UK00001B/14/P